**The Commons
in the Seventies**

The Commons
in the Seventies

Edited by
S. A. WALKLAND and MICHAEL RYLE

For the Study of Parliament Group

Fontana/Collins

First published in Fontana 1977

Copyright © The Study of Parliament Group 1977

Made and printed in Great Britain by
William Collins Sons & Co. Ltd, Glasgow

Contents

Introduction

The first edition of this volume, *The Commons in Transition*, published in 1970, enjoyed some success as a collective product of the Study of Parliament Group at a time when reform of Parliament was much discussed and when the changes of the 1960s had not yet reached the textbooks. It summed up, although certainly with no unanimity amongst the contributors, the nature and impact of recent innovations in the House of Commons, by academics and present and former officials of the House for whom the changes had immediate practical concern. What *The Commons in Transition* gained in relevance it probably lost in the short perspective which, of necessity, it had to take. Six years later this second edition seeks to remedy this. It has also become possible to assess the success or failure of some of the changes in the Commons procedures and practices that were being made when the last volume was published.

In many ways, however, it has been more difficult to produce this second volume. It was not simply possible merely to update the essays of *The Commons in Transition*. One main reason is that since that was written three founder members of the Group, Professors Hanson and Wiseman and Sir Edward Fellowes, have died, and they were collectively responsible for five of the essays. New areas of Parliamentary activity, such as European legislation and the work of the Expenditure Committee of the House of Commons have obviously had to be dealt with, and with a lengthening perspective the understandable concentration of the first volume on the commitee structure of the Commons has been offset by essays on the Members of the Commons themselves and on the floor of the House. As well as producing a more balanced coverage, these essays reflect the interests of some of the younger and newer members of the Study of Parliament Group, whose membership has grown and diversified in the last six years.

But other and more fundamental difficulties are apparent in the essays collected here. It is some considerable time since Parliamentary government in Britain was subject to the same pressures which are assailing it now, and in this respect the situation has changed even in the few years since the publication of *The Commons in Transition*. Although it was stressed in the Introduction to the previous volume that the Study of Parliament Group is seldom unanimous, except in its wish to see a vigorous Parliament in Britain, there was at that time some considerable shared optimism amongst the contributors and a marked uniformity of interpretation of recent events which it has been impossible to reproduce in this book. As will be evident from some of the essays, the Study of Parliament Group has not been able to insulate itself from some of the current controversies over the political state of Britain and the impact of politics on the vexed question of Parliament's efficacy. And as the opening and closing chapters, by the two editors, show, there may now be emerging deep differences about the very purpose and functions of Parliament. We believe that it can only be good for Parliamentary studies and for the constructive discussion of reform of the House of Commons, for these differences to be clarified and exposed. Too long, perhaps, have basic assumptions and historically ingrained attitudes remained unquestioned, and we hope that the very differences apparent in this book will help to focus the debate, not obscure it. This, however, makes it all the more necessary to stress that neither the essays nor the editorial contributions are to be regarded as other than expressions of individual opinion. The Study of Parliament Group has no collective view on these matters and accepts no responsibility for the views here expressed, still less for any factual error which may appear. If, as a result, the book lacks a certain coherence this partly reflects the fact that at the present time a consensus on the current state and likely future of Parliamentary government in Britain is not possible.

At the time of writing a new Procedure enquiry by the House of Commons has started, but with no clear directions or guidelines. It is likely that these essays will be published before the Procedure Committee reports, since they apparently intend to conduct a fundamental and full review. Again, different views are possible about what the Report should recommend, and there is total uncertainty about what will be accepted by the Government. That there is still great scope for improvement is agreed by many, but it is more than likely that these essays will still be very relevant when the Committee has reported.

The editors would like to thank the contributors for their ready response to the invitation to produce these essays, and also Mr R. B. Woodings, of Fontana, for his generous help.

SAW

MTR

August 1976

1 The Commons in the Seventies – a General Survey

MICHAEL RYLE

Introduction

Any assessment of the effectiveness of an institution must involve not only judgements about the actual performance of that body but also an understanding of the functions it is intended or might be expected to perform. To adapt Professor Joad's well-known key to clearer thinking, 'It all depends on what you expect . . .' Much of the current criticism of Parliament may in part reflect a failure to appreciate what roles Parliament may reasonably be expected to perform – what might be called mistakes in perceived functions.

The criticism is admittedly widespread. The critics include some journalists, broadcasters, academics, lawyers, businessmen, 'the man I was talking to in the pub last night' and MPs themselves. Their criticism commonly includes the following: holding Parliament responsible for the nation's ills; blaming the Commons for not preventing some foolish act of government; complaining that Parliament has not given the country a lead in one direction or other; finding fault with the content or drafting of a new Act and blaming Parliament for passing it in that form; complaints of time-wasting and over-lengthy debate on the one hand, or of hasty decisions on the other; condemnation of the Commons for not being more 'businesslike'; and finally criticism of Members for sometimes being rowdy, excited, or abusive – or (on other occasions) for being dull, passive, cynical and lacking the vigour of Parliamentarians of yesteryear.

Of course some of these broad criticisms are not wholly erroneous. Few would claim that the House of Commons functions perfectly. Nor can it be totally exonerated from responsibility for the nation's malaise. As Professor Bernard

Crick has argued,[1] an alert and effective House of Commons (and how it should display those qualities is a matter we will come to) should be a help, not a hindrance, to good government. And of course there are other criticisms of the way the House works at present which may be far more valid. But there is, I believe, a basic fallacy at the heart of much of the contemporary criticism: namely that Parliament, and particularly the Commons, is blamed because it is expected to be, in some sense, 'governing the country' and they are thought not to be doing this at all well. And this, as I will argue, is a fundamentally false expectation. (Incidentally, it is significant that the House of Lords, whatever else they may be criticized for, are seldom blamed for the economic ills of the country or for passing bad laws, because it is generally recognized that they have no powers of economic management and do not make laws – good or bad; here the perceived functions are more closely matched to the reality.)

It is not surprising that people are frequently mistaken in their perception of the functions of Parliament. We were all brought up on school books which described how 'Parliament makes the laws'. Constitutional writers such as Bagehot have freely used the term 'Parliamentary government'. It is a central tenet of our constitutional description that ministers are subject to Parliamentary control, and that the House of Commons votes money to the Crown and gives legislative sanction to taxation. The heart of my argument is that these are all true statements, but only in very special – and frequently misleading – senses. Take 'Parliamentary government'. This suggests that Parliament itself governs and exercises a direct power, while the reality is that others (Prime Minister, Cabinet, civil service – and, indirectly perhaps, trade unions, business interests, foreign bankers, etc.) govern or exercise power; but are required to do so *through* Parliament.

Thus much of the criticism of Parliament, and particularly of the House of Commons today, flows, I believe, from this fundamental mistake in their perceived functions. Parliament is wrongly blamed for bad government because Parliament does not govern. To put it baldly: the government governs; Parliament is the forum where the exercise of government is publicly displayed and is open to scrutiny and criticism. And the Commons does not control the executive – not in any real sense: rather the executive control the Commons through the exercise of their party majority power.

In the remainder of this chapter, I wish to examine more fully the role or roles (for packaging every concept into one can add to confusion) of the House of Commons and to show how, in the 1970s, they are performed through the medium of the traditional processes of the House and its committees. Later chapters in this book will then look at these different processes and aspects in more detail. But, in my view, it is against this perception of the functions of Parliament – as a critical, not a governmental, body – that the effectiveness of Parliament in the seventies must be assessed.

The Influence of the House of Commons

It may seem stuffy to analyse the several roles of the House of Commons in the 1970s, in the way Bagehot did a century ago. One suspects things have become more complicated. Certainly Members are drawn from much wider social and economic fields and bring a great variety of motives and inspirations to the work, as well as styles, techniques, experience and specialist knowledge. Probably the Members of the House today are as well – and widely – informed as ever in our history. Certainly they themselves see themselves – and the House as a whole – performing a number of different functions. But the one thing neither the House as a whole, nor the majority of individual Members, is primarily concerned with is exercising the powers of government itself.

The Government, through its ministers, plays the primary active part in the House. The Government declares its policies – or draft policies – in the form of White and Green Papers, ministerial statements, etc. The Government lays before the House its proposals for implementing many of those policies in the form of bills, and, through the exercise of its control of the majority in the House, ensures that those bills nearly always become law in much the form the Government itself wishes – or at least with only such amendments as it is prepared to tolerate.[2] The government presents Estimates of the money it requires to pay for its policies and for other inherited responsibilities of the executive; and the Commons vote this Supply without a single change (other than those proposed by ministers). Similarly the Chancellor of the Exchequer presents his proposals for new or changed taxation, which the House normally endorses. And finally, the government – ministers and civil servants together – implement their policies and act over the vast range of executive authority with little need to refer to Parliament at all. In other words the powers of government are enormous; they decide what they want to do, they use their control of the Commons to ensure that they receive the necessary formal Parliamentary authority to do what they desire, and they then do it: the powers of Parliament, in this sense, are very slight indeed.

Where, then, lies the importance or the influence of Parliament? I have described the Commons as a forum for the public exercise of government, but is it no more than a football stadium, where the crowd may cheer or boo, but have only limited influence on the game? No, it goes beyond this for three reasons – all of them stemming from one essential relationship, namely the fact that the proceedings of the House are public and are publicized and that it is to the voting public that, in the end, ministers are accountable. Governments may face with equanimity the criticism of the opposition: they expect it and, indeed, would be frequently embarrassed if they did not receive it. They may even be prepared to receive a certain amount of rough handling from some of their own back-benchers – provided they ultimately respond to the crack of the whip. But no government of any political complexion can face, without concern, a loss of sympathy, confidence or support by the electorate as a whole. The ultimate power in our democratic system is exercised through the ballot box. Therefore, in so far as the House of Commons can influence – and be seen to influence – electoral opinion, and particularly party opinion, its own reactions to government proposals and actions must be taken seriously by ministers. And in so far as Parliament is seen to be reflecting public opinion, or opinion in the parties, then its own reactions to government must similarly be found significant. To sum up, the influence – and this is a more appropriate word than 'power' – of the House of Commons derives from its ability to speak to and to speak for the people. It is, as Lloyd George said, the sounding board of the nation.

It is therefore as a critical forum, not as a governing body, that the House of Commons must be assessed. As Leo Amery wrote in *Thoughts on the Constitution*, 'the main task of Parliament is still what it was when first summoned, not to legislate or govern but to secure full discussion and ventilation of all matters'. It is in this sense that Parliament is the custodian of our liberties. These liberties are not only protected by preserving certain features of the constitution, but also by ensuring that ministers always have to explain and publicly justify their policies and their actions.

It is by these tests, therefore, that the functioning and influence of the House of Commons must be assessed – not by the extent to which the House contributes to the preparation of legislation, for example, or is able to sanction or veto expenditure, but rather by the extent that legislative proposals are fully ventilated and expenditure is subjected to detailed, and informed, discussion. And the significance of the ancient pillars of Parliamentary procedure – the various readings of bills and the voting of Supply, for example – is not that they give the House power to decide for or against bills (except on private Members' bills) or to decide how much money should be voted for government spending, but rather that they ensure the opportunity to debate or otherwise consider ministers' proposals. The Government may secure the approval they require in the end but the procedures of the House should 'secure full discussion and ventilation of all matters'. It is in this sense that Parliamentary procedure is the cement of our constitution. Let us now look at how the cement is holding the fabric together in the 1970s.

Opportunities and Techniques

For the House to operate effectively as a critical forum two requirements must be satisfied. First there must be adequate opportunities for all the main elements in the House – the Government, the official opposition, minority parties and back-benchers on both sides, acting individually or collectively – to take the initiative in bringing business before the House and raising matters which concern them. The second requirement is that there must be effective techniques for scrutinizing government and calling ministers to account. This involves not only debate but also techniques for informing Members – and people outside Parliament – about the policies and acts of government and also the background to such policy decisions.

Take opportunities first. The Government must clearly have the lion's share of opportunities to enable them to bring forward their own legislation. I will not enter the largely unresolveable argument as to whether there is too much or too little legislation, but one point is worth noting. The volume of legislation is not necessarily directly related to the amount of time available for its consideration. Between 1970 and 1975 the volume of legislation (measured by pages on the statute book) increased by about 20 per cent; yet the time spent on government legislation in the House (admittedly I am ignoring the increasing time spent by Members in standing committees) remained broadly the same over those years.[3] Correspondingly if less time were given for consideration of legislation it might not mean fewer bills, but simply that they received less debate.

In addition to legislation the government have other opportunities for initiative in presenting their policies to the House, such as during the debate on the Address in reply to the Queen's Speech at the beginning of each session, the Budget speech and debate, debates on motions to approve or take note of White Papers setting out government policy, motions to approve delegated legislation subject to the affirmative procedure, and ministerial statements.

The official opposition have their opportunities for bringing issues of the day of their choice before the House, and so they may choose policies or actions of the Government to be debated which would otherwise remain out of the spotlight. They also have the chance to deploy publicly their alternative policies. They normally put down two amendments to the

Address, which are debated for one day each. They have the choice of the subject for debate on the twenty-nine Supply days. They table occasional motions of censure for which the government traditionally give time. Occasionally – in recent years only about once a session – they may initiate an 'emergency' debate under Standing Order No. 9. They can put down 'prayers' against Statutory Instruments of their choice. And, to some extent, they can press ministers during Question Time on issues of their own choosing.

The main opportunity, however, is on Supply days and it is interesting to see how they are used. In 1971–2, the Labour Opposition chose to debate the following topics:

Education	Royal Navy
Northern Ireland	Land and house prices
Pensions	UNCTAD
Development areas	Steel industry
Public expenditure	Industrial training
Signatures of EEC Treaty	Yorkshire and Humberside
Unemployment (3 times)	Food prices
PAC Reports	Pound sterling
Rhodesia (twice)	Industrial relations
Coal industry	North West Region
Chronically sick and disabled	Scottish Affairs
Royal Air Force	Wales
Army	

In 1975–6, the Conservative Opposition chose the following:

Development in the EEC	Foreign affairs
Off-shore oil	Public expenditure (twice)
Motor vehicle industry (twice)	Housing (rented accommodation)
Devolution	British Rail commuter services
PAC Reports	International trade
Services for the mentally ill	Elections to European Assembly
Municipal trading and direct labour	Nationalization
Fishing industry	

Children and Young Persons   Royal Air Force
  Act 1969   N. Ireland security
Local government   Child benefits
Royal Navy   Immigration
Army   Pay and prices policy
Sale of council houses

Although these lists cover only two years, it appears that
both parties in opposition have tended to choose topics of
current concern or with immediate political appeal. Certain
matters are regularly debated while other aspects of government are ignored. In particular, some of the big-spending
departments are left out – in neither year, for example, was
the NHS debated. There seems little evidence of either
opposition planning, over the session, a regular and systematic
coverage of the whole area of government. But this is not
surprising. The Government have opportunities to parade their
successes; the opposition, naturally, wish to focus Parliamentary and public attention on those aspects of government
where ministers seem to be failing or where the opposition
have attractive alternative policies to offer.

Minority opposition parties have far less opportunity for
bringing matters of their choosing before the House. Their
amendments to the Address are not normally selected for
debate. On only two occasions in recent years, in 1974 and
1976, have the Liberals had a Supply Day although the
Scottish, Welsh and Ulster Unionist parties also each had half
a Supply Day in 1976. These parties have little opportunity
to have 'prayers' debated and even during Question Time
their opportunities are severely limited by their numbers.
However, at least for the Scottish and Irish parties, there are
a number of occasions when they can advocate their policies
on legislation, including delegated legislation, affecting their
countries which has to be brought before the House by the
Government. And, of course, there are Questions to the Scottish, Welsh and Northern Ireland Ministers.

Private Members, however, have certain clearly defined
opportunities for taking the initiative in getting subjects of
their choice before the House. And there is a sense in which

they play a distinct and important role, apart from their activities in support of their parties. All back-benchers, where ever they sit in the House, have a duty to represent their constituents and to articulate their anxieties and protect or further their interests. They do this in numerous ways – by tabling amendments to bills, by Questions, both oral and written, through Adjournment debates, by 'prayers' against Statutory Instruments and in debate on any bill (including private legislation) or other topics brought before the House.

There are, however, a number of specific occasions which are recognized as private Members' occasions. These include debates on motions for the adjournment of the House for the four sessional recesses, debates on the second readings of two or three Consolidated Fund Bills each session (when ballots are held to determine the priority in which Members may raise matters of which they have given notice), the eight Fridays and four half Mondays which are now set aside for private Members' motions (priority again being determined by ballot) and the twelve Fridays on which private Members' bills have priority. Professor Richards discusses these opportunities in Chapter 6.

Opportunities are, however, only half the story. Effective scrutiny of government and public airing of issues also requires the use of Parliamentary techniques that enable Members to get the essential facts, to deploy these effectively in debate, and to get the main matters and arguments over to the wider public outside in a way that will engage public attention.

It is a matter of continuing argument how much information is necessary. On the one hand, it is sometimes argued that Members are unable to exercise effective scrutiny of government unless they are armed with detailed knowledge about the background to, and reasons for and against, every government decision. Some people have even argued that Members should be assisted by large teams of research assistants – a sort of counter civil service – so that they are at least as well informed and briefed as ministers. Others have argued that if Members are too well informed they cease to be effective critics. The challenge to ministers that is inherent in the confrontation nature of British politics can be blunted if the clarity of party dogmatic disagreement is blurred by the sophistication of statistical analysis. Consensus politics resulting from an objective search for truth would be dull politics and let ministers off too lightly. Over concern with a search for facts could deliver MPs into the hands of experts and make them remote from the people they represent. The expertly advised decisions of ministers, it can be argued, should be tested, in part at least, by their acceptability to the electorate, and that means by political criteria, not by further expertise.

The argument continues, and where the balance should be struck will surely be at the heart of the broad enquiry into the procedures and practices of the House now being undertaken by a select committee. It is true that there are dangers in expecting Members to be fully informed before daring to criticize ministers; if that requirement were adhered to, many cases of maladministration and of the liberties and rights of individuals would never be raised at all, and that would include those where the minister concerned was, in the end, shown to be in the wrong after all. There is something attractive about the political Davids – like Wilberforce, Shaftesbury or, more recently and on a smaller scale, Fenner Brockway – who, armed only with political wit, integrity and a sense of purpose, have been prepared to take on several Goliaths at once – strong pressure groups, ministerial indifference and bureaucratic inertia – whether or not they won. But government today has become so complex and many of the issues so technical that if Parliament is to match the decision-taking processes of government – which includes detailed study of the relevant information – with anything like an effective critical scrutiny, then the House must be able to inform itself to some extent. Even in the last century the great social reformers were rarely successful when they first raised the issue. Extensive fact-finding by select committee enquiries – which also helped to change public opinion – was required before the slave trade was abolished or the Factory Acts could be passed. And today it appears impossible for Parliament properly to examine major decisions involving many million pounds of public money, such as, for example, the decision to develop and build and fly Concorde, or even other matters, not involving much expenditure, such as immigration controls, without detailed examination of the facts and arguments. It would clearly be wrong for Members to be limited, in the supply of information, to that which ministers choose to make public without request, plus whatever they may learn from the Press and other outside sources. Parliamentary processes must, therefore, to some extent, be designed to enable the House as a whole, committees, or individual Members to seek for and obtain further information relevant to the issues before them.

The sum of information on any topic may be likened to water in a well. In varying degrees, according to the subject, the Government themselves will draw up and distribute much water/information to the thirsty public. They publish White and Green Papers – the latter a useful innovation in recent years – make statements in the House and issue Press releases both on their proposals for policy changes or future legislation and on how legislation is working out in practice (by means of numerous annual reports, for example). Ministers will also volunteer such additional information as they think desirable in the course of debate on bills or motions in the House and in standing committees.

Ministers are also willing to draw up more water if specifically requested. There is much information that ministers will willingly give if asked for by Members in the course of debate or, of course, by means of Parliamentary Questions. (Questions for written answer are most important in this respect, and their numbers have grown spectacularly in recent years.)

There is a further range of information which cannot, or will not, be readily given in general debate or even in answer to Questions. Some of this ministers may be happy to have published but it is complex and voluminous. Some needs considerable explanation and qualification if it is to make sense and not mislead people. But some ministers may not be anxious to give, especially not if it is to be published, but may be obliged to give if asked persistently and pressed to do

so. For extraction of these precious drops the select committee technique is essential. It is easy in debate in the
House or even in answer to Questions for a minister to
avoid giving information if he wishes so to do, or indeed in
such a context he may not be able to do so; a committee
which can request detailed papers and whose Members can
persist in asking searching Questions is far harder to deny.
Here ministers and civil servants representing them may be
obliged to give much information (some of it admittedly in
confidence and not for publication) that would otherwise
remain concealed on departmental files. Furthermore such
committees have, through other witnesses, alternative sources
of information which sometimes force a government to come
clean (or cleaner), if only so as to defend their policies or
decisions from misinformed criticism. A truly significant
extension of the work of select committees of enquiry, not
only in number but also on the range and depth of their
investigations – examining, for example, the problems of the
British motor industry and the value and control of government assistance to British Leyland and Chrysler – has been
one of the most important developments (or redevelopments,
for it was also done in the last century) in the House of
Commons in the later 1960s and in the 1970s.

Two other recent developments have also given Members
more effective access to information, much of it published but
requiring digesting and analyses. First the growth of the
House of Commons Library's research services has enabled
Members to be better briefed on many topics that come up
for debate. And secondly the increasing employment by
Members of personal research assistants may well have worked
to the same end. Finally the Parliamentary Commissioner
(Ombudsman), acting on behalf of Members, has enabled the
facts to be brought out about individual cases – often of
considerable significance to wider administrative or policy
decisions – that would otherwise not have emerged.

At the end of these processes, however, there still remains
much information at the bottom of the government's well that
will never be drained. In some fields, such as defence, this
may include the most important facts of all; elsewhere there

will remain much information of only incidental and temporary significance.

How far down the well the House should dip will remain a matter of argument. Totally open government would almost certainly mean timid and temporizing government. But equally, without some openness by ministers, and at least the techniques for seeking to secure the production of further information, we would have government behind closed doors, which is a total negation of the British Parliamentary system. The price of liberty is eternal vigilance and the price of democracy is eternal scrutiny. And the ever increasing extent, power and complexity of government requires that that scrutiny be more and better informed.

The House of Commons and the Public

The full exercise of opportunities for Parliamentary criticism and the development of effective techniques for getting information and expressing that criticism is not, however, sufficient. As already argued, Parliament's influence depends on its contacts with a wider public – both outward and inward. Again there is a continuing argument on how far this should go, which will no doubt also be reflected in the deliberations of the Procedure Committee. Some will argue that the House, in some sense, is a workshop, where Members should be left alone, without close participation by the public even as spectators, to get on with their work in the way they think proper. This view has, of course, great historical authority; after all for many years the proceedings of the House were not reported and most of the work of select committees has been conducted in private. On the other hand many people are increasingly aware of the danger of the House becoming a mere debating society where Members speak to other Members (although without, perhaps, any great expectations of ever influencing each other) but where the debates are little heeded outside. (This, it may be thought, is one of the problems of the House of Lords.)

In the later 1960s and the 1970s there have been limited, but significant, developments in this regard. In various ways the activities of Parliament have become more 'open', especially in regard to select committees. Until about 1965 no select committees had heard evidence in public for many years; now the great majority of hearings are open to the public (except when strictly confidential evidence is being given). Advance notices are also published in the Press of meetings of select committees and many committees issue Press statements about their work. As a result, select committees are much more extensively covered by the 'media' than they used to be (encouraged, of course, by the greater news-worthiness of some enquiries and the growing practice of taking evidence from ministers).

Another revived committee practice (the significance of which may have been too little noticed) has been the holding of 'grass-roots' enquiries. Committees such as the Select Committee on Education between 1967 and 1970 and that on Race Relations and Immigration have returned to the nineteenth-century style of enquiry by hearing much evidence away from London, and sometimes outside the UK, from witnesses directly concerned with the subject of enquiry. For example, when looking at the question of immigrants' relations with the police the committee were not content to take evidence from Home Office officials, senior police officers, the Race Relations Board, leaders of immigrant communities and other witnesses at national level, but they spent a number of days in several towns with large immigrant populations meeting informally, as well as taking evidence from, local police officers, community spokesmen, churchmen, social workers, etc., and many ordinary people, immigrant and indigenous, who represented no one but themselves. In Notting Hill, for example, they held an informal session one evening in a local café with a number of young immigrants, hearing their point of view at first-hand.

There may be dangers in this type of enquiry (how typical is the evidence, etc.), but from the point of view of the House's contact with the public the value is two-fold. First, an organ of Parliament goes away from Westminster and concerns itself – and is publicly seen to concern itself – with local problems of interest to many people. And naturally there is extensive coverage in the local Press and on local radio or television. As a result one side of the work of the House gets full publicity and the public at large are made aware of the way the committee are looking at the issues before them. And, secondly, Members are very directly made aware of what many people are thinking about these issues. More enquiries on these lines could do much to improve the dialogue between Parliament and the public.

Against the growth of publicity for select committee work, however, must be set the increasing difficulty for the Press in covering all the committee activities. It is not uncommon nowadays for about eight standing committees on bills and five or six select committees to sit on the same day, and many of them at the same time. This makes it extremely difficult for the general Press to cover the work of all these committees, and many meetings go unreported.

As far as standing committees and the House itself go there has, until recently, been little change. All their meetings are, of course, in public, but the great majority of the electorate are quite unaware of their debates except through the Press and radio and television news. However, after a number of experiments, committee reports, debates and votes, the House has now decided to permit the proceedings of the House to be broadcast on radio. Judging by public reaction to the broadcasting experiment there is widespread interest in the broadcast of debates and, when this becomes permanent, it may do more than anything done so far to enable Parliament to speak to the people. The question of television – both much more powerful and influential but also much more fraught with dangers in the eyes of some Members – will no doubt come up again. But if sound broadcasting succeeds this will undoubtedly change the argument in regard to television.

Last, and most important, one must refer to the role of the individual Member. His are, of course, the constant ears and eyes of the House. With varying degrees of success he measures public opinion in his constituency, or within his social, professional, business, industrial or otherwise specialist community, or he acquires relevant knowledge and briefing by reading the Press and specialist journals. Or he is briefed by pressure groups or experts. And to varying degrees he conveys this opinion, this information and these views to the House. He thus articulates the anxieties of the people. Similarly, by his reaction to events, through his activities within his party, by his contacts with ministers and other Members and finally by his public writing and speeches, both within the House and outside, he plays his part in mobilizing public opinion in favour of or against the government, their policies, and their actions. But even then the process is not complete without the action of the media in reporting, both locally and nationally, the proceedings of the House and its committees.

Thus it can be seen that, at every stage, the House, if it is to succeed in speaking both for and to the electorate, requires also the operation of a free Press (and one that spans at least as wide a range of political belief as is represented in the House) and of politically constructive broadcasting services. Parliament and the media must work in partnership – not necessarily harmoniously, not necessarily with one or the same voice, but at least with a realization that they are furthering the same aim: the effective working of Parliamentary democracy.

To a large extent this is achieved today. It may be thought that the pundits on *Panorama*, speaking to millions, have much more influence than any Member speaking in the House to a handful of Members and a few visitors in the gallery. But the important fact is that the topics that are discussed on television current affairs programmes are nearly always either matters which have come up in the House or are due to do so, or are matters which will be raised in the House following mass publicity by the media. The House remains the ultimate forum for the public discussion of the issues of the day. But without the Press, radio and television to feed it and to disseminate it, its proceedings would be much less effective.

The partnership is essential. It is, therefore, worrying that so much of the comment about Parliament in the Press demonstrates a mistaken perception of the functions of Parliament, leading to damaging and misleading criticism. It is even more worrying when there is no comment at all. It would also be a matter for concern if the House appeared to take the Press for granted and to do little to help the media to present its debates to the public; perhaps the debates are too often not really of interest to the public. It may well be that one of the challenges to the House of Commons in the next decade will be to devise procedures and practices that will make it easier for the House and its committees to present themselves to the wider public outside.

Some Recent Developments

The following chapters in this book consider in detail the current working of the House in its different aspects. It may be helpful here to refer to some of the most significant recent developments and to examine the relevance these have to the central concept of the House as a critical forum.

To all who work – as Members or staff – at the House of Commons, by far the most important change in recent years in the operations of the House (as opposed, that is, to the political scene) has simply been the growth of business. This has proved the case whatever party has been in power. It is, it may be thought, a function of two factors: first the volume of business, namely legislation, introduced into the House (and in measuring this, substance, i.e. political importance, is as significant as the number of pages or sections), and second, the time and effort that Members are prepared to devote to its consideration, and to other Parliamentary work.

There has been growth on both counts. Although, as Gavin Drewry shows, the *number* of government bills introduced each session has not grown markedly, the *length* of bills has increased (Parliament enacted 1416 pages of public Acts in 1963 and 2248 pages in 1973 – but in both cases this includes consolidation measures) and, though this is essentially impressionistic, the number of controversial bills introduced each Session appears to have been greater in recent years. There has also been a growth of delegated legislation, the consideration of which is also discussed by Gavin Drewry. And recent years have added the need to examine a massive volume of European 'secondary legislation', which is the subject of Professor Coombes's chapter.

As far as Members' own contribution is concerned, the greater willingness of Members to play an active part is shown primarily by two things: first, the great growth of written questions (perhaps partly resulting from the employment of research assistants) to which Sir Norman Chester draws attention; and, second, the extension of select committee activity, to which Nevil Johnson refers, which is largely work that Members themselves choose to do, rather than work, such as that on bills, which is thrust upon them.

Whatever the causes, the results are experienced by Members (and staff) in three ways. First, a great growth in the sittings of committees. In Session 1951–2 there were 66 meetings of standing committees and 278 meetings of select committees and their sub-committees; in Session 1971–2 the corresponding figures were 399 and 628. Second, by a lengthening of the sitting day; the average length (including Fridays) was $8\frac{3}{4}$ hours in 1951–2 and $9\frac{1}{4}$ hours in 1971–2. And, third, there has been in recent years a particularly hectic period in June and July which has frequently threatened (and occasionally violated) the treasured period of the summer Recess, and has lengthened the Session: the House sat on 157 days in 1951–2 and on 180 days in 1971–2.

This is not the place to consider possible changes in the sittings arrangements of the House. But the growing volume of business of all kinds does pose the question as to whether the House is using the available time in the best way for the critical scrutiny of the policies and activities of government. Dr Borthwick examines this problem in relation to the use of time on the floor of the House and draws attention to the high and rising percentage of time devoted there to various stages of government bills. Much of this is debate on the Report stage, often on detailed matters only of immediate interest to a few Members. And yet every Leader of the House will testify to the demand for debates on major issues, on the floor, to which he cannot accede because of shortage of time. It may be hoped that the Procedure Committee will review the use of time on the floor of the House.

Use of time is not the only issue. The use of techniques should also be questioned. For example, it may be asked whether the House is making the most sensible use of its committee system. Should, for example, select committee techniques be used in examining some bills, as Professor Griffith suggests (and as, indeed, the Procedure Committee recommended in 1971[4])? And is the way the present select committees are used and the subjects they are concerned with – which question is discussed by Dr Ann Robinson and Nevil Johnson – the best way of using this important tool of House of Commons scrutiny?

This last question becomes of increasing importance in view of the significant developments in the select committee field in the last ten years which Nevil Johnson and Dr Robinson describe. These include the hearing of ministers as well as civil servants, public hearings, the use of specialist advisers, a considerable increase in both the volume of evidence heard and published and in the length of the committees' reports, and, to some extent, the entry of select committees into more controversial areas of the political arena. This development of select committees clearly shows the House operating as a critical body. These committees are not making governmental decisions nor even legitimating the acts of government, but they are increasingly requiring Members and officials to explain and justify their policies and actions. Furthermore, as Johnson indicates, they have begun to concern themselves more with review of legislation or with urging the need for legislation, and their work in this way has proved influential.

The other major area – apart from legislation – where the House exercises a legitimating role (i.e. its formal authority is required), but where it takes no real decisions, is in the control of public expenditure. Dr Robinson discusses this in Chapter 7. Here I only make two broad points. First, the issue of public expenditure lies at the heart of government. Its level – and hence the level of taxation – and its allocation between services and purposes is the very stuff of politics. And yet the House has no systematic processes for the examination of expenditure policy across the board and over a period of years. Of course there are many regular opportunities for discussing expenditure – on the Budget debate and on Supply Days for example, and in addition, after Chancellors of the Exchequer have announced expenditure cuts or have produced their annual Public Expenditure White Papers (giving a forward look at government spending for five years ahead), debates are held, which are often lively and politically significant (in the 1975–6 session the government were defeated in one such debate). Yet none of this matches the more systematic and relatively sophisticated methods of the government in planning and determining public expenditure that have been developed in Whitehall since the Plowden Report, and, in particular, the annual PESC exercise. In this field the only significant Parliamentary development has been the establishment of the Expenditure Committee, the General Sub-Committee of which does look at the Government's own methods of planning and control in a critical way.

A second notable feature of the House's procedures in relation to expenditure control or criticism is the way scrutiny of 'expenditure' tends to be separated out as a separate issue – through the institution of Supply Days, money resolutions, the Expenditure Committee, etc. – rather than being looked at as part of a continuing and interrelated process together with policy formulation, legislation, delegated legislation and administrative action. The House, for example, has separate committees for examining bills, Statutory Instruments and the Estimates, although the public expenditure decisions that will flow from an Act and which will be reflected in the Annual Estimates of future years cannot be separated from the decision on the bill itself. However this has been the pattern of the House's regard for public money for many years. Now that Supply Days have ceased to be occasions for controlling Government spending, perhaps the interrelationship between policy and legislative decision on the one hand and expenditure planning and allocation on the other needs to be reconsidered in the House of Commons.

Conclusion

This is not the place, and I am not the person, to advance views on the reform of Parliament. In this chapter I have simply attempted to provide a conceptual analysis of the function of Parliament as a critical, rather than governing, body, which seem to me to make more sense of some of the House of Commons operations in the 1970s than some of its critics will allow. And I have tried to illustrate, with some examples, how the House performs this function. However, few people are complacent about the working of the House of Commons today, even regarded in this light. There is a widespread belief that the House has failed to develop techniques and procedures to enable it to match the growing complexity and power of government with effective and continuing critical scrutiny. There is also a feeling in many quarters that the House is in danger of growing out of touch with, and has lost the sympathy of, its own immediate power base, namely the public by whom it is elected.

These matters are yet again under review at the time of writing. This review is given added impetus by the additional strains that may be put on the House if we are to enter a long period characterized by narrow party majorities, by a growth of minority and national parties, and perhaps by minority governments. Again it is not for me to comment or speculate on these changes (my fellow editor, Stuart Walkland, gives his own view on the role of the House under these circumstances in the final chapter). However, it may well be that, whatever the extent of the changes involved in these new features of British political life, much of the work of the House will go on much as before. Governments will still require majorities in the House for their legislation, for their expenditure and for their taxes. And all elements of the House – particularly the official opposition, the minor parties and back-benchers – will continue to have opportunities to require the government publicly to explain and account for their policies and actions before it gives formal sanction to these requests.

This, in my view, is the way the House has traditionally

worked (and we have had minority governments before, without the role of the House being radically changed). This is how it works in the 1970s. And, personally, I am convinced that the House of Commons, provided it develops effective and critical procedures to match the power of government, and provided it always speaks both for and to the people, will continue to be the lively, effective and influential body that our system of Parliamentary democracy requires.

2 The Members of Parliament

MICHAEL RUSH

The House of Commons is substantially middle class in its composition and, with one possibly significant exception to which we will return later, this remains true no matter how class is defined. Moreover, it is, to paraphrase Dunning's motion, a trend which has grown during the twentieth century, continues to grow and, some would say, ought to be diminished. This having been said, it could be dismissed as interesting but of little real significance. After all, the fact that the House of Commons is in many respects unrepresentative of the electorate is well known. This has long been true in socio-economic terms, but it is, of course, also true in electoral terms.

For example, even between 1931 and 1970, when the combined vote of the Conservative and Labour Parties averaged 91 per cent of the votes cast at general elections,[1] only in 1931 and 1935 did either party receive an absolute majority of the votes cast, although one of them always received an absolute majority of the seats in the Commons. It is likely, however, that the majority of the electorate was unaware of the relationship between votes and seats and, even if they were, showed little or no concern about it until the much greater electoral distortions of February and October 1974. By producing a minority government in February 1974 and the first post-war majority government with less than 40 per cent of the votes cast, these two elections, more than all the pleadings of those who had long campaigned for proportional representation, showed vividly how the electoral system favoured the two major parties at the expense of their minority rivals.

Obviously the electoral system is a major factor in determining the composition of the House of Commons, notably in almost certainly producing a greater turnover of seats than would occur under proportional representation, since under the simple plurality it requires only a small swing of the electoral pendulum to produce substantial gains for one major party and losses for the other. Thus for every 1 per cent electoral swing between Conservative and Labour between sixteen and eighteen seats change hands. This factor became even more important as the electorate appeared to become more volatile in its behaviour during the sixties and seventies, generally producing larger swings than those of the four general elections between 1950 and 1959 and, more particularly, swinging from one party to the other over a much shorter time span. The Conservative majority of a hundred in 1959, 'built up' over four elections, was eradicated in a single election in 1964 and replaced by a similar Labour majority in 1966, which was in turn overthrown by a strong swing to the Conservatives in 1970, who in turn again lost office in February 1974.

However, as a factor directly affecting the *turnover* of the House of Commons from one election to another, the swing of the pendulum should not be exaggerated, although it has assumed greater importance with increased electoral volatility. It is important to bear in mind the fact that the majority of the seats in the Commons – at least two thirds – are 'safe' seats, held securely election after election by one or other of the two major parties. For the Members holding these constituencies election and re-election is normally a formality, always provided the Member is not refused readoption by his local party, or disowned by the national party organization, or chooses to part company with his party, all of which are comparatively rare occurrences. Once elected for such a constituency a Member will normally continue to be re-elected until he decides to retire from Parliament. On average, in the post-war period MPs whose parliamentary careers have ended with voluntary retirement have served approximately sixteen years, although the range is considerable as some Members serve as long as thirty or forty years in the House. Sometimes, of course, death intervenes before retirement, usually causing a by-election, or a Member resigns or accepts a peerage, again usually causing a by-election. Nonetheless, no matter what terminates his membership of the Commons, the career of an MP sitting for a 'safe' seat will normally span several general elections.

The turnover of the House of Commons is therefore the product of three factors: the swing of the electoral pendulum resulting in the defeat of sitting Members, the retirement of MPs, and by-elections. It has been calculated that the average turnover of MPs from one Parliament to another since 1945 is 21 per cent, but this may be very low when elections follow swiftly in succession, as they did in 1950 and 1951, when it was 12 per cent, and February and October 1974, when it was 7 per cent. Of the average 21 per cent turnover, 7 per cent has been due to the defeat of sitting MPs, 8 per cent to retirement and 6 per cent to by-elections.[2]

A more fundamental factor than turnover in determining the composition of the Commons, however, is the process by which MPs are selected. This is, of course, the responsibility of the political parties, but this responsibility rests largely on the local constituency parties rather than the national party organizations or the national leadership. In practice the national party can usually veto the candidature of a candidate it does not like, but can seldom ensure the selection of a candidate it favours, and even the negative power of veto is used most sparingly. Exceptions, apparent or otherwise, in which the national party has had some influence, such as the selection of Sir Alec Douglas-Home for Kinross and West Perthshire, following the disclaimer of his peerage and appointment as Prime Minister in 1963, or the selection of Patrick Gordon Walker at Leyton in 1965, following his defeat at Smethwick in 1964, are, at best, exceptions which prove the general rule. A major responsibility for the composition of the House of Commons therefore lies with constituency parties – a fact which holds true in almost every constituency regardless of party or the relative safeness or marginality of the seat. This is so because the majority of *candidates* stand on behalf of and are selected by local constituency *parties*, and in only a very small number of constituencies is any sort of independent or non-party candidate likely to be elected. Indeed, in many cases the traditional party

loyalties of the electorate are such that the effective choice
lies between the Conservative and Labour candidates, although
the increased success of the Liberals, the Scottish National
Party and the Plaid Cymru in recent elections has provided
a wider choice in a significant minority of constituencies.[3]

What sort of House of Commons in socio-economic terms
is produced by these factors? How unrepresentative of the
electorate is the House of Commons? To answer these questions we now examine the sex, age, education, occupations
and social class of all MPs elected at the three general elections of 1970, February 1974 and October 1974. Table 1
gives a breakdown of these MPs according to party affiliation.

In spite of the inroads made by the third parties, the
Commons remained overwhelmingly dominated by the Conservative and Labour Parties in the three elections. The
Liberals, with other third party and independent MPs, comprised just over 5 per cent of the 821 MPs elected, but it is
important to note that in October 1974 this proportion was
6·1 per cent compared with only 1·2 per cent in 1970. Moreover, third party intervention was sufficient to cause a minority
government following the February election and leave Labour
with a majority of only three after the October election. The
extent to which the two elections presage a fundamental and
long-lasting change in the party system is beyond the scope
of this chapter, but should any change occur it could have
some affect on the socio-economic composition of the House
of Commons. Yet, as we shall see, although there are significant differences in the socio-economic backgrounds of MPs
from different parties, there are greater differences on the
whole between MPs and the electorate which returns them to
Westminster.

In socio-economic terms the most unrepresentative characteristic of the House of Commons is the presence of so few
women MPs: the largest number of women ever elected to
Parliament was in 1964, when twenty-nine women became
MPs, but these comprised a mere 4·6 per cent of all MPs.
In 1970 and in February and October 1974 the proportions
were 4·1 per cent (26), 3·6 per cent (23) and 4·2 per cent (27)
respectively. There is little doubt that prejudice against

TABLE I: Party affiliation[1] of the MPs elected in 1970, February 1974 and October 1974.

Party affiliation	Number	%
Conservative	395	48·1
Labour	376	45·8
Liberal	15	1·8
Scottish National Party	11	
Plaid Cymru	3	
United Ulster Unionist Council	12	
Social Democratic & Labour Party	1	
Social Democratic[2]	1	
Independent Labour[3]	2	4·3
Independent[4]	1	
Unity[5]	1	
Independent Unity[6]	1	
Mr Speaker[7]	2	
Total	821	100·0

Notes:
1. Where a Member was elected under more than one party label at different elections, the party label under which he was last elected has been used. This applies to only five MPs.
2. Dick Taverne, former Labour MP for Lincoln, who was refused readoption by his local party, resigned his seat in 1972 and won the ensuing by-election in March 1973. He retained the seat in February 1974 but lost it in October 1974.
3. S. O. Davies, former Labour MP for Merthyr Tydfil, who was refused readoption by his local party on grounds of age and who fought and won the seat as an Independent, but died in 1971, and Edward Milne, former Labour MP for Blyth, who was also refused readoption by his local party and fought the seat as Independent Labour, winning it in February 1974 but losing it in October 1974.
4. Frank Maguire, elected for Fermanagh and South Tyrone in October 1974.
5. Frank McManus, elected for Fermanagh and South Tyrone in 1970 and defeated in February 1974.
6. Miss Bernadette Devlin (Mrs McAliskey), elected for Mid-Ulster in 1969 and defeated in February 1974.
7. Mr Speaker King (now Lord Maybray-King) in 1970 and Mr Speaker Lloyd (now Lord Selwyn-Lloyd) in February and October 1974.

women candidates and MPs exists among the selectors in many local parties, though it is probably prompted less by simple misogyny and more by an apparent reluctance to believe that women are just as capable as men of being effective Members of Parliament. Such evidence as exists, however, suggests that an equal, if not more important, factor, is that of *supply* – simply that considerably fewer women actually seek selection as parliamentary candidates.[4]

The area in which there is the closest socio-economic correspondence between MPs and their constituents is that of age, but even here the contrast is marked and the phrase 'closest correspondence' is hardly appropriate.

TABLE 2: Age of MPs elected in 1970, February 1974 and October 1974.

Age[1]	Conservative	Labour	Liberal	Other	Total
	%	%			%
Under 30	1·0(4)	1·3(5)	–	4	1·6(13)
30–39	13·4(53)	13·3(50)	4	9	14·1(116)
40–49	34·2(135)	30·6(115)	7	11	32·6(268)
50–59	28·3(112)	26·9(101)	3	5	26·9(221)
60–69	16·5(65)	19·1(72)	1	3	17·3(141)
70 or over	6·6(26)	8·8(33)	–	2	7·4(61)
Not known	–	–	–	1	0·1(1)
Total	100·0(395)	100·0(376)	15	35	100·0(821)

Note: 1. Age was calculated according to the Member's age at the time of the last general election at which he was elected, e.g. for an MP who was elected in 1970 and retired or was defeated in October 1974, his age was taken as in February 1974; for an MP elected in all three elections his age was taken as in October 1974.

Table 2 shows that nearly three fifths of all MPs elected between 1970 and 1974 were aged between forty and fifty-nine, approximately a sixth were under forty and nearly a quarter were over sixty. Compared with the adult population only two age groups (30–39 and 60–69) were represented in similar proportions among MPs. The youngest age group (under 30), consisting of 21 per cent of the adult population, accounted for less than 2 per cent of MPs, and the oldest group (70 or over) were considerably under-represented. The two middle age groups (40–49 and 50–59) were represented in the Commons in twice the proportion found in the adult population. All this, however, is hardly surprising. On the whole, local parties expect would-be MPs to have had some experience in both work and politics before they are prepared to select them for constituencies which are 'safe' for the party concerned or at least marginal and therefore 'winnable'. Thus the commonest age at which MPs are *first* elected to Parliament is between thirty and forty-nine, with a considerable concentration between thirty-five and forty-five. On the other hand, most MPs now retire in their sixties, although a few septuagenarians continue to stand for re-election. In addition some local parties begin to place pressure on their MPs to retire once they have reached or are approaching normal retiring age.

There is little difference in the age distribution between the parties in the three elections and the median ages of Conservative, Labour and Liberal MPs in October 1974 was 47, 49 and 35 respectively,[5] although a higher proportion of Labour MPs were aged sixty or over. This is in contrast to the situation which prevailed in 1964 and earlier, when Labour MPs were on average significantly older than their Conservative colleagues. As recently as 1959 and 1964 the median age of Labour MPs was seven years older than that of Conservatives.[6] This convergence of age distribution between the two major parties is probably due to two major factors: first, the willingness since the mid-sixties of constituency Labour parties to adopt more candidates under forty and, second, the introduction from 1964 of a pension scheme for MPs, which reduced the necessity almost certainly felt by a number of Labour Members to postpone retirement from Parliament.

If age marks the closest correspondence between Members and their constituents, however, then the contrast found in other socio-economic characteristics is likely to be sharp indeed. How far this is the case in terms of education is clearly shown in Table 3.

TABLE 3. The educational background of MPs elected in 1970, February 1974 and October 1974.

	Conservative %	Labour %	Liberal	Other	Total %
A. Level of full-time education					
Elementary	0·5(2)	7·7(29)	–	–	3·8(31)
Secondary	25·1(99)	22·4(84)	4	11	24·1(198)
Elementary/ secondary plus	4·8(19)	16·2(61)	1	2	10·1(83)
University	69·6(275)	53·7(202)	10	22	62·0(509)
Total	100·0(395)	100·0(376)	15	35	100·0(821)
B. University education					
Oxford	28·6(113)	15·1(57)	4	2	21·4(176)
Cambridge	24·0(95)	5·6(21)	2	3	14·7(121)
Other univ.	12·9(51)	33·0(124)	4	17	23·8(196)
Service coll.	4·1(16)	–	–	–	2·0(16)
Non-univ.	30·4(120)	46·3(174)	5	13	38·0(312)
Total	100·0(395)	100·0(376)	15	35	99·9(821)
C. Attendance at public school					
Public school	76·7(303)	19·1(72)	11	7	47·9(393)
Non-public school	23·3(92)	80·9(304)	4	28	52·1(428)
Total	100·0(395)	100·0(376)	15	35	100·0(821)

More than three fifths of the MPs elected at the three elections were university graduates, and over a third were graduates of either Oxford or Cambridge. Compared with this, between 3 and 4 per cent of the adult population are university graduates. Similarly, in the early seventies Oxford and Cambridge accounted for less than 10 per cent of the undergraduate population and, even allowing for the fact that these two universites would account for a higher proportion of graduates prior to the post-war expansion of universities, they remain considerably over-represented. The contrast with the population at large remains when attendance at public school is examined: nearly half the MPs attended public schools, compared with approximately 4 per cent of the adult population.

There are, of course, notable differences between the parties: more university graduates are found among the Conservatives and the overwhelming majority of Conservative graduates are from Oxford and Cambridge, whereas the majority of Labour graduates are LSE or provincial university products; the majority of those who attended public schools are Conservatives, but even the Labour proportion of public-school products is between four and five times the national average. There has, however, again been a convergence between the two major parties: between 1918 and 1935 approximately a fifth of Labour MPs were graduates; in 1945 this rose to a third and it is now more than half. Similarly, between 1918 and 1935 less than 10 per cent of Labour MPs had attended public schools; by 1945 it had risen to 22 per cent, falling only marginally to 19 per cent in the seventies.

This same pattern of contrast with the adult population and convergence between the two major parties is also found in the occupational background of MPs. (See Table 4.)

Nearly two thirds of the MPs elected in these three elections were members of the professions; nearly a third pursued various business occupations; rather less than a fifth had various miscellaneous occupations such as journalist, social worker or professional party worker; and little more than an eighth were routine manual or non-manual workers. Compared with the electorate the figures speak for themselves: with only one MP in eight a worker and over two thirds engaged in the professions or business, the House of Commons is hardly a microcosm of the working population.

There is also, of course, a contrast between the two major parties in that the overwhelming majority of businessmen are Conservatives and all but four of the workers Labour

TABLE 4. Occupations[1] of MP elected in 1970, February 1974 and October 1974.

Occupation	Conservative	Labour	Liberal	Other	Total
	%	%			%
Professions	30·9(122)	42·8(161)	9	17	37·6(309)
Business	57·0(225)	5·1(19)	4	13	31·8(261)
Workers	1·0(4)	27·6(104)	–	3	13·5(111)
Miscellaneous	11·1(44)	24·4(92)	2	2	17·1(140)
Total	100·0(395)	99·9(376)	15	35	100·0(821)

Note: 1. Occupations have been classified according to the Member's principal occupation prior to election. Many MPs, especially on the Conservative side of the House, accept company directorships and develop various business interests after their election and an analysis based on such considerations would produce significantly different figures, although these would not invalidate the principal conclusions of the occupational analysis that follows.

MPs. Moreover, although both parties, especially Labour, draw heavily on the professions, lawyers are the principal Conservative and teachers the principal Labour professional group. Of greater significance, however, is the extent to which the two parties have again converged since 1918. Between 1918 and 1935 over 70 per cent of Labour MPs were routine manual or non-manual workers, the majority being manual workers in fact; by 1945 this proportion had fallen to little more than 40 per cent; and by the 1970s to less than 30 per cent. Taking the figures on education and occupation as a rough indication of social class, there is little doubt that the House of Commons is now predominantly middle class in its socio-economic composition, and this is confirmed more explicitly by an analysis according to the Hall–Jones scale of occupational prestige.

The Hall–Jones scale of occupational prestige ranks occupations in seven classes, one of which is sub-divided into two. Some four fifths of the adult population are found in Classes 4–7. In contrast to this 90·8 per cent of Conservative MPs and 53·4 per cent of Labour MPs are found in Classes 1 and 2,

TABLE 5. Analysis of the occupations of MPs elected in 1970, February 1974 and October 1974 according to the Hall–Jones scale of occupational prestige.

Class	Conservative	Labour	Liberal	Other	Total
	%	%			%
Class 1	47·4(187)	28·2(106)	9	13	38·4(315)
Class 2	43·5(172)	25·2(95)	6	16	35·2(289)
Class 3	8·1(32)	23·2(87)	–	3	14·8(122)
Class 4	0·5(2)	10·4(39)	–	1	5·1(42)
Class 5a	–	2·1(8)	–	1	1·1(9)
Class 5b	0·5(2)	6·4(24)	–	–	3·2(26)
Class 6	–	4·5(17)	–	1	2·2(18)
Class 7	–	–	–	–	–
Total	100·0(395)	100·0(376)	15	35	100·0(821)

Note: Short definitions of the classes on the scale are as follows:
Class 1 – professionally qualified and high administrative;
Class 2 – managerial and executive (with some responsibility for directing and initiating policy);
Class 3 – inspectional, supervisory and other non-manual (higher grade);
Class 4 – inspectional, supervisory and other non-manual (lower grade);
Class 5a– routine grades of non-manual work;
Class 5b– skilled manual;
Class 6 – manual, semi-skilled;
Class 7 – manual, routine.

and only 1 per cent of Conservative MPs and 23·4 per cent of Labour MPs in Classes 4–7.

Class is, of course, a controversial term and no doubt different figures would be produced by different definitions, particularly if subjective class identification were used. Many Labour Members are by most definitions of class clearly middle class, but many are also first or second generation members of the middle class and if an analysis based on parental or family background were undertaken more Labour MPs would be classified as working class. Unfortunately, it has not been possible at this stage to conduct such an analysis, but even so it is important to bear in mind that an important contrast between Labour MPs who are first- or second-generation members of the middle class and many of their pre-war predecessors would remain: many of these predecessors were working class no matter what definition is used; many latter-day Labour MPs would, whatever their familial antecedents or indeed their subjective feelings, be widely *regarded*, certainly by many of their constituents, as middle class rather than working class.

The socio-economic convergence of the two major parties which has taken place since the rise of the Labour Party as a major electoral force is marked, however, by a greater movement on the part of the Labour Party than the Conservatives. It is true that since 1900 the Conservative Party has seen the disappearance of the 'country gentleman' and a very considerable decline of its aristocratic element, and both groups have been replaced by an influx of businessmen and members of the professions, but much greater changes have occurred among the ranks of Labour MPs. The reasons for these changes in the composition of the Parliamentary Labour Party are undoubtedly complex and it is particularly difficult to distinguish between the significance on the one hand of *demand* – what sort of individuals constituency Labour parties wish to adopt as prospective MPs – and *supply* – what sort of individuals are offering themselves as prospective MPs. However, some of the important factors are easy enough to delineate, even if their relative significance is difficult to assess.

Some factors undoubtedly influence the recruitment of parliamentary candidates regardless of party. One of the most important is that some occupations facilitate a political career, sometimes because it is possible to resume that occupation should a political career be interrupted or terminated, sometimes because it is possible to pursue that occupation on a part-time basis at the same time as a political career, sometimes because that occupation provides the individual with the financial security and time to lay the foundations of a political career, and in many cases some combination of these. Other factors probably affect the Labour Party more than the Conservative Party. For instance, the enormous widening of educational opportunities has helped to create conditions of greater social mobility and given many people a university education, or some other form of further education, which in earlier generations would have been denied them. On the whole, this widening of educational opportunities has benefited the middle class, rather than the working class, but it has opened up the lower echelons of the middle class to political recruitment, particularly by the Labour Party. At the same time, working-class individuals who, forty or fifty years ago, would have risen to the ranks of the PLP through the trade-union movement, have, in some cases, found different routes to the House of Commons. Others, who have retained their links with the union movement have, nonetheless, secured middle-class jobs. There has also been a decline in the ability of industrial trade unions to dominate the selection process in particular constituencies and, in some cases, faced with competition from able and articulate non-union candidates, unions have themselves supported candidates whose links with the unions do not stem from their occupations. This is particularly true of the two general unions, the TGWU and the NUGMW, who have increasingly sponsored MPs from the professional and managerial classes. Furthermore, although the proportion of trade-union-sponsored MPs rose slightly in the sixties and seventies, compared with the fifties, and now constitutes 40 per cent of all Labour MPs, this increase is largely accounted for by the practice of industrial unions sponsoring middle-class candidates and more particularly by the increased activity of the 'white collar' trade unions, whose proportion of union-sponsored MPs has risen from 8 per cent in 1964 to 21 per cent in October 1974, and many of whose candidates are middle class rather than working class.

Probably one of the most important factors, however, in accounting for the middle-class composition of the PLP is the impact of increased social mobility over two or three generations which has provided the Labour Party with recruits, who have all the attributes of a middle-class background in terms of education and occupation, but who also have some claim to working-class origins – origins which may well explain why these individuals sought to become Labour rather than Conservative MPs. It is also likely that many constituency Labour parties find it difficult to resist selecting well-educated and often highly articulate middle-class individuals in preference to less well-educated and sometimes less articulate individuals from lower down the social scale.

Whatever explanation accounts for the substantially middle-class composition of the House of Commons, it remains pertinent to ask whether the socio-economic characteristics of MPs have any importance in determining anything. Elite and class theorists would, of course, reply that we need look no further than establishing that a dominant elite or class exists in the legislature and that this is significant in itself. The problem with elite and class theories, however, is that they tend to rely heavily on *prima facie* or circumstantial evidence that a group of individuals with common socio-economic characteristics hold positions of power without necessarily establishing that there is any relationship between the *exercise* of power and these common socio-economic characteristics. Furthermore, it is not always clear whether such theorists are arguing that elites or ruling classes exercise power consciously or subconsciously in response to their elite or class membership.

It is not necessary to subscribe to elite or class theories, however, to argue that the socio-economic composition of the House of Commons could be of some significance. It may, for example, be significant because people *believe* that the degree to which the Commons is socio-economically representative of the electorate is important. Thus, if a view develops that there are too many or too few male or female, young or old, graduate or non-graduate, public school or non-public school, working-class or middle-class Members of Parliament, then this could be an important factor in determining the attitude of people towards Parliament. Certainly there are those who believe that the Commons would be improved if it were a microcosm or more nearly a microcosm of the electorate. Or again, if some relationship, causal or predictive or both, could be established between the socio-economic characteristics of MPs and their behaviour and attitudes, then the socio-economic composition of the Commons would clearly be of importance.

It hardly bears repeating, however, that the most important

determinant of political behaviour in the House of Commons is party and that there is no evidence that the socio-economic composition of the House has any bearing on a Member's choice in the division lobbies, although it may help to explain why he supports one party rather than another. Of course, if MPs were little more than lobby fodder then their socio-economic backgrounds are perhaps relevant only in providing the requisite number of suitably docile and loyal Members, but, if the role of Parliament and of individual MPs goes beyond the division lobby, then, depending on the nature of that role, the socio-economic composition of the House assumes greater importance. Indeed, even assuming that MPs are primarily lobby fodder, sustaining their parties in government or opposition, in one important respect the socio-economic composition of the House is of considerable importance: whatever the reality of the constitutional dependence of the government on the House of Commons, the fact that the persons who form the government are drawn almost entirely from the Commons cannot be over-emphasized. In causal terms this relates to the process by which candidates are selected, but the Prime Minister is by and large confined to the pool of talent in his party in the Commons when he comes to form his government or subsequently reshuffle it.

The role of Parliament and of the individual Member is not a matter on which there is general agreement, either in respect of what those roles are or what they ought to be. But as far as the House of Commons is concerned it is possible to argue that it performs a number of important political functions, apart from that of ministerial recruitment, including the legitimizing of governmental policies and actions, the representation of the electorate, the authorization of taxation and public expenditure, the provision of a channel for the redress of grievances, the passing of legislation, and, perhaps above all, the scrutiny of and provision of a means by which the public can be informed about the government's policies and activities. It can be further argued that each Member may fulfil several of these functions individually, over and above their collective performance by the House itself. Even assuming the acceptance of these roles, however, it remains a matter of dispute as to how effectively they are performed, whether collectively or individually. Nonetheless, however imperfectly they may be performed, it is likely that their performance will be affected by the types of MPs who are elected. The relationship between the socio-economic characteristics of MPs and their activities and interests in the House of Commons remains as yet largely unresearched, but it may be of significance in determining or predicting the attitudes of MPs towards their roles as Members of Parliament. There is, in fact, some evidence that in this area of attitudes towards Parliament the views of MPs cut across party lines.

One of the features of Parliamentary developments in the sixties was the increasing reformist mood inside and outside the House of Commons, a mood which produced an expansion of select committee activity and an even greater expansion of the services and facilities available to MPs. In their study, *The Member of Parliament and His Information*, Barker and Rush found some association between the background of MPs regardless of party, and the extent to which they favoured expanded information facilities, the greater use of specialized select committees and a desire to have the help of a research assistant.[7] Following the election of 1970 Barker and Rush also found strong support among newly elected MPs for specialized committees and for the view that MPs ought to be full-time or nearly full-time Members.[8] The reformist atmosphere of the sixties was also reflected in an unprecedented expansion of the services and facilities available to MPs, including a considerable increase in their salaries and allowances – a process which, in spite of increasing economic difficulties, continued in the early seventies. MPs now receive a salary of £6062, a secretarial allowance, free postage and telephone calls on Parliamentary business, various travel allowances and a subsistence allowance when Parliament is sitting. Rooms or 'desk-spaces' are available for all MPs and extensive information services are provided by the House of Commons Library.[9]

There is little doubt that the attitude of MPs, especially more recently elected Members, towards their Parliamentary role has become more demanding and this is reflected in the increase in the number of full-time or nearly full-time MPs. The demands on Members have also increased as the constituency 'welfare officer' role has increased, as select committee activity has expanded, and as governments have introduced, if not always more legislation, certainly longer and more complex bills, quite apart from the impact of Britain's entry to the EEC, with its flood of Community regulations. As early as 1971 the Boyle Committee reported that the average number of hours per week spent on Parliamentary business by individual MPs was 63,[10] and this figure has almost certainly increased. Barker and Rush suggested that the attitudes of MPs towards Parliament may owe a good deal to their Parliamentary experience, especially when they were first elected,[11] and in this context the Parliamentary experience of those elected in the three elections of 1970–4 may be pertinent.

TABLE 6: Parliamentary service of MPs elected in 1970, February 1974 and October 1974.

First elected	Conservative	Labour	Liberal	Other	Total
	%	%			%
Prior to 1945	2·8(11)	1·1(4)	–	1	1·9(16)
1945–9	4·3(17)	13·6(51)	–	1	8·4(69)
1950–9	34·2(135)	16·5(62)	2	3	24·6(202)
1960–9	21·0(83)	35·9(135)	6	7	28·2(231)
1970 or later	37·7(149)	32·9(124)	7	23	36·9(303)
Total	100·0(395)	100·0(376)	15	35	100·0(821)

Note: In a minority of cases MPs experienced a gap in their parliamentary service, although in most cases this did not last longer than a single Parliament.

Table 6 shows that nearly two thirds of the MPs elected in the three elections were first elected in 1960 or later, with a further quarter elected in the fifties, leaving only 10 per cent who first entered Parliament before 1950. By October 1974 only two MPs, G. R. Strauss (Labour Member for Lambeth-Vauxhall since 1929) and John Parker (Labour Member for

Dagenham since 1935), had been members of pre-war Parliaments. In numerical terms, therefore, the House of Commons
is now dominated by MPs elected in the sixties and seventies
and their attitudes towards what Parliament should do and
what they as individual MPs should do may be crucial.

The reformers of the sixties wished to see a House of
Commons which was capable of effectively scrutinizing the
executive and some advances towards that goal were achieved.
However, the continued impact of the adversary system, with
its stress on governmental control of the House of Commons,
tended to frustrate the reformers' fuller ambitions. Of course,
it is possible that the two-party system has begun to break
down in a way which will profoundly affect the adversary
system, but unless or until that happens the choice may lie
between the adversary system in its present form and more
effective scrutiny of the executive: between governments
which more often than not insist on having their way in the
Commons and governments which are prepared to modify
their programmes and policies in the light of parliamentary
criticism.

In this context there is no evidence that Parliament or the
nation would necessarily be better served by a House of
Commons which was a microcosm of the electorate, but it is
at least arguable that a House which contained more women,
fewer graduates (or at least a wider spectrum of graduates),
fewer products of public schools and a greater variety of
occupations, would have the advantage of drawing on a
broader and deeper pool of knowledge and experience and
would add rather than detract from Parliament's ability to
scrutinize the executive. And yet so much depends on what
the late Harry Hanson called the *purpose* of Parliament, for
the socio-economic composition of the House of Commons
has little relevance unless Parliament has a sense of purpose.

3 The Floor of the House

R. L. BORTHWICK

What happens on the floor of the House of Commons is a reflection of the prevailing temper and style of our political system. It is a result of history and the consequences of the preceding general election, thereby compelling us to remember that we must view the matter in political as well as more narrowly procedural terms. For most of the post-war period we have been accustomed to the idea that Britain had a two-party system which produced a Government whose job it was to govern (whatever the relationship between the proportion of its votes in the country and its seats in the House) and an opposition whose task it was to act as a critic but whose prospects of defeating the Government were not nearer than the next election. The two general Elections of 1974 cast doubts on the continuing validity of these assumptions. As this is written we may be in a transitional stage as regards the role of the House of Commons. The continuance of the twin features of a pure (or almost so) two-party system and a government little likely to be defeated on the floor of the House can no longer be so confidently assumed. Against this background it is important to analyse what has happened on the floor of the House in recent years, and to suggest what might or should happen in what remains of the 1970s.

How does the House spend its time? Inevitably no session is typical but the two examined here have the virtue of having run for a whole year (unlike some others recently). Session 1972–3, during a Conservative Government, was the third session of the 1970–4 Parliament and ran from 31 October 1972 to 25 October 1973. The second example, the first session of a Parliament, was during a Labour administration and ran for just over a year, from 22 October 1974[1] to 12 November 1975. Ideally one would have liked sessions more nearly equal in length. 1972–3 comes nearer to be a typical session, at 164 sitting days compared with the 194 days of the 1974–5 session.[2] In 1972–3 the House sat for a total of just over 1457 hours and an average sitting of 8 hours 53 minutes. In 1974–5 the House sat for just over 1828 hours giving an average length of sitting at 9 hours 26 minutes.

In the table that follows there are a number of categories that may appear somewhat arbitrary.[3] For example, the main elements in the miscellaneous category are Questions and Ministerial Statements. It includes also the time taken on requests for the adjournment of the House under S.O. No. 9, on the introduction of private Members' bills under the Ten minute Rule, as well as on other minor procedural matters. Equally, as Professor Richards has noted,[4] one cannot always make the categories watertight: matters relating to the European Economic Community, for example, are under-counted in the table because the subject can occur on other procedures such as debates on government motions or Supply Days, as well as on the special procedure devised for handling European matters.[5]

Of the items listed in this table, several are considered elsewhere – for example, government and private Members' legislation, and Questions – so that consideration of them can be briefer here than they would otherwise merit. Question Time accounts for the bulk of the miscellaneous category. It is restricted to rather less than an hour a day and the House has resisted pressure to expand that time. Perhaps the most striking thing to emerge from the figures is the very substantial share of the House's time occupied by Government legislation. In both the sessions examined it is by far the largest single item: in 1972–3 it accounted for almost 32 per cent of the time (exactly that if one includes time spent debating a guillotine resolution); while in 1974–5 just under 38 per cent of the time (just over with guillotine resolutions included) or a little under 700 out of the 1828 hours that the House sat. The latter figure may be inflated by the fact that this was the first session of a Parliament and of a government with a very heavy legislative programme, but it would seem that around one third of the time of the House is spent

Distribution of time on the floor of The House of Commons

	SESSION 1972-73		SESSION 1974-75	
Miscellaneous[1]	hrs – mins 206-10	per cent 14·1	hrs – mins 262-22	per cent 14·4
Government Bills	465-35	31·9	688-49	37·7
Government Motions	176-00	12·1	175-16	9·6
Private Members' Bills	63-05	4·3	57-18	3·1
Private Members' Motions	50-41	3·4	54-34	3·0
Statutory Instruments	109-11	7·5	94-11	5·2
Supply	155-21	10·7	163-44	9·0
Daily Adjournment	80-14	5·5	89-13	4·9
Recess Adjournment[2]	29-52	2·1	29-21	1·6
S.O.9 Adjournment	3-10	0·2	3-13	0·2
Second Reading Con. Fund Bills	41-48	2·9	54-47	3·0
Ways & Means Debates	21-35	1·5	42-10	2·3
Allocation of Time orders	1-56	0·1	11-29	0·6
Debate on the Address	38-23	2·6	38-42	2·1
Private business	14-20	1·0	18-10	1·0
Measures	–	–	8-06	0·4
EEC business	–	–	36-41	2·0
TOTAL	1457-21	99·9	1828-06	100·1

on government legislation in each session. By contrast, private Members' legislation occupies a rather small share of the time of the House: around 60 hours in each of the sessions, though, as noted earlier, this does not include the time spent on many Tuesdays and Wednesdays in the session when private Members are allowed to seek to introduce bills under the Ten minute Rule procedure.[6]

Apart from its treatment of legislation, the House of Commons devises for itself a number of opportunities to hold debates. These occur in different types of business: for example, delegated legislation; Ways and Means debates when a budget is discussed; the second reading of Consolidated Fund Bills;[7] and the 29 days each session allocated for Supply debates. Other procedural devices to enable debates to take place include the Address in Reply to the Queen's Speech, discussion of which traditionally occupies the opening days of a session; motions in government time, usually but not always initiated by the Government itself; debates on European secondary legislation (which, procedurally, are somewhat similar to debates on delegated legislation); and debate in time specifically set aside for private Members' motions. In addition there are Adjournment debates: these may be one of the kinds of motions debated in government time (or on Supply Days) and as such belong in the group above. But there are three other types: the whole day debate prior to each Recess; the half-hour debate which terminates each day's proceedings;[8] and the emergency debates held under S.O. No. 9. No tidy classification is possible; nor is it possible if one considers the sources of debate. Three groups have some prescriptive claim on the debating time of the House: the Government, the opposition and back-benchers, but in practice much proceeds by agreement. For example, it is not uncommon for a major debate to straddle time provided by both the Government and the opposition: thus in July 1975 the House had a two-day debate on the White Paper 'The Attack on Inflation', the first day of which was government time and the second a Supply Day. Three months before that the House spent three days debating the government's decision to recommend, in the referendum of June

1975, that Britain remain a member of the European Community: for this the first and third days were provided by the Government while the second was a Supply Day. Early in 1976 the House held a four-day debate on devolution; here again there was mixed provision, one of the four days being a Supply Day.[9] Moreover, time that formally belongs to one group may in practice be given to another, as with the second reading of Consolidated Fund Bills.

Non-legislative debates are based on three types of motions. Substantive motions are the most concrete. Typically, governments seek approval of their policies in such motions, opposition parties move expressions of regret at omissions or make suggestions for more sensible courses of action. Alternatively, on a Supply Day for example, the motion may be critical of the government who will then propose a more acceptable (from their point of view) set of words as an amendment. Less clear are motions, much favoured by governments, inviting the House to 'take note' of this or that document, though even these may have amendments moved to them.[10] Least precise of all in terms of wording is the debate based on a motion for the adjournment of the House. It may, of course, be an advantage in certain situations not to have a more precise motion before the House. In what is probably the most famous example in this century, the debate of May 1940, the absence of a more precise motion probably helped broaden support against the Government, while in less dramatic circumstances it may be useful to facilitate a very wide-ranging debate (as on devolution early in 1976) or to permit all sides of a divided party to come together, as when the Labour Government was seeking a vote of confidence in March 1976. It may be useful, however, to consider some of these types of debate in a little more detail.

The debate on the Address in Reply to the Queen's Speech normally occupies the first six working days of a session.[11] Conventionally the first part of the debate is devoted to a general discussion of the government's programme, followed by debates on amendments from the Opposition on particular aspects of that programme. Even on the general debate, however, there is usually agreement to concentrate on particular topics. In November 1975, for example, only the first day of the debate was truly general: the second was devoted to a discussion of industry and the third to the National Health Service. For the remaining two days, debate was based on amendments moved to the Address but again each day had a theme: education on one and economic affairs on the other. For most of the post-Second World War period the only amendments called in this debate have been those tabled by the official Opposition.[12] In the changed party conditions of the mid-1970s this situation has, not surprisingly, been challenged. The matter was considered by the Procedure Committee in 1974–5 (in relation to all debates). The problem is aggravated by the rules of the House which 'prevent a second amendment being called if proceedings on the preceding amendment are not completed before the moment of interruption'.[13] The Procedure Committee recommended a modest experiment to cope with this procedural tangle. This was, on the debate on the Address to allow the Speaker to call a second amendment for division after the first had been disposed of, even though the moment of interruption (i.e. 10 p.m.) had then passed. This was done on the final day of the debate on the Address in November 1975 and the experiment repeated in the devolution debate in January 1976. This episode illustrates the way in which the confident two-party assumptions about the running of the parliamentary system come up against changed political realities. Such clashes are likely to be a feature of the parliamentary scene for the next few years.

Around 10 per cent of the time of the House has been spent in recent years on debates in government time with approximately the same amount of time devoted to Supply Days. Thus these two account for about one fifth of the time the House sits and provide the forum for the major non-legislative debates in the session. In recent years several subjects such as Northern Ireland, Europe and devolution have been the subject of debates lasting more than one day, but usually a single day suffices. Third parties secure only a minor slot here as far as formal arrangements are concerned: for example in 1974–5 the official Opposition gave the

Liberals one of their Supply Days.

Other procedures permit what are in effect general debates; for example, the Ways and Means Resolutions following a Budget provide an opportunity for a substantial debate. In 1974–5 a total of seven sittings were devoted to the contents of two Budgets;[14] while in 1972–3, four sittings were devoted to the single Budget in that session. Statutory Instruments too provide an opportunity for substantive debates. Many of the debates in this area are, of course, on rather narrow issues but in recent sessions there have been a number of major exceptions. Two in particular deserve mention: Rhodesia, where the need for annual renewal of the sanctions resolutions has provided the opportunity for a major debate, and Northern Ireland, which for much of the 1970s has put considerable strain on this and other areas of the House's procedure. In 1974–5 the House spent 25 hours on delegated legislation relating to Northern Ireland; well over one quarter of the total for this class of business. Some of the routine discussion of Statutory Instruments has now been removed to a Standing Committee.[15] On Europe[16] the House is hesitatingly developing procedures to cope with a new situation. The timing and form of these debates too have given rise to considerable concern.[17]

Adjournment Debates

As noted earlier the House has four types of Adjournment Debate, the first of which, the peg on which to hang a broad discussion, has already been dealt with. The second is the half-hour debate which is the closing item of business on each day the House sits. As a *regular* feature of the House's day (and certainly as a *guaranteed* half-hour) it is a product of the Second World War. As a result of its safeguarded status it has become a popular outlet for back-benchers. It has suffered somewhat on the first few days of the week by the frequency with which the House sits late. But no matter how long the House sits it will spend half an hour solemnly debating (albeit that the House in this context is no more than a tiny handful of people) some matter of, usually local, interest.[18] In 1972–3 on only six days when an Adjournment debate might have been held was it not, while in 1974–5 only three opportunities were not taken. Although it is a guaranteed half-hour, if other business finishes before 10 p.m. (Monday–Thursday) or before 4 p.m. on Fridays, any unused time is available for the Adjournment debate. To a considerable extent the debate tends to be constituency-oriented. Often, it represents a further, if not final, stage in the process of grievance-raising that may have begun with correspondence with Ministers and continued with a Parliamentary Question. A regular part of the Question Time routine is for the dissatisfied questioners to give notice that they will seek to raise the matter on the adjournment. Whether this happens depends not only on the Member's seriousness but also on two other factors: his success in the weekly ballot for four out of the five slots each week or his good fortune in being chosen by the Speaker to fill the Thursday position. The Speaker's discretion gives him a useful power to enable what he considers deserving topics to be aired.[19]

It is difficult to be sure how useful these half-hour debates are. They usually take place in an almost empty House and are therefore of little use for informing other MPs directly; their timing limits their potential for national media coverage (though no doubt the subject matter usually ensures local attention). If we judge by the infrequency with which a slot is unused they are undoubtedly useful to MPs: they enable them to raise topics and compel governments to justify themselves at greater length than is possible at Question Time. To that extent it is a modestly useful device.

By tradition, the final day on which the House sits before each of the four Recesses in the year is devoted to a series of private Members' debates. The actual motion setting the dates for the Recess is usually moved some days beforehand and is now debated for about 2–3 hours on each occasion. Until the 1950s (and even occasionally in the 1960s) this motion was agreed to without debate but it now provides an opportunity for a diverse series of points to be made around the theme that the House ought not to be in Recess for the period planned. The actual Adjournment debate itself lasts for 4–5 hours and provides for discussion of a series of pre-arranged topics, with a general understanding that the length of each discussion will be limited. Normally there is time for seven or eight mini-debates of between 35 and 40 minutes each on average. The topics raised can be extremely diverse; to take an example at random: at the Whitsuntide Recess debate in 1975 they ranged from the problems of the valve industry to housing in London, from railway services in north-east Kent to the Severn-Trent Water Authority.

The debates on the second reading of each Consolidated Fund Bill provide a further opportunity for private Members. Here the topics are chosen by ballot and the whole affair is much more protracted: almost invariably giving rise to an all-night sitting. In 1972–3 of the four debates, two lasted until after 9 a.m. on the following day, while in 1974–5, where again there were four debates, three lasted until after 10 a.m. on the following morning. Not only does the House sit longer than in the pre-Recess debates but each mini-debate tends to last longer. Thus the four debates in 1972–3 enabled a total of 44 topics to be raised for an average of rather less than an hour, while in 1974–5 47 topics were raised at rather over an hour each on average.

To return to Adjournment motions, the last type we have to consider is in some respects the most interesting. This is the 'emergency' or 'urgency' adjournment under the procedure provided for in S.O. No. 9. It represents one of the last vestiges of the freer, from the back-benchers' point of view, House of Commons that existed prior to the 1880s. It encapsulates what remains of the right of the private Member to move the adjournment of the House to discuss a definite matter of urgent public importance and as such, of course, is potentially disruptive of the business programmes carefully worked out by the front benches. Since restrictions were first imposed in this area in 1882 there have been two tendencies at work: the first has been to limit the occasions on which debate under the procedure is permitted, while the second has been to minimize the disruption caused when such a debate is granted. Under the first heading there developed increasingly restrictive interpretations of what each of the

terms in the Standing Order meant, while under the second
there was a move away from immediate interruption to having
the debate later on the same day and a change to first limiting
the debate to three hours and then providing that any sitting
interrupted for such a debate could be extended by a period
equal to the length of the interruption. In 1967[20] a further
refinement was introduced when it was agreed to hold any
debate granted at 3.30 p.m. on the day following the application (applications successful on Thursday were to stand over
till the following Monday), though in cases of extreme urgency
debate at 7 p.m. the same day remained possible.

Much concern about the difficulty of obtaining debates
under S.O. No. 9 has been expressed in the last thirty years.
The Procedure Committees of 1945–6 and 1958–9 considered
the matter but neither led to changes. In 1966–7 the Procedure Committee, in line with the prevailing mood of
modernizing the House, suggested replacing the traditional
phrase 'a definite matter of urgent public importance' with
the words 'a specific and important matter that should have
urgent consideration'. This change was accepted by the House
as were other modifications designed to make it easier to
secure such debates. It was felt that such debates enabled the
House to respond to current concerns and so it was agreed
to set the Speaker free of precedents and of the requirement
to give reasons when applications were refused.[21] Initially
there seems to have been some improvement: from 1959–60
to 1965–6 when there were on average 10·8 applications per
session of which 0·7 were allowed, in 1967–8 there were 20
applications of which 4 were successful, but in 1972–3 only
1 out of 32 applications was allowed and in 1974–5 it was
1 out of 30.[22] Nor does it appear that being able not to give
reasons for a refusal has helped very much. The figures above
suggest that it has not made debates easier to obtain and
Speaker Lloyd has himself had second thoughts on the matter:
'I was a member of the Select Committee on Procedure and
this discretion was to some extent my own idea. I have subsequently regretted it because it put a great burden on the
Chair.'[23] Such explanations as there have been in recent years
have centred on whether it is right to disrupt the programme

of the House; few such potential disruptions have appealed to the Speakers. Given the substantial pressure on the time of the House one can sympathize with their position.

Private Members' Motions

Private Members' legislation being considered elsewhere in this book,[24] it is sufficient to note here that in the sessions 1972–3 and 1974–5 it accounted for about 60 hours on the floor of the House.[25] Of the 20 Fridays during a session set aside for private Members' business, the practice in the 1970s has been to divide them 12 to Bills and 8 to motions. (In 1974–5 there were actually 12 Bill Fridays and 9 motion Fridays.) This compares with a split 10–10 from 1950 and a period from the mid-1960s when Bills were favoured with a 16–4 split, until the present division was established in 1970. In addition, since 1959 private Members have had four half-days (at present Mondays) when their motions have precedence up to 7 p.m. The selection of topics for both Friday and Monday debates is determined by means of a ballot. Quite how valuable these debates are is not easy to decide. One can illustrate the range of topics covered. In 1974–5, for example, the main debates on Fridays covered such things as Natural Referenda, the plight of the small businessman, the insurance industry, the rating system and public health. On the four Monday debates the topics dealt with were juvenile crime, the arts, grammar and direct-grant schools, and finally a double bill of a Bill of Rights for the United Kingdom and the problems of one-parent families. As with other aspects of private Members' activity on the floor of the House, one can say that while its impact is not dramatic it nevertheless represents a useful outlet and a way of airing topics that might otherwise remain undebated in the House.

Problems

All that happens on the floor of the House has as its background the constraint of time. Time is not neutral, it is both the weapon of those not in Government (no longer can we speak confidently of *the* Opposition) and the limitation which governments do their best by various devices to overcome. For the various oppositions it provides a bargaining counter with government since so much of what happens on the floor of the House has to be the product of agreement. (It is true of course that governments have resources normally to overcome some opposition, for example, by imposing allocation of time orders but, while the introduction of these is not so time-consuming as formerly, nevertheless there are limits to the extent to which such resources can be used.)

Arguments about time are not merely procedural: usually that is but a subsidiary argument to the political one about the content and volume of the demands made on the Parliamentary system. That the volume of these demands has increased in recent years there is little doubt: that it is right they they should increase, touches an issue which it is beyond the scope of this chapter to deal with.[26]

The House has from time to time introduced changes in its procedures designed to ease the pressure on the floor of the House. In the post-war period, Standing Committees have been developed in a number of ways: first to take the great bulk of contentious legislation, secondly, to enable more discussion to take place of the affairs of first Scotland, then Wales and more recently token gestures towards Northern Ireland and the English regions. Thirdly, there have been Committees to debate, in effect, the Second Reading (and more rarely Report stages) of Bills off the floor of the House – akin to a procedure developed for Scottish legislation early in the post-war period. Finally, one of the perennial problems in the 1960s in this context seems to have been solved: the treatment of the Finance Bill. After a number of not very happy experiments in the late 1960s it now seems well established that each Finance Bill can be split, with the more technical sections being taken in Committee off the floor of the House: the system seems to have survived dire warnings about the constitutional impropriety of such a procedure. More recently, as we have already noted, provision has been made to debate the 'merits' of Statutory Instruments in a Standing Committee. Other devices enable items of business to be kept within bounds: the limitations on the debates under S.O. No. 9 is one example; others include the limitations on time for prayers against Statutory Instruments and the rules for debating European secondary legislation, although in this last category it could not be claimed that there exists much satisfaction with the time available or the timing of the debates. For Parliamentary Questions the solution has been to make no extra time available on the floor of the House.

It is not only the weight on the Parliamentary timetable that causes concern but also the organization of that timetable. This has two aspects: the pattern of the Session and of the Parliamentary day. The Parliamentary year in its autumn-to-autumn form dates only from the 1920s: until then the Parliamentary year and the calendar year coincided though the former was shorter, running normally from February to November or December. The present arrangements no doubt suit governments, which explains a good deal about both that and the parliamentary day. Neither seems particularly well designed for non-ministerial or full-time MPs. Certainly there seems little prospect that the House might decide to sit for fewer days during the year.

The 'normal' meeting times of the House each day have remained virtually unchanged[27] since soon after the end of the Second World War. In practice the time for adjourning has not been closely adhered to on the first four days of the week in recent sessions. The formal times would give an average sitting, taking the week as a whole, of 7½ hours. In 1972–3 the average length of a sitting was 8 hours 53 minutes and in 1974–5 it crept up to 9 hours 26 minutes. Another way of looking at the matter is to examine the time at which the House rose. In 1972–3 (excluding Fridays and other days on which the House met at 11.00 a.m.) the House rose before midnight on 69 days and after midnight on 62 days. In 1974–5 (with the same exclusions) the House rose at midnight or before on 62 days and after midnight on 95 days. In 1974–5 an enquiry by the Procedure Committee into the subject of 'Late Sittings' avoided the central issues on the grounds that it had been superseded by the government's announcement of a more fundamental enquiry into the working of the House. One year later that enquiry had not even started. Now that it has it will not be able to avoid dealing with this issue for demands for more conventional hours of work on the floor of the House are probably growing in strength. In addition there is the related issue of whether the hours, as well as starting and finishing too late, are in any case too long. No doubt attention will once again be drawn to the provision in Standing Orders enabling the House to adjourn to enable Committees to meet. Once before the House wiped this provision from its books only to restore it in the post-war euphoria of 1946. Thirty years later it has still to be used for the first time.

One means of using time better, if not necessarily saving it, is to have a time limit on speeches on the floor of the House. The arguments in favour of this are that it would enable more Members to contribute to debate and perhaps make debates more lively by encouraging briefer contributions. The idea has been around throughout the twentieth century and an experiment in the form of a period during debates set aside for brief speeches was advocated by the 1958–9 Procedure Committee. Nothing came of that and recent Committees have been more sceptical: for example, the 1974–5 Procedure Committee poured cold water on the idea.[28] In fact a good deal happens informally. We have already noted the arrangements which enable debates on Recess Adjournment or Consolidated Fund Bill Second Readings to work, through limitations on length of speeches. In other areas too the Speaker has much discretion: most obviously by rewarding the terse and punishing the prolix. There is little doubt that compared with, say, the beginning of the century, speeches have become shorter. Yet reading Hansard one is left with an impression that they could, with advantage, become even shorter and many could remain undelivered.

Much time is spent by private Members complaining that governments are insufficiently careful about their rights. Governments not surprisingly see matters otherwise: their concern is with governing, in which the House is perceived as an accomplice rather than an independent source of power. The test must be what happens: if enough Members felt strongly then governments could be checked: whether it be over the abolition of a select committee, the release of documents or which minister shall appear before a select committee. More than fifty years ago a perceptive foreign observer remarked that 'while many private members loudly bewail their wrongs, they make no organized effort for mutual protection.'[29] In essence this remains true and while of course the force of party is not lightly to be set aside nor the fact that the House *qua* House can provide few career rewards,[30] the complaining back-bencher cannot have it both ways. In this context the House is rarely a cohesive unit. To develop such a feeling is not easy, given the tradition of party versus party, major parties versus minor parties, and front-benchers versus back-benchers; it is made more difficult by the survival of the rather curious convention of the privileges of Privy Councillors. This convention is nowhere formally laid down but it operates so that in debates the Privy Councillor has an advantage over the ordinary back-bencher in his claims to be called to speak. Over the years Privy Councillors have become more tactful in exercising their privilege and it no longer operates with the force it once did, yet that it survives at all is remarkable.

Commentators on the American Congress sometimes lament the low importance accorded to floor proceedings in the House of Representatives and even in the Senate. A contrast is drawn with what happens, or is believed to happen, in the British House of Commons. There are obvious reasons for the floor assuming greater importance in the House of Commons than in a legislature which is so largely committee-centred. In drawing attention to this contrast, one is pointing to a choice which has faced (though which has not always been faced up to by) the House over the last decade and which provides an essential background to an understanding of the House's role in the 1970s. This choice is simply whether the House is to remain floor-oriented or is to become, to a greater extent, committee-oriented.

The importance of the floor of the House needs to be considered on two levels: the factual and the mythical. On the first level the floor has an obvious importance in that not only does legislative procedure give primacy to proceedings there, the decision in principle on a bill at second reading being both logically and chronologically prior to Committee proceedings on it, but also, and perhaps ultimately more important, the floor is the forum for holding governments accountable and for witnessing the ultimate tests of political strength. Whatever the day-to-day reality of these last points, from them flow a number of things, notably that parliamentary reputations are made (or equally important, are believed to be made) on the floor of the House. On the mythical level one can point to the belief that all power resides on the floor of the House (that legislation is written, governments seriously scrutinized there and so on). This view implies also that Committee work is less important, that debates 'ought' to be well attended and that oratory rates ahead of knowledge in the list of desirable parliamentary qualities.

Of course not all who are wary of moves on the part of the House towards a greater committee involvement are necessarily worshipping a mythical constitution. Many of those who have been outspoken in their suspicion of committees and in their defence of the virtues of the floor have tended nevertheless to exaggerate the strength of the latter and the dangers of the former.[31] It is also perhaps significant that the best-known members of this school of thought are men whose parliamentary skills are shown to advantage on the floor rather than in committee. Such people tend to stress the centrality of debate in the House as a feature of our political life (what might be called the 'grand inquest of the nation' school), and to view what happens on the floor of the House as important particularly in terms of a clash between parties – a choice of ideologies. Implicit in this is a defence of the two-party system, yet paradoxically it is precisely when the two-party system is strongest that the House as such is weakest. At the same time members of this school are suspicious of committees and their further development. They see committees as open to the twin dangers of collaboration and colonization: collaboration between opposing parties who ought to be articulating clear and conflicting choices and colonization of back-benchers who are offered fragments of information, which then marks them off from their fellows. That this latter point is a danger is clear from American experience, that it is an argument against a developed committee system is not. It assumes that information can better be gained (and be therefore more widely shared) on the floor of the House; at best a doubtful assumption.

This argument is likely to go on for a long time; witness for example the frequent complaints in the last decade that debate on the floor of the House is being adversely affected by the demands of committees or that intolerable demands are being placed on MPs by the volume of committee meetings. This is of course connected with another debate about whether MPs should be part-time or full-time but it reveals also something about the career perceptions of MPs. So long as it is believed (and so far there is no reason to suppose incorrectly) that political advancement depends more on performance on the floor than in committee, then the incentive for an MP to devote a substantial part of his energy to committee work is likely to remain weak.

What lies behind the stronger defences of the floor as the centre of parliamentary activity is the belief that it is only there that the executive can be checked effectively because it is only there that the full force of the party battle can be brought to bear. But there are in practice severe limits to the extent to which the executive can be exposed on the floor of the House and secondly because of the predictability of normal parliamentary business it is unlikely to be at the centre of our national concern. It is in fact only when the outcome is open to some doubt – on private Members' business, when the Whips are for some other reason removed, when there is a substantial rebellion or when there is an uncertain parliamentary situation, that public attention is focused on debate and there is a possibility of debate actually influencing the vote at the end of it. In that sense adversary politics, so eagerly defended by those who commend the floor in parliamentary life, are not necessarily favourable to making the Chamber itself effective as the centre of Parliamentary activity.

The critics of committees see in them two further dangers: the creation of two classes of members (an extension of the colonization argument) and the tendency to take things out of politics. In part the first is a price that has to be paid (though equally it could be argued that not all are equal in floor debate). The second point rests on the assumption that the only valuable arguments are those which occur between parties. What Committees may do of course is not to take issues out of politics so much as to consider them in ways that do not fit conveniently into traditional party slots.

Of course there have been times when the floor has been vital to political activity. The blocking of House of Lords reform in the late 1960s is a much quoted example (though whether the consequences of that particular activity were beneficial is more doubtful). But this was precisely where normal party lines did not hold and where the Powell-Foot school was able to make common cause. Such clear examples are rather rare and it seems doubtful whether one can erect a theory of Parliamentary effectiveness on them, though one might predict that they are likely to become more frequent in the future.

When one has finished describing what happens on the floor of the House and discussing some of the problems raised by that description one is left with the most difficult problem of all. This is to decide what impact proceedings on the floor of the House have, what the point of it all is. This in turn leads one into the treacherous marshes of the viability of Parliamentary Government. Without embarking on any cataclysmic predictions for the House one can fairly say that the answers to this kind of question depend on answers to other questions: the future shape of the party system and the relationship between the House of Commons and the world outside.

While one may discount much conventional speculation of the 'House is not what it was' variety, it remains doubtful whether the present arrangements in the House are the most effective. Such changes as the House has made over the years have, so far as the floor is concerned, been limited. Much that happens there reflects adversary politics. The House sits for long hours, but do its deliberations justify this? The quality of legislation almost certainly does not reflect the hours which the House devotes to the subject. Its proceedings at Question Time are often not of the sort which encourages confidence outside, while it has a collective faith in debate for its own sake irrespective of the value of that debate. In short the House runs some danger that people cease to listen or, to put it the other way round, perhaps the House is talking to no one but itself. In part, this results from the relative insularity of proceedings: the House has undergone a protracted courtship with radio and television.

It would be naïve to suppose that it is possible or even desirable to make the House of Commons the focus of wide public attention. Equally it would be exceedingly self-centred for the House to believe that merely to spend more time on this or that would help very much. It may be that to devolve some of the work of Parliament to regional assemblies will help a little. It is doubtful whether it will make much difference unless some hard questions about the point of proceedings on the floor are asked: floor managers, like nature, abhor a vacuum. Of course the future shape of business in the House is not a mere academic question: it is primarily about power, and procedure and structure will reflect that power. In so far as governments have power, they are unlikely to give it up but, equally, in certain political situations they may find themselves seriously weakened. The dilemma is a painful one and the House of Commons as it faces new party combinations, new relations via live broadcasting with the outside world, may have to develop new ways of conducting its affairs. Already one can see signs that governments face more difficult problems on the floor of the House than they have for many years. The public expenditure defeat for the Government of March 1976, although not of permanent significance in itself, represents a way of life to which the House may have to accustom itself. At the very least it seems likely that the usual channels will have to be broadened and business on the floor will be less predictable. This will make life more difficult for governments, but the floor of the House may become more compelling for those who like spectator sports.

4 Legislation

GAVIN DREWRY

Legislation wears many different disguises. Apart from the familiar public general Act, of which there are various sub-species, a quick glance along the shelves of any law library or through the pages of *Erskine May's Parliamentary Practice* reveals the existence of private Acts, provisional order confirmation Acts and Church of England Measures; then there is delegated legislation, which can be sub-divided into categories which include statutory instruments, by-laws and rules of court procedure, and each of these can be further categorized according to such criteria as the procedure to be followed for promulgation and scrutiny; European secondary legislation, again of several distinct types, impinges increasingly upon the work of the United Kingdom Parliament and upon the lives of those represented in it. And the word legislation commonly crops up in such phrases as 'judicial legislation' or 'legislation by administrative circular', emphasizing that it is a distinctive *process* as well as being the printed product of a process, and sometimes in contexts which make clear the author's disapproval of judges or administrators straying into territory allegedly forbidden to them by virtue of a 'doctrine' of separation of powers. This chapter is concerned almost exclusively with public general Acts initiated by the government; other facets of legislation are dealt with elsewhere in this book.

Even in its narrow sense, emphasizing what happens when Parliament converts a Bill into an Act, the legislative process can be examined from a variety of different angles. Professor J. A. G. Griffith, in his chapter on legislation in *The Commons in Transition*, wrote from the standpoint of an academic lawyer with a particular interest in constitutional and administrative law. Some political scientists might prefer to adopt a comparative approach or to discourse upon the difficult problems of delineating the legislative process from other kinds of governmental activity such as administration or policy-making. This writer – a hybrid lawyer and political scientist – does not intend to stray down the paths already marked out by Professor Griffith; and while this chapter touches upon the general characteristics of legislation as a process, it does so only so far as is necessary to locate Parliament's part in that process.

The central object of this essay is to examine recent legislative history, partly because it is interesting in its own right and partly because it has a bearing upon the central purpose of this book, which is to speculate upon the present and future state of parliamentary government in the United Kingdom in an era of grave constitutional and political uncertainty.

The Background

This book's predecessor, *The Commons in Transition*, was first published at a time when the cautious euphoria generated among advocates of parliamentary reform by the Crossman reforms of the mid-1960s was beginning to ebb away. It was conceived in the shadow of a number of reports by the Commons' Select Committee on Procedure, one of which bore the portentous title, *Public Bill Procedure, Etc.*[1] That report suggested a number of procedural changes, some of which – for example, that the third readings of Bills should normally be taken without debate, and ways of improving the technical scrutiny of statutory instruments – resulted in modest but sensible reforms. But, as Professor Crick pointed out, the Committee failed 'to redraw the shape of the wood amid the tangle of fine new saplings, mature timber and decaying trees'.[2]

The 1970s have seen a continuing search for the Eldorado of procedural rationality. In 1971 the Procedure Committee carried on the work of its predecessor and produced a bigger report called *The Process of Legislation*;[3] in 1975 the Renton Committee, working from a different angle, reported on *The Preparation of Legislation*.[4] Large-scale procedural enquiries were launched in both Houses in 1976. But, important though they are in their own ways, it is a general and perhaps inevitable failing of exercises of these kinds that they do little to grapple in a detached way with fundamental problems arising out of a legislative process based upon theories of parliamentary sovereignty and realities of strong executive government.

Mr Edward Short (then Leader of the House of Commons) correctly identified the importance of these questions during his opening speech in the major debate on parliamentary procedure which took place on 2 February 1976;[5] but predictably, his own suggestions for reform (in so far as they related directly to the legislative process) were aimed mainly at improving the government's capacity to push through an ambitious legislative programme. Thus he mooted the idea of extensive 'framework legislation', to give ministers even wider powers than at present to make delegated legislation; and he favoured the idea of taking the report stages of Bills 'upstairs' in standing committee in order to relieve pressure on the floor of the House. Equally predictably, the opposition spokesmen and back-benchers who contributed to the debate stressed the desirability of more searching scrutiny of government bills and deprecated the tendency for legislative initiative to slip further and further away from Parliament.

It is clear that any parliamentary reform cannot please everyone. Governments are loath to make rods for their own backs by conceding changes which, in the eyes of opposition and back-benchers, will make legislative scrutiny more 'effective'; but they may sometimes offer such concessions as a trade-off against counter-concessions which will make their own lives easier. The opposition will not press too vigorously for a change in the balance of power between Parliament and the executive, because (given the present electoral and party system) before long it will be in office itself. There is a tacit consensus among most parliamentarians, not only about the 'rules of the game', but also about the need for effective government and about the limits of responsible opposition. The smooth working of Parliament depends, as we shall see, upon the smooth working of 'the usual channels'. And when we come to examine the legislative process in the 1970s, one thing which will quickly become clear is that not only is legislative *procedure* founded upon a thinly camouflaged consensus but also, notwithstanding recurrent nightmares about a cycle of events in which successive governments, in an age of 'adversary politics', spend their time repealing the enactments of their predecessors, a similar consensus is the norm for the *substance* of legislation. But before examining these matters in greater detail it is necessary to take a preliminary look at Parliament's role in the wider legislative process.

Parliament and Legislation

The House of Commons spends at least half its time talking about legislation[6] and a considerable amount in addition talking about matters which may give rise to legislation and matters arising, directly or indirectly, from past legislation. Yet it is a commonplace that Parliament is not a law-making body, save in the important but strictly formal senses recognized by the courts and by constitutional theory. As Walkland succinctly puts it:

> The legislative process in Britain is now complex: it comprises deliberative, Parliamentary and administrative stages, over all of which executive influence is predominant. Legislation is now an almost exclusively executive function, modified, sometimes heavily, by practices of group and Parliamentary consultations.[7]

And:

> In so far as there is a 'deliberative' stage in the legislative process, this is now found much earlier than the Parliamentary stages, in the interplay between political parties, pressure groups, Departments and the Cabinet, which together form a complex decision-making structure, involving a variety of social and political forces.[8]

Thus today's conventional wisdom is that the parliamentary stages of the legislative process are, for purposes of getting policies converted into laws, the least creative ones; that Parliament has relinquished any capacity for legislative initiative it may once have possessed to the executive in its midst; that Parliament 'legitimates' but does not 'legislate'. Such views, expressed thus crudely, conceal a large number of value judgements and begged questions and cannot fairly be used as slogans to justify a dismissive attack upon parliamentary government; it is arguable that 'legitimation' is an essential function in any ordered society, and that a facility for public ventilation of policy issues cannot be brushed aside merely because it falls short – even a long way short – of a Utopian view of what representation and democracy are all about.

But, in this instance conventional wisdom does accord with the facts of life. On the principle that one picture is better than a thousand words, the legislative process can usefully be portrayed diagrammatically as involving four interlocking and overlapping functions (see figure 1): 1, Inspiration; 2, Deliberation and Formulation; 3, Legitimation; 4, Application – plus a capacity for 'feedback', or learning by experience. If one accepts this as broadly accurate then it can be seen that the role of Parliament (in so far as the latter is separable from the executive which sits in it) impinges hardly at all on 1 or 4. It has slightly more of a part to play in 2, both overtly in so far as limited facilities exist for debates on White Papers, etc., and more covertly in the day-to-day interaction of MPs and ministers, for example in party committees and in tea-rooms and bars. And the Finance Bill is an important exception, the secrecy of its preparation giving peculiar importance to its parliamentary stages, during which substantial changes are often made following pressure group representations which, in the case of other Bills, are normally taken into account much earlier;[9] the norm is for formulation and legitimation to be kept apart. Parliament's key role in legitimation derives, as has already been hinted, more from widely believed theories of representative government than from any realistic assessment of its impact upon legislation.

Private Members' bills, discussed in another chapter, are a somewhat aberrant departure from the picture of the legislative process sketched above; and it is arguable, in any event, that the minority of back-bench Bills which actually reach the statute book (and many that fail are propaganda exercises rather than law-making ones) do so only with Government approval and can thus be regarded as a peculiar species of Government Bill.

Before leaving this matter a note of caution must be sounded. Although it may be accepted that Parliament's role in the legislative process is pre-eminently a passive one, in which Parliamentarians sit back and eat what is given to them, there are significant exceptions where the menu is changed as a result of complaints, or where the waiter is forced to take away an unpalatable dish: some of these will be encountered both in the sections that follow and in the chapter on standing committees.

But the most important caveat lies in the nature of parliamentary 'influence'. As Bachrach and Baratz pointed out in a famous article, power is something with two faces; it is necessary to look not only at decisions, but also at non-decisions, at why some issues never emerge into the public political arena at all.[10] The number of concessions forced from ministers in the form of Bills abandoned or amendments carried may not amount to very much, but we do not know how often an idea fails to get beyond the 'inspiration' stage or through its 'formative and deliberative' stages because of the daunting prospect of having ultimately to justify an unpopular policy in public.

Legislation, 1968-76 : Some Facts and Figures

Quantifying a phenomenon is only a first step to understanding it; statistics of the legislative process need to be interpreted with considerable caution, though they provide a useful starting point for discussion. Some of the raw statistics on public Bill legislation in recent sessions are set out in Table 1.

The *number* of measures enacted remains more or less constant from Session to Session: even the very heavy Sessions of 1974-5 and 1975-6 were not outstandingly deviant cases in this respect. This is no accident, for in planning the Session's programme the Future Legislation Com-

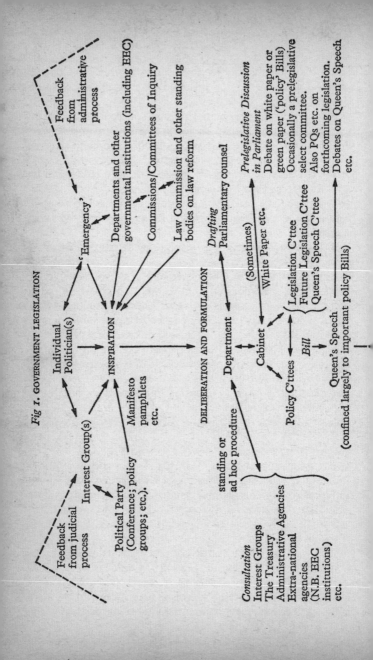

Fig 1. GOVERNMENT LEGISLATION

Feedback from judicial process

Feedback from administrative process

Interest Group(s)

Individual Politician(s)

'Emergency'

Departments and other governmental institutions (including EEC)

Commissions/Committees of Inquiry

Law Commission and other standing bodies on law reform

Political Party (Conference; policy groups; etc.).

Manifesto pamphlets etc.

INSPIRATION

DELIBERATION AND FORMULATION

Drafting
Parliamentary counsel

Department

Cabinet

(Sometimes)
White Paper etc.

Policy C'ttees

{ Legislation C'ttee
Future Legislation C'ttee
Queen's Speech C'ttee }

Bill

Queen's Speech
(confined largely to important policy Bills)

Prelegislative Discussion in Parliament
Debate on white paper or green paper ('policy' Bills)
Occasionally a prelegislative select committee.
Also PQs etc. on forthcoming legislation.
Debates on Queen's Speech etc.

standing or ad hoc procedure

Consultation
Interest Groups
The Treasury
Administrative agencies
Extra-national agencies
(N.B. EEC institutions)
etc.

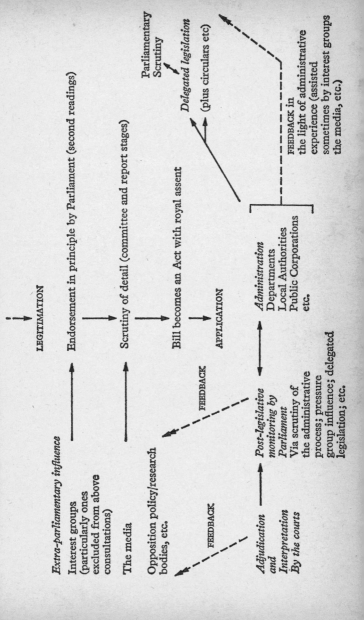

LEGITIMATION

Extra-parliamentary influence

Interest groups
(particularly ones
excluded from above
consultations)

The media

Opposition policy/research
bodies, etc.

*Post-legislative
monitoring by
Parliament*
Via scrutiny of
the administrative
process; pressure
group influence; delegated
legislation; etc.

*Adjudication
and
Interpretation*
By the courts

Endorsement in principle by Parliament (second readings)

Scrutiny of detail (committee and report stages)

Bill becomes an Act with royal assent

APPLICATION

FEEDBACK

FEEDBACK

Administration
Departments
Local Authorities
Public Corporations
etc.

Parliamentary
Scrutiny

Delegated legislation
(plus circulars etc)

FEEDBACK in
the light of administrative
experience (assisted
sometimes by interest groups
the media, etc.)

TABLE I

Public Bills, 1968–76

Session	Acts Passed	Government Acts			Government 'failures'		Major Divis- ions[3]	Backbench Acts	Backbench 'failures'[2]	
		Consolid- ation	Consolid- ated Fund	Other	Number	% of Bills introduced			Number	% of Bills introduced
1968/9	63	4	3	44	4	7·2%	8	12	93	88·6%
1969/70[1]	53	3	3	32	25	39·7%	10	15	74	83·1%
1970/1	88	11	4	61	1	1·3%	15	13	64	83·1%
1971/2	76	9	4	46	2	3·3%	10	17	63	78·8%
1972/3	72	7	4	46	0	—	9	15	75	83·3%
1973/4[1]	15	2	2	11	23	60·5%	5	0	52	100·%
1974[1]	42	5	3	27	8	18·6%	2	7	41	85·4%
1974/5	83	18	4	51	9	11·0%	19	10	85	89·5%
1975/6	88	13	3	56	5	6·5%	11	16	75	82·4%

Notes: [1]Denotes short session

[2]Excludes Ten minute Rule Bills refused leave (In any event the statistics do not distinguish different categories of back bench bill, some of which are only propaganda exercises)

[3]Fifty or more votes against the Bill or in favour of a reasoned amendment.

mittee of the Cabinet must, among other things, take into account Parliament's capacity to do the work in the time available (bearing in mind possible procedural short-cuts such as guillotines, and the possible political difficulties of using such devices with any frequency). And this capacity, although incrementally enhanced by periodic procedural reforms, does not alter much from one Session to the next; though it is dependent to some degree upon the government's varying capacity to command a clear majority both on the floor and in standing committee. Some events requiring legislation – for example, the collapse of Rolls-Royce, or the fast-changing ramifications of the tragedy of Northern Ireland – cannot be planned for very far in advance, but the overall picture remains one of careful government planning, not just in respect of single Sessions but also over the anticipated span of a complete Parliament. The main threat to legislative productivity is the premature curtailment of a Session by a general election: this can be seen in the figures for 1969–70, 1973–4 and 1974.

By the same token, the incidence of government bills which are introduced but which fail to become law is very low, other than in Sessions where premature dissolution results in part of the programme (usually the most contentious part, in respect of which the opposition will not co-operate in agreeing an abbreviated timetable) having to be abandoned: 1974–5 was an exception where, arguably, too much was attempted, and, perhaps ominously, there were similar signs of ministerial over-ambition in 1975–6. Here is a good illustration of the fact that statistics may tell only half the story. A 'failure' may arise for no other reason than that the government introduces a bill late in the Session as, in effect, a discussion document, and to advertise its determination to legislate next Session. It may also happen for the purely technical reason that, in the interests of speed, two identical bills are debated simultaneously in both the Lords and the Commons, the No. 2 version of the measure being withdrawn when it has served its purpose; this happened to the Community Land (No. 2) Bill in 1975.

The three substantial examples of government 'failures'

during this period (other than ones which occurred in shortened sessions) are exceptions which underline the almost inviolate norm of government 'success'. The first was the Parliament (No. 2) Bill in 1969, where the government was thwarted in its attempt to reform the House of Lords by an unlikely coalition of Conservative traditionalists and Labour left-wingers. The second was the House of Commons (Redistribution of Seats) (No. 2) Bill, also in 1969, where the House of Lords carried, and maintained despite Commons' insistence upon rejecting it, a wrecking amendment to a Bill intended to protect the Government from any legal repercussions from its refusal to revise parliamentary boundaries as recommended by the independent Boundary Commissioners. The third instance was the Trade Union and Labour Relations (Amendment) Bill in 1975 (*post*), where the House of Lords insisted upon amendments to exempt newspaper editors from closed-shop provisions to a point where it began to look as though the Parliament Acts 1911 and 1949 might have to be invoked to overcome their resistance.

In any event, in the same way that parliamentary 'influence' may be covert as well as overt (*vide ante*) so government 'failure' cannot be measured simply in terms of bills failing to become Acts.[12] Legislative ideas may be killed before they become bills (sometimes, though very rarely, at an advanced stage, and amid great publicity, as with Mrs Castle's plans to reform industrial relations law in 1969). Sometimes a bill emerges from Parliament having been amended in ways objectionable to the government, though this is rare in circumstances where the government has a working majority in the Commons and can mobilize that majority to reverse setbacks suffered in standing committee or the House of Lords.[13] The norm is for government bills, once they have survived the mainly pre-parliamentary formulative stages, to become law, and to do so in substantially the same form as that in which they are introduced; and this norm, the electoral events of 1974 notwithstanding, apparently remains almost as firmly entrenched in the mid-1970s as it ever has been.

In calculating legislative productivity it is necessary to take account of the varying physical *bulk* of each Act, and here it is important (particularly in recent years) to distinguish consolidation measures from the rest. This is because consolidation bills (as their name suggests) incorporate the substance of several earlier enactments, and are often very large measures in consequence; a recent example is the Criminal Procedure (Scotland) Act 1974, containing 464 sections and ten bulky schedules. Table 2 indicates the average size of different categories of measure enacted in three full sessions; apart from demonstrating the bulkiness of consolidation measures, these figures show that, for equally obvious reasons, successful private Members' bills tend to be much smaller than government bills.

TABLE 2

The average size of public Acts

Session	Consolidation Acts No. Average size			Other Govt. Acts[1] No. Average size			Back-bench Acts No. Average size		
		Sections	Schedules		Sections	Schedules		Sections	Schedules
1971/2	9	68	– 6	46	25	– 3	17	5	– ½
1972/3	7	38	– 3	46	23	– 4	15	7	– 1
1974/5	18	56	– 5	51	24	– 4	10	8	– 1

[1]Excludes Consolidated Fund Acts

In the session 1974–5, no less than 43·5 per cent of the sections of Acts placed on the statute book were a consolidation of old laws. Such measures are of very little relevance to the debate about whether parliamentary procedures are seriously overloaded, because their consideration takes place almost entirely in a Joint Committee on Consolidation Bills, but they have an important part to play in tidying up the statute book for the benefit of statute users.

In so far as the rather crude figures in Tables 1 and 2 tell us anything about the phenomenon of parliamentary 'overload', which has been much discussed in recent years, they suggest that the picture has not changed very much over the last few sessions and certainly not to a point where Parliament is

suddenly being asked to cope with problems of an unprecedented order of magnitude, though the sessions 1974–5 and
1975–6 were both heavy ones, unusually replete with large and
contentious Bills, and future hindsight may indeed reveal the
onset of a disturbing trend towards overload. But, of course,
these statistics deal with *outputs*[14] and do not answer the
complaint sometimes heard from ministers – such as Mr Short
(*vide ante*) – that governments have to economize in their
inputs of proposed legislation, to the detriment of the public
interest and of the keeping of election promises, because
Parliament has reached saturation point. It is clear, in any
event, that we have to go a long way behind these kinds of
statistical evidence to uncover the real story of the legislative
process in the 1970s.

But before moving on, we might usefully look at one additional feature of Table 1 which highlights something which
will be touched upon in a later section. The final column
of the table gives the number of government bills which were
subjected to substantial opposing divisions at second and/or
third reading in the House of Commons, the definition of
'substantial' being 50 or more votes against the main question
and/or in favour of a reasoned amendment. It is at once
apparent just how few bills are opposed in principle. The
incidence of divisions fluctuates from Session to Session, and
the figures for 1970–1 and 1974–5 lend some support to the
commonsense expectation that a government's most contentious policy proposals are pushed through as early as
possible in a new Parliament (and, perhaps, that a newly
dethroned opposition, smarting from recent defeat, is likely
to seek solace by nuisance tactics in the division lobbies). But
even these sessions do not seriously undermine the principle
that the *substance* of legislation (as well as the working of
legislative *procedure*) is founded upon consensus rather than
conflict, with most bills – by definition, the ones which attract
the least public attention – being of a non-partisan and
'departmental', 'administrative' or consolidation type. This
theme will be mentioned again in the concluding section.
Meanwhile, we will turn from the statistics to examine the
substance of public legislation in the 1970s.

Legislation, 1968-76: The Highlights

Having said that most legislation is uncontentious and administrative in character, it may seem perverse to illustrate recent legislative history through 'highlights' which are definitionally atypical. The cases cited here are landmarks; but the legislative process in the 1970s will be remembered for the European Communities Act 1972 rather than for the Island of Rockall Act 1972 and others like it, except by those who happen to live on Rockall. In any event, the exciting exceptions cited here serve to underline by contrast the more banal realities of the day-to-day legislative grind.

Of course this selection of 'highlights' is a personal one. Most of the great political events of an era are reflected, sooner or later, in public Bill legislation. This selection includes no Finance Bills (in a period which saw the advent of VAT and CTT); it omits the measures which transformed the structures of local government, the National Health Service and the courts; there is no discussion of the Bills arising out of the abortive decisions to build a Channel Tunnel and a third London airport; where are the crucial issues of wage and price control, food subsidies, Northern Ireland, pensions, the EEC referendum, consumer protection, the National Enterprise Board and 'community land'?

The items were selected with a view to capturing some of the flavour of major policy legislation in the 1970s. All are important, both in the substance of the laws produced and, in many cases, in showing what happens when a creaky legislative machine, dependent upon the good will and good sense of those operating it, comes under pressure.

The Industrial Relations Act 1971[15]: The passage of this measure was remarkable for the intensity of emotion evinced by Labour MPs whose party had recently gone through considerable trauma over Mrs Castle's White Paper, *In Place of Strife*. During a debate on a timetable motion on 25 January 1971 the sitting had to be suspended after 40 Labour MPs had clustered around the Speaker's chair chanting protests against the Bill. Three days later, when the first guillotine fell, 18 Government amendments and 24 clauses were approved without debate, but subject to 22 consecutive divisions occupying five hours and accompanied by the singing of 'The Red Flag'. This pattern was repeated on several further occasions and the committee stage (taken on the floor of the House because of the Bill's importance) was completed with only 39 out of about 160 clauses having been considered and with none of the schedules debated at all. A five-day Report stage ended with a sitting lasting 21 hours and 41 minutes, the longest since 1881, which included a record 63 divisions. Much of the real scrutiny was left to the House of Lords (where the small contingent of Labour peers suffered considerable stress through a number of all-night sittings). Altogether, there were 238 divisions in the Commons, 138 in the Lords, and 34 more when the Commons finally considered the Lords' amendments.

The unruliness of the Opposition's protests did little to enhance the image of Parliament in the world outside and laid Labour Members open to the charge of encouraging the unions to break the law when the Act eventually became operative. The Bill's passage shows just how far the day-to-day working of the parliamentary process depends upon at least a minimal degree of procedural consensus. There must be serious doubt whether the Bill underwent proper scrutiny of its detailed and complex provisions; but this does not account for its manifest failure to sweeten industrial relations. That failure is more attributable to the stubborn, even reckless, determination of the Heath Government to override trade-union resistance without first ensuring that it had the public support necessary to do so successfully; an important lesson to remember in considering the importance of the 'legitimating' role of Parliament in the legislative process.

The Immigration Act 1971[16]: In contrast to the Industrial Relations Bill, the almost equally controversial Immigration Bill, establishing a common framework of immigration control for aliens and Commonwealth citizens, showed parliamentary scrutiny in its best light. There was well-informed and informative debate at all stages, some significant and constructive cross-voting in Commons standing committee, and the Government was forced to concede amendments on a number of points. As with the Industrial Relations Bill, there was a rare second reading division in the Lords, where a wide-ranging debate emphasized the interesting catholicity of the membership of the upper House (though it is seldom harnessed in common cause to such good effect). A voluntary principle was inserted into the provisions for repatriation and the provisions for compulsory registration with the police were restricted to aliens. This is a rare and important instance of the deliberative and formulative stages of the legislative process, involving constructive and useful suggestions for amendment being made by informed interest groups, focusing upon the parliamentary stages rather than taking place exclusively in the secretive corridors of Whitehall.

The European Communities Act 1972[17]: Although with the possible exception of the Scotland and Wales Bill this was perhaps the most momentous single item of legislation in recent memory, in form it was a 'framework Bill', comprising just 12 clauses, 4 schedules and a financial memorandum, providing extensively for secondary legislation. Its passage was marked by considerable pre-legislative debate both inside and outside Parliament, spread over many years and several successive administrations, and at the end of the 1970–1 Session the Conservative government had secured a comfortable Commons majority of 112 in favour of entry, and a massive one of 393 in the Lords (where 509 peers voted in the largest division in the House for fifty years). Three days were set aside for Commons second reading, which was carried by 309 votes to 301. The committee stage, though guillotined, took 173 hours and was the occasion for 88 divisions, over 200 amendments being discussed. There was unprecedented cross-voting at all stages,[18] but although the Government's majority fell to single figures sixteen times during the committee stage alone, it did not concede a single amendment; its success was virtually guaranteed when three members of the Shadow Cabinet, including Mr Roy Jenkins, resigned in April 1972, providing a rallying point for about 60 Labour pro-marketeers.

The debate was generally of high quality and the Opposition, while opposing the bill as fiercely as its divided ranks and previous shifts of policy permitted, avoided violent and undignified tactics of the kind used against the Industrial Relations Bill. Many MPs saw the bill as having crucial implications for the power and sovereignty of the Westminster Parliament; and it is undoubtedly true that one of the main problems facing the Commons in the 1970s has been its difficulty in adapting itself to the European dimension of public policy (see Chapter 10).

Housing Finance: The complicated Housing Finance Act 1972[19] introduced the concept of 'fair rents' into public sector housing. Its passage was again marked by fierce opposition and produced a debate in standing committee which lasted, notwithstanding the late imposition of a guillotine, for a record 57 sittings. The Government made several concessions during its passage through Parliament.

But the most eventful part of the Act's political life occurred after the Royal assent. Several Labour-controlled local authorities refused to raise existing council rents to the 'fair rent' level, thus unlawfully subsidising council tenants. Some 400 of the defiant councillors eventually gave up the struggle, though not before being called to account by their district auditors; but the councillors of Clay Cross in Derbyshire held out to the bitter end and suffered financial surcharges and consequent disqualification from public office. When Labour returned to power in 1974 it was faced not only by its long-standing pledge to repeal the 1972 Act but also by a resolution of the 1973 Party Conference that the defaulting councillors should be relieved of all penalties incurred in defying the Act. The former was achieved, though only after a fierce struggle, by the Housing Rents and Subsidies Act 1975; realizing the second objective proved even more troublesome.

In March 1975, a storm of protest broke out when the Government published its Housing Finance (Special Provisions) Bill, designed to replace the surcharge procedure in this context by provision for recovery of the deficiencies through locally collected revenues and to terminate the disqualifications imposed upon the Clay Cross councillors (but not to refund surcharges already imposed, which were the basis of the disqualifications). The Opposition insisted that the Government was encouraging unlawful conduct on the part of anyone politically opposed to particular Acts of Parliament, and there was clearly some unease even among some sections of the Parliamentary Labour Party about what was being done; in the end, some back-bench defections thwarted Government attempts to reverse a Lords' amendment removing the provisions which would have terminated the Clay Cross councillors' disqualifications (by now an academic exercise because they were also disqualified for matters which had nothing to do with the Housing Finance Act). So the parliamentary scrutiny of this legislation did force the Government to justify itself, and ultimately forced an amendment which reflected the degree of unease generated by this explicitly political Bill.

Reversing the Industrial Relations Act: The minority Labour Government came to office in February 1974 pledged, as part of the much vaunted social contract, to repeal the Industrial Relations Act 1971, retaining only the provisions for unfair dismissal. The difficulties they encountered in so doing demonstrate the problems of legislating without a guaranteed Commons majority and the potential powers possessed by the House of Lords, particularly when the Government lacks an adequate power-base in the elected chamber.

Although the Conservatives opposed the Trade Union and Labour Relations Bill,[20] published on 30 April 1974, it was by then evident that the main part of the 1971 Act had been an embarrassing failure; in any event, it was noticeable in the early days of the new Parliament that the Opposition was not anxious to force a general election. The Bill inevitably suffered one or two setbacks in a standing committee where Labour was outnumbered by the other parties, but it was not until the Report stage in June that any serious embarrassment occurred, and then only through a bizarre accident.

In several divisions on report the Government narrowly escaped defeats, and a couple of amendments were defeated only on the Speaker's casting vote. But after the Bill had gone to the Lords it was discovered that a minister, Mr Harold

Lever, had been 'nodded through'[21] the tied divisions even though he was no longer in the precincts of the House. The Bill had to be brought back to the Commons and the amendments formerly lost were deemed to be carried. These amendments, plus others inserted in the Lords which the Government was unable to reverse, undermined the Act's crucial 'closed shop' provisions; so the Government decided to try again in the 1974–5 Parliament.

A short Trade Union and Labour Relations (Amendment) Bill was quickly introduced into the new Parliament and as it progressed through the Commons the opposition to it increasingly focused upon the broad issue of the right of conscientious objection to belonging to a union and the narrow and symbolic one of the possible effects of a closed shop upon editorial freedom in the mass media. By the time the Bill got to the Lords the Government had agreed in principle that some kind of 'code of practice on the freedom of the Press' should be worked out within the newspaper industry, and an amendment to that effect was inserted; but Lord Goodman, Chairman of the Newspaper Publishers' Association, carried a further amendment embodying an explicit four-point charter of journalists' rights, and this amendment was later extended to give right of recourse to the civil courts for breaches of the charter. The Government was still conciliatory, but unwilling to accept the Goodman formula. The Bill went to and fro between Lords and Commons until, in a historic debate on 11 November 1975, their Lordships finally insisted upon their amendments. So the Bill was lost at prorogation.

The Government, bearing in mind that the Parliament Acts 1911 and 1949 might have to be brought out of cold storage to overcome the Lords' resistance, reintroduced the Bill in a form which included only those amendments which had been agreed by the two Houses, and carried a motion substituting a debate on 'suggested amendments' (i.e. ones which embodied the previous Session's compromise on the Press charter) for the usual Committee and Report stages. Once the Opposition had failed to get a majority in the Commons for its amendments and the Government had carried its 'suggestions', their Lordships decided to call it a day and Lord

Goodman's final amendment was lost by 109 votes to 71. The Lords did insert an amendment allowing conscientious objection to union membership, but the Commons threw it out and the Lords did not insist.

The Labour governments of the 1970s suffered a lot of aggravation at the hands of the House of Lords, though this was the first outright confrontation between the two Houses since the wrecking of the Redistribution of Seats Bill in 1969 (*vide ante*). For the most part a Labour Government with a large and contentious legislative programme probably gains more than it loses from the second chamber, in terms of valuable and relatively non-partisan scrutiny of its bills, the anomalous composition of the House notwithstanding.[22] As for the substance of this confrontation, it is no coincidence that their Lordships should have chosen to hazard their own future on a narrow issue with a high emotive content and one which, by its very nature, was certain of banner headlines and sympathetic editorials.

Procedural wrangles in the 1975–6 Session: Apart from the clash between Lords and Commons, there was a major controversy in April and May 1976 about the Government's right to a majority in standing committees, after a number of deaths and the defection of Mr John Stonehouse had deprived it of an overall majority in the Commons. The Opposition accused the Government of cheating and the issue was ultimately settled in a somewhat uneasy spirit of compromise; but the controversy over this was as nothing compared with the fury generated over the Aircraft and Shipbuilding Industries Bill, a nationalization measure regarded as a central plank in the Government's programme.

The Bill won a second reading by only five votes and then underwent 58 sittings in standing committee (breaking the record set by the Housing Finance Bill, *ante*). As soon as it came out of committee a Conservative MP, Mr Maxwell-Hyslop, submitted to the Speaker that although it had so far been subject to ordinary public Bill procedure, it was in fact a hybrid Bill because it inconsistently excluded one company from the schedule of shipbuilding firms to be nationalized, while including that company's commercial competitors.[23]

After some consideration the Speaker ruled that *prima facie* this was indeed a hybrid Bill; whereupon the Government sought to avoid going back to square one (it argued that the consequent delay would cause great damage to the industry) by moving that the relevant Standing Orders relating to private business – i.e. giving private interests affected by the Bill a chance to make representations before a select committee – be dispensed with. At the end of an acrimonious debate on 27 May 1976 an Opposition amendment to the Government motion was defeated on the Speaker's casting vote. Then the Government's motion was put, and instead of a tied result which would in this case have required the Speaker to vote *against* the motion, in order to maintain the *status quo*, it was surprisingly carried by one vote. At once there were allegations that a Government supporter had voted in breach of a firm pairing arrangement, and disorder broke out in the Chamber; amid violent scenes reminiscent of those during the Industrial Relations Bill, the sitting was suspended.

The immediate outcome was a complete breakdown of the 'usual channels' between Government and Opposition, and a consequent threat to the Government's uncompleted legislative programme. Later in the session the Government (having by now regained its slender overall majority through by-election successes) applied 'multiple guillotines' to five of its most important and controversial Bills – provoking further outcries. The Aircraft and Shipbuilding Industries Bill was lost in the Lords and had to be reintroduced in the next Session.

The merits of the case are not entirely clear-cut. On the one hand, Standing Orders expressly designed to protect private interests were set aside. On the other hand, it is the House of Commons which made the rules of legislative procedure, and by the same token it can unmake them; it is one of the realities of power politics in a 'winner takes all' system that any Government commanding a majority in the Commons can change the rules. But if they are changed too often and in circumstances which smack of political expediency rather than of principle then the whole parliamentary system, founded as it is upon consensus about how the game shall be played, is seriously threatened.

New Procedures for Scrutiny of Delegated Legislation

It would be a grave omission in an essay on legislation to say nothing at all about delegated legislation, though this short section can be only a token offering on so vast a subject. It has long been accepted as a fact of life that primary legislation, in the shape of public Acts, cannot cover every contingency and that Parliament must delegate extensive law-making powers to ministers and other bodies. But the case for delegation is fundamentally undermined if it can be shown that the procedures for monitoring delegated legislation either in its technical aspects (for example, whether a Statutory Instrument is *infra vires* its parent Act and whether it is properly drafted) or on its political merits, are deficient. Parliamentary procedures for scrutinizing delegated legislation have been extensively revised during the 1970s, but it is this writer's view that these procedures remain grossly inadequate.

There is, in particular, a grave and continuing absence of adequate facilities for debating 'Prayers' to annul instruments subject to the 'negative' procedure. The 1970–1 report of the Procedure Committee, *The Process of Legislation (ante)* stated that:

> . . . the failure of Governments of both major Parties to find time to debate Prayers has led to a breakdown of part of the process of legislation . . . Your committee believe it to be of cardinal importance that the House should appreciate the gravity of the inroads into its power of control of legislation.[24]

Following the First Report of the Brooke Committee on Delegated Legislation,[25] a body which was established in response to one of the Procedure Committee's recommendations, a Joint Committee on Statutory Instruments was created out of the House of Commons Select Committee on Statutory Instruments and the House of Lords Special Orders Committee, to rationalize the technical scrutiny of instruments. This aspect of the function of Parliament in monitoring delegated legislation is generally acknowledged to work relatively well (though it still does not extend to considering the enabling powers conferred by primary legislation).

More crucially, in March 1973 it became possible to refer consideration of the merits (as distinct from the technical quality) of uncontentious instruments subject to the 'negative' and 'affirmative' procedures to a specially constituted standing committee on Statutory Instruments; and this facility has recently been extended to European secondary legislation and to Church of England Measures. In the 1975–6 session no fewer than five separate standing committees were convened for these purposes.

While it is certainly true that some useful discussion of delegated legislation has taken place in these committees, it is clear from a perusal of *Committee Hansard* that, contrary to what was said when they were first set up, the main beneficiary of the change has been the Government itself, which has managed to move discussion of many of its affirmative resolutions off the floor of the House (though it is not certain whether the time 'saved' is used wholly for Government purposes). In two and a half years from March 1973 to the end of the 1974–5 session the standing committees considered 23 prayers (the overwhelming majority having been tabled by the official Opposition) and 149 affirmative resolutions; in the same period 20 prayers and 215 affirmative resolutions were taken on the floor of the House. It is clearly open to question, moreover, whether the form of these proceedings – a 'take note' motion with no opportunity for an effective vote in the committee or for subsequent debate on the floor of the House – gives adequate opportunity for meaningful pronouncement upon the merits of either affirmative or negative instruments. It is clear that if the Procedure Committee's warning was well-directed in 1971, then that warning merits repeating, for nothing in principle has changed. The inadequacy of these procedures is probably the strongest argument of all against Mr Short's advocacy of 'framework Bills' (*ante*).

Conclusion: A Suggested Basis for Reforming Public Bill Procedure

This essay has attempted to take an overview of legislation in the 1970s, taking as given – though by no means ideal – a model which assigns to Parliament an essentially passive, legitimating role in the legislative process. But clearly that role is of some practical as well as theoretical importance in that the 'viscosity'[26] of parliamentary procedures, and the energy and skill of the Opposition in opposing, sets limits upon the capacities of governments to realize their legislative ambitions; and the latter have, in recent times, been considerable.

Legislative procedures and conventions in Parliament tend to be geared to passing 'normal' Bills; some of the case-studies demonstrate how quickly alarming cracks begin to appear when abnormally troublesome measures are fed into the machine. And it is then that ministers wax eloquent about reforms, which, when they are examined carefully, turn out to be ways of thinning Parliament's already watery viscosity, or of by-passing altogether the more irksome parts of parliamentary scrutiny, thus enabling governments to get their way more easily. Even given the necessity for firm government, such eloquence should be viewed with suspicion by anyone who believes, as does this writer, that imperfect parliamentary scrutiny and a modest requirement for policy to be justified in public is better than even less scrutiny and an even feebler requirement for public justification.

It is too much to ask of an academic that he keeps his own oar out of the issue of 'reform', though here the dictates of space will spare the reader more than brief inconvenience. In the procedure debate on 2 February 1976 (*ante*), Mr John Peyton, Opposition spokesman on House of Commons affairs, said:

It has long seemed to me that if we taxed our ingenuity we could have some system of classifying legislation. In the course of my labours in that dreadful place called the Department of the Environment, I recall the fact that legislation was urgently necessary to ensure the safety of reservoirs. It is ridiculous that such matters should be held up because of party politics. If the public are in jeopardy, as they well might be from such a cause, it is of the utmost importance that the matter should be dealt with without delay.

But he did add a note of caution:

> ... if such legislation is to be given a privileged and easy passage, will not this unduly weaken the Opposition in that it will make it easier for the Government to get through the more offensive and obnoxious portions of their legislation?[27]

As indicated earlier, most legislation is technical and uncontroversial in character; yet public Bill procedure takes no account of the difference between the Reservoirs Bill and the innovatory Housing Finance Bill. There is an important distinction – one which has, with only a few minor setbacks, survived the efforts of this writer and his research colleague[28] to find exceptions to it among all public Bills studied over several parliamentary sessions – between *administration* Bills which carry on a well-established line of policy (for example, by correcting anomalies discovered in the course of applying an earlier piece of legislation or by correcting details to take account of changed circumstances such as the falling value of money), and *policy* Bills which are genuinely innovatory.[29] In principle the former should be dealt with quickly,[30] but all too often a great deal of time is taken reopening long settled issues of principle: the bulk of legislative scrutiny should be directed at policy Bills, but this does not always happen. No doubt there would be difficulties in operationalizing the distinction in procedural terms, but it seems to me to be a line of attack well worth exploring.

5 Standing Committees in the House of Commons

J. A. G. GRIFFITH

Standing Committees are usually thought of in the context of the committee stage on public Bills.[1] But there are half a dozen other uses in addition.

Thus a standing committee of sixteen to fifty Members may be nominated to consider the second reading of a Bill and to make a recommendation that the Bill ought to be read a second time.

The motion to refer a Bill to a second reading committee may be vetoed by twenty Members. This means that, at least, the motion must have the support of the official Opposition as well as the government but it means also, in these days, that a group of other Members may prevent the motion being carried.

The object of this procedure is to save time on the floor of the House by having non-contentious bills read a second time 'upstairs'. It has had only a very limited success though in recent sessions more bills have been dealt with in this way. Its impact can be considerable only if the official Opposition, and others, are willing to interpret 'non-contentious' fairly widely.

So also the Report stage of a Bill the second reading of which was taken in committee may itself go to a standing committee. The motion for committal may be vetoed by twenty Members. Only one Bill has been dealt with in this way.

Again, if the Speaker is of opinion that the provisions of any public bill relate exclusively to Scotland, he gives a certificate to that effect. On the order for the second reading, a motion may be made by a minister that the bill be referred to the Scottish Grand Committee (which is a standing committee), but if at least ten Members object, the Speaker declares that the noes have it. A Bill so referred is considered by that Committee in relation to the principle of the Bill and is reported to the House as having been so considered. Normally it will then be sent directly to a Scottish standing committee for committee stage.

The Scottish Grand Committee consists of the Members representing Scottish constituencies together with not less than ten nor more than fifteen other Members nominated by the Committee of Selection having regard to the approximation of the balance of parties in the committee to that of the whole House.

In addition, the Scottish Grand Committee may consider Bills on report – but it has never done so. It may also consider Scottish estimates and, subject to a veto by ten or more Members, other referred 'matters'.

Bills and other 'matters' relating to Wales may be referred to the Welsh Grand Committee consisting of all Members sitting for constituencies in Wales, plus five other Members. If any motion were moved referring a Bill to this Committee for second reading, twenty Members could veto it.

The Northern Ireland Committee was set up in 1975 to consider matters referred to it. Twenty Members are added to the Irish Members.

A standing committee on regional affairs was also appointed in 1975 to consider, subject to a veto by twenty Members, any matter referred to it. It consists of all Members for English constituencies, together with five others.

Finally, in recent years, it has become increasingly difficult for Members, who wish to move 'prayers' for the annulment of statutory instruments, to find time to do so. For this reason, among others, standing orders now provide for the appointment of one or more standing committees to consider any instruments referred to them. Twenty Members may veto the motion to refer.

In addition to members of this committee, any other Member of the House may speak in the committee but may not vote. Normally the debate on an instrument may not continue for more than $1\frac{1}{2}$ hours (or $2\frac{1}{2}$ hours for instruments relating to Northern Ireland).

I now turn to the most important use to which standing committees are put.

The Committee Stage of Bills

1. *Function*

Standing Orders require that when a public bill (other than a Consolidated Fund or an Appropriation Bill or a bill confirming a provisional order) has been read a second time, it shall stand committed to a standing committee unless the House otherwise order. And in the majority of cases it is so committed. In recent years it has been the practice to send part of the Finance Bill to a standing committee and to retain part on the floor of the House but no other bill is so split. Consolidation bills go to a joint committee with the Lords. Scottish bills are generally sent to a Scottish standing committee.

'The function of a committee on a bill,' says Erskine May, 'is to go through the text of the bill clause and, if necessary, word by word, with a view to making such amendments in it as may seem likely to render it more generally acceptable.' There are two difficulties in this formulation. The first is that it conceals the fact that each clause and each schedule must be put to the committee for its approval whether or not any amendment to the clause or schedule has been moved. The debates on clause stand part are a special characteristic of Commons' procedure in the sense that they are not logically necessary. If detailed examination of a bill is thought desirable, then the power to move amendments is almost an inevitable corollary. But it does not follow that each clause should be debatable. This is not to say that the debates on clause stand part are undesirable but only to notice that they take place, are an important part of the procedure, and are not part of Erskine May's formulation.

The second difficulty is the assumption that the purpose of going through the text of a bill is to make amendments that will render the bill more generally acceptable. This confuses a number of different matters. Amendments may have one

C.I.S. – D

or more of a great variety of purposes. Whether moved by the Opposition or by a Government back-bencher, an amendment may be intended to cause political mischief, to embarrass the Government, to discover what are the Government's real intentions and whether (in particular) they include one or more specific possibilities, to placate interests outside Parliament who are angered by the bill, to make positive improvements in the bill the better to effect its purposes, to set out alternative proposals, to initiate a debate on some general principle of great or small importance, to ascertain from the Government the meaning of a clause or sub-section or to obtain assurances on how they will be operated, to correct grammatical errors or to improve the draftsmanship of the bill. If moved by the Government, the purpose of an amendment is most likely to be to correct a drafting error or to make minor consequential changes, to record agreements made with outside bodies which were uncompleted when the bill was introduced, to introduce new matter, or occasionally to meet a criticism made by a Member either during the second reading debate or at an earlier part of the committee stage, or informally.

Not all of these purposes, if fulfilled, are likely to make the bill 'more generally acceptable'. Apart from the trivialities of minor errors, the occasions of an amendment falling within that phrase are when an Opposition amendment is accepted by the Government or when a Government amendment goes some way to meet an objection. This of course, may, at the same time, make the bill less acceptable to some of the Government supporters. This is not to say that committee debates seldom, if ever, result in the improvement of a bill. It is to say, however, that very many amendments are not put forward with that purpose, and of those that are, not all have that effect.

More importantly, much of what takes place during committee on a controversial bill is an extension and an application of the general critical function of the House and there is little or no intention or expectation of changing the bill. The purpose of many Opposition amendments is not to make the bill more generally acceptable but to make the Government less generally acceptable.

This great variety of functions that a committee may perform reflects also the great differences between the activities of different committees. When several standing committees are sitting at the same time, an observer who moves from one room to another may pass at once from a crowded and heated political debate on some major social problem when tempers are short, Opposition Members obstructive and Ministers intransigent, to a quiet, highly technical discussion conducted by ten or a dozen Members, many of whom, at any point of time, seem not to be wholly absorbed in the proceedings. In mood, in spirit and in purpose, these two sorts of activity are very far apart.

The business of conducting a bill through committee as the Member-in-charge requires a Minister to have a detailed understanding of the provisions of the bill. He must know not only the purpose of each clause and its relation to other clauses and the bill as a whole, but also why the draftsman has used certain words or phrases. Sometimes a Minister's understanding of legislative language is not complete and he is obliged to say that he is advised that the words used and not other words are necessary to achieve the purpose sought. It follows that when amendments are tabled the Ministers must be carefully briefed as to their meaning, their purpose, and their effect. He must know what he can accept either with profit or at least without loss, what he can give way on and to what extent, what he must resist to the end.

For the performance of all these functions, the Minister is advised and instructed by his department. His relationship with his back-bench supporters in committee is of less importance. He wishes, of course, to carry them with him and he hopes to be able to rely on them to support him with their vote in divisions. When the bill is taken on the floor of the House, the relationship is no different from that of a Minister making a statement of general policy on behalf of the Government on any non-legislative matter. If the party machinery has worked well, Members who are interested will have argued the general issues in party groups or, if the issue is important and central to the party's policy, more generally, even perhaps at party conferences. Members may have served on select committees which were concerned with the issue. Or they may, for constituency or other reasons, be wholly familiar with it and need no help from their Minister. And, in the case of standing committees, as we shall see, they may have been nominated for membership of the committee because of the positive help they can give the Minister from the back benches.

At the same time, Members of Parliament are not by nature subservient. Their loyalty to their party may make them hesitate at length before they vote against their front bench in committee, as in the House. And, more often than not, their hesitation will end in their continuing to support their leaders. But this does not mean, when they are Government supporters, that they will speak only when asked to by the Whips or that they will refrain from moving amendments that may cause the Government some embarrassment.

The extent to which the Minister in charge of a bill, as Minister, will seek to organize his party supporters in standing committee varies greatly from Minister to Minister and from bill to bill. On a contentious and complicated measure, the Minister may call regular meetings to explain the purposes of the different parts of the bill and the way in which he intends to deal with it in committee. And then the opportunity will arise for Members to give their views. But this suggests a degree of formality of proceedings which is misleading. Even when such meetings occur, Members will approach the Minister informally, to give him information, to make suggestions, to urge particular courses of action. Certainly any impression of a tightly-knit group of backbenchers meeting, with the Minister, to decide how the bill shall be handled would be false. Apart from the fact that a much looser association normally governs the relationship between Ministers and back-benchers in their ordinary dealings in the House, whether on legislation or other matters, the Minister has a duty to his department and to the Government which transcends his obligation to his party supporters. He is first a Minister and only secondly one of his party's front-bench spokesmen. In this sense the line that separates Ministers from all other Members of Parliament is more strongly drawn than the line that separates the Government side of the House from the Opposition side. Being a member of the Government cuts a Minister off from his party colleagues because, however accountable he may be to his colleagues and to the House, his primary responsibilities are to the Executive arm. In legal terms he is one of Her Majesty's Ministers and not a servant of the House; and this reflects his constitutional and political position also.

Ministers do not, therefore, regard the organizing of their supporters in a standing committee as a primary or even as a particularly important part of their duties. To ensure support there is seldom any need to do so; to try to force total unanimity when this does not exist would be folly. Too much emphasis has been placed by too many commentators on the pressure brought to bear on Members of Parliament by the Whips' Office to toe the party line. Of course there are important occasions when the pressures are strong. But the emphasis distorts the general pattern of relationships within a party. Members begin by sharing common beliefs with their party colleagues and it is this, combined with party loyalty, which makes for agreement far more than consideration of the consequences of disagreement.

The need to organize is more obvious when in Opposition. There are no departmental advisers to provide information and briefing. On important bills, the affected interests outside Parliament will be anxious to help in the hope of bringing further pressure to bear on the Government to accept amendments. And if they are powerful they will be well and expertly staffed and will have or will engage lawyers to draft amendments so that all Opposition Members need do, if they are so minded, is to sign the amendment provided and hand it in to the Public Bill Office. At times, this servicing by professionals and experts comes close in its drafting and in its briefing to the service provided for the Minister by his department.

Sometimes those who lead for the Opposition will set up working parties of their own drawn from outside, affected interests and also draw on teams of lawyers from outside Parliament. These groups may meet regularly to prepare the Opposition case in detail against the bill when it is in committee. And in this way the Opposition provides its own civil service, helped by research departments at party headquarters.

So also those leading for the Opposition may regularly meet with their supporters, on a standing committee, or specially selected group if the bill is committed to the whole House, and may seek to divide amongst them the task of moving amendments. But, again, the danger in writing of all these arrangements is to overstate the case. Not infrequently, opposition to a bill is hardly organized at all but carried almost entirely by one or two front-bench spokesmen, with others making back-up speeches when they choose. The organization, if that is not too strong a word, is then highly informal and haphazard. In addition, Opposition back-benchers frequently engage in their own individual activities and put down amendments without, necessarily, informing their front bench.

How far any arrangements are made depends on the nature of the bill, its size and complexity, how far it is a measure in its essentials agreed to by Government and Opposition, and on the personal approach and tactics of those on the Opposition front bench in committee.

The job of the Minister in charge of a bill in committee, assisted by the committee Whip, is to ensure that it is reported to the House with all its principles and the great mass of its details preserved and, according to the length and complexity of the bill and the extent to which it is contentious, with reasonable speed. The Government's timetable allows for accidents but if several of its bills are kept longer in committee than had been allowed for, difficulties will begin to arise and the whole programme will be threatened with disruption.

What the Opposition seeks to achieve is more various

depending on its attitude not only to the bill itself but also to the Government generally. It follows that the Opposition may be seeking to achieve different objects on different days, at different stages of the bill, on different clauses. And the unexpected often happens. An amendment no bigger than a man's hand may suddenly be used to twist the Government's arm. The personal attitude, real or imagined, of a Minister or an Opposition spokesman may antagonize the other side to such an extent that progress on the bill is effectively ended for a time. If it appears, rightly or wrongly, that the Minister or junior Minister has a brief that he imperfectly understands, perhaps because, through no fault of his own, he has to deal with a subject usually entrusted to others of his colleagues, tempers on the Opposition side may become a little short.

More important than any of these to the progress of a bill, to the attitude of Government to Opposition and Opposition to Government, are political events that may be wholly irrelevant to the subject-matter of the bill. Even a bill supported by both sides of the committee may give rise to angry debates or to obstruction if, for some reason, perhaps in the field of foreign policy or economic affairs, the political atmosphere in the House and outside suddenly thickens and the political fight sharpens. Members of each side begin to show personal distaste for those on the other and the surface courtesy which helps the House to go about its business disappears. Then bills that would otherwise have followed a moderately peaceful or moderately contentious course in committee become the occasion for acrimony and anger. And little progress is made. Even procedural changes, if they appear to be attempts to push Government business through at an unwonted pace, may give rise to obstruction in order to defeat that purpose — as happened in response to morning sittings. On other occasions debate on uncontentious bills may be prolonged to make it more difficult for the Government to make progress on some other, strongly opposed, measure. This took place when the Industrial Relations Bill 1970–1 and the European Communities Bill 1971–2 were before the House.

2. *Membership*

A standing committee normally consists of a chairman appointed by the Speaker and Members nominated by the Committee of Selection. As many standing committees may be appointed as are necessary for the consideration of bills or other business. Each committee is formed separately for each bill so although we may read that Standing Committee A in 1970–1 'considered 6 bills and held 44 sittings', the reality is that six different groups of Members sitting under different chairmen were designated successively as Standing Committee A. Seven or eight standing committees are commonly necessary. In addition, in each Session two Scottish standing committees are usually necessary to examine Scottish bills. In all but one of the standing committees Government bills have precedence, most private Members' bills being sent to Standing Committee C where they have precedence. It is a duty of the Speaker to allocate bills among the committees, but in so doing he has regard to the priority wished by the Government.

The Committee of Selection nominates the Members (not less than 16 nor more than 50) to serve on each standing committee and is required to have regard to the qualifications of those Members and to the composition of the House. The Committee of Selection consists of eleven Members, of whom three are a quorum. Its Members are nominated each session by the House which in this case means by the party Whips. The chairman is a member of the Government party.

As every schoolboy knows, governments for the first 74 years of this century enjoyed overall majorities in the House except in 1924 and in 1929–31. And so they enjoyed overall majorities in standing committees. Thus at the beginning of 1970–1 Session the Conservative Party had 330 seats; the Labour Party 287 seats; the Liberal Party had 6 seats; 1 seat each was held by Members being Independent Irish, Independent Labour, Protestant Unionist, Republican Labour, Scottish Nationalist, and Unity; in addition was the Speaker. This resulted in the allotment of the following numbers of Conservative and Labour Members of standing committees:

Number of Members on standing committee	Conservative	Labour
16	9	7
20	11	9
25	13	12
30	16	14
35	19	16
40	21	19
45	24	21
50	27	23

If it were wished to include a Liberal Member or one of the independent or unsupported Members, this could be done either by the Government or (more likely) the Opposition giving up one of their places or by increasing the membership of the committee.

But the election of February 1974 resulted in the Labour Party having 301 seats, the Conservatives 296 seats, the Liberals 14 seats ond others 24 seats. For the next seven months, the Government had to be content with half the total number of seats in standing committee. In October 1974 the Government narrowly regained its overall majority in the House and so obtained a majority of one in standing committee. But by April 1976 the Government had suffered casualties and lost its overall majority. After argument in the House and the Selection Committee, the Government agreed to revert to an equality of membership.

Certain Members are inevitably members of a standing committee. These are the minister in charge of the bill; and one or more of his junior ministers, with perhaps ministers from other departments, depending on the size and complexity of the measure. It is the practice for the Parliamentary Private Secretary of the Minister in charge also to be a member; and for a Government Whip to be nominated. Similarly, on the Opposition side, one or more official spokesmen will be members nominated by the Shadow Cabinet; and they will discuss with the Chief Whip which other Members would be helpful on different aspects of the bill because of their particular knowledge or their experience of its subject-matter or their constituency. Such Members who are specialists and experts on particular matters – such as housing and planning, or defence, or health services – appear frequently as Opposition back-bench members of standing committees, nominated by the Whips.

The number of places on a standing committee for which a true competition exists may therefore be relatively small. But this is subject to two considerations: first, the larger the committee the greater the number of places to be competed for; and secondly, the keenness of the competition, whatever the size of the committee. For it must not be supposed that Members commonly vie for committee membership. Sometimes this is so. Membership of the Standing Committee on the Finance Bill is sought after, particularly by Conservatives. Opportunities can arise to plead the case (and, if one's own party is in power, with some hope of success) for the relief from taxation of special groups of persons. Committee membership for bills on controversial social issues (such as immigration or housing) is also sought after. Generally there will be no shortage of Conservative candidates for committees on bills concerned with agriculture or of Labour candidates for committees on mining bills or those affecting other regional industries. But committee members are not easily found for the large number of unexciting bills which pass through the House of Commons each Session.

Standing committee work, except for the main protagonists, can be tedious, and time-wasting. This is particularly so for government back-benchers who, although they are often discouraged by the committee Whip from speaking as this tends to slow down progress, must be present or at hand in case of divisions. And so the Chief Whip will find the recruitment of members for standing committees more difficult when the party is in power than when it is in opposition; and usually he has fewer back-bench Members to choose from.

Each party claims that it seeks to get 'a fair spread' of opinion within the party represented on the more popular or controversial committees. And each tends to believe that the other is more ruthless. The concept itself is too vague for any precise assessment. But it is certainly true that under the Labour Government 1964–70 the 'Left' was represented on standing committees for bills concerned with housing, prices and incomes, nationalization and others where their views on certain clauses were known to be opposed to Government policy. No doubt they also felt themselves inadequately represented on other committees. Similarly under the 1970–74 Government the Conservative membership on the Standing Committee for the Immigration Bill 1971 contained Members usually associated with the right wing on this issue, e.g. Mr Enoch Powell, and others usually regarded as liberal, e.g. Sir George Sinclair. It would have been interesting to see how far the 'fair spread' principle would have been applied by either Government or Opposition parties had the European Communities Bill 1971–2 been sent to a standing committee.

3. Value, defects and possible reform
If the value of the proceedings in standing committee on Government bills[2] is judged by the extent to which Members, other than ministers, successfully move amendments, then the value is small. It has been as rare for ministerial amendments to be rejected as for other Members' amendments to be successfully moved against government opposition. Party discipline is largely maintained in standing committee. Not surprisingly when the latter rarity occurs it is often on bills concerned with matters of the highest social controversy like race relations or immigration policy. For it is on such matters that the Whip is most likely to be defied.

On the other hand, minor reforms are quite often successfully achieved by persuading the Minister to 'look again' when the matter is before the committee and not infrequently[3] he may propose some compromise on report.

But more important than the making of amendments is the scrutiny to which ministers and their policies are subjected. Committee rooms are not large and do not have that sense of space and support which can be felt on the floor of the House (though that also can no doubt be at times a very lonely place). For hour after hour and for week after week a minister may be required to defend his bill against attack from others who may be only slightly less knowledgeable than himself. His departmental brief may be full and his grasp of the subject considerable but even so he needs to be constantly on the alert and any defects he or his policy reveals will be very quickly exploited by his political opponents.

All this of course is much sharpened when, as may be the situation for some years to come, the government has no majority, or only the barest, in standing committee because it cannot command a true working majority in the House. The possibility of successful amendment becomes greater and the scrutiny more effective. If we do move into a period of minority governments, then far fewer contentious Government bills are likely to be introduced. Those that do find their way to standing committee will be open to stronger attack – subject however to this constraint that the Opposition may not be anxious to present the Government with issues which the Government might take to the country with success. Attacks must to some extent be more restrained when likely to be lethal. A numerically-weak government can often find itself in a strong position because the Opposition when willing to strike may be afraid to wound or when willing to wound may be afraid to kill.

The conflict in standing committee between Government and Opposition often seems, and often is, highly formal. Positions are taken up, attitudes are struck and roles are played, almost as much as they are on the floor of the House itself. And some of the weakness of the Opposition lies in that narrow difference between a good knowledge of the details of the matter in hand and a very good knowledge. The Government enjoys the latter because the department has so much the better means for acquiring knowledge. And ministers do not, in committee, readily and easily lay more of their cards on the table than they must. So the scrutiny of ministers has about it a measure of superficiality based on an inadequacy of information. And one reform which has been considered and even on a few occasions applied, is to subject ministers and civil servants to the kind of detailed examination which takes place before select committees. In 1970–1 the Second Clerk Assistant and the Clerk of Public Bills submitted to the Select Committee on Procedure a memorandum which in part considered select committees in relation to public bills. I am here concerned only with the memorandum so far as it dealt

with the submission of public bills to select committees
after second reading, not with pre-legislation committees. The
memorandum summarizes the position thus:

The procedure in a Select Committee to which a public
bill has been committed after Second Reading differs
according to whether a Bill is Hybrid or not. In the case
of the majority of Bills which are not Hybrid, procedure
follows a standard pattern. The Committees concerned are
given power to send for persons, papers and records, and
this power enables the Committee to take evidence on the
Bill. When the evidence has been concluded the clauses of
the Bill are considered. The rules which govern the admissi-
bility of amendments are the same as those in a Committee
of the whole House or a Standing Committee, but the
Chairman does not have the power of selecting amendments
nor of accepting closure. Proceedings on the Bill form part
of the deliberations of the Committee and are not open to
the public; nor are speeches for or against amendments
recorded (as they are in Standing Committee) though the
decision on each amendment is recorded in the minutes in
the same manner as in Standing Committee Minutes. After
the Committee have gone through the Bill, it is open to
them to consider and agree to a special report informing
the House of any matters in relation to the Bill, to which
it is thought the attention of the House should be drawn; in
recent years it has been customary for Select Committees
to make a special report of this nature, though there is no
obligation upon them to do so.[4]

It has not been the practice to refer to select committees
bills which form the principal part of the Government's
legislative programme. I wish to consider the feasibility of
so doing. I assume that the major measures which are, for
the reasons discussed above, usually sent to a committee of the
whole House, would continue to be sent there. I assume the
same for the minor measures which are similarly committed
and indeed their number might well be increased. What I am
therefore considering is the replacement of standing committee
procedure (including that part of the Finance Bill usually so
committed) by a new procedure.

Under this new procedure, the bills sent to select committee after second reading would be, in large or small part, controversial between the parties. The atmosphere would often be partisan and votes would need to be taken from time to time. The select committee would therefore need to be composed, as standing committees are at present, of members in numbers reflecting the party strengths in the House. The select committee would usually be composed of ten to twelve members.

I envisage the proceedings of this committee as falling into two distinct stages. In the first stage, its function would be to take evidence on the bill clause by clause. Throughout the bill the principal witnesses would be the Minister in charge of the bill, or a junior Minister deputizing for him; the departmental advisers; and the draftsman of the bill. Ministers would not, therefore, at this stage, be members of the committee. Any member of the committee might ask questions of any witness and request the production of any document or of any other information. These powers would require controls to prevent abuse. It would be necessary for the chairman of the committee to act not as the chairman of a select committee normally acts (that is, as its leader), but as the chairman of a standing committee acts (that is, as a neutral). He would be empowered to refuse to allow questions to be put, as falling outside the scope of the clause under discussion or as being repetitious or as otherwise being out of order. He would also be empowered to refuse to put the request for the production of particular documents or the calling of particular witnesses on the ground of their *prima facie* irrelevance or the likelihood that they would merely duplicate other witnesses. Moreover the Minister (who, or whose deputy, would be entitled to be present throughout the proceedings), would be permitted to instruct any departmental adviser who gave evidence not to answer a particular question but to answer it himself or to refuse to do so.

The select committee would have power to call for written or oral evidence from any other person or body; and any person or body might submit written evidence to the select committee.

The chairman would have power to accept or not to accept

a closure motion to end discussion on a clause. In order to reduce the likelihood of one or two committee members taking an undue length of time in questioning a witness, the chairman would normally invite members alternately from the majority and minority members of the committee to put their questions. To prevent or limit obstruction the guillotine would be available.

The proceedings would normally be open to the public and would be recorded in Committee Hansard, as would the documents and information submitted unless they were classified and the Minister requested that they be not published. No amendments would be moved at this stage of the proceedings. At the end of the first stage, the Minister might, if he thought fit, amend the bill and, if he did, the bill would be reprinted as amended, with a detailed explanatory memorandum on these amendments.

The second stage of the committee would be conducted by the same committee except that the Minister or Ministers would now be added members, an equal number of Opposition Members being added. Amendments might be tabled and the whole process would follow that of standing committees with the following modifications. The chairman's power to select amendments would be exercised more forcefully than at present and in particular he would be empowered not to select amendments that in his opinion were designed to probe matters already adequately probed during the first stage. So also where amendments were tabled which raised matters of principle already adequately discussed during the first stage, the chairman would have power either to select them for a division only, or to curtail discussion, much more strictly than at present, in particular by ruling that he would permit only two or three speeches (including the reply of the mover of the amendments) from each side of the committee. He might also need to use his power to accept closure motions more freely.

The justification for this increased control by the chairman at the second stage is, of course, that Opposition speakers in particular would already have had opportunities to raise with the Minister and his departmental advisers many of the questions that they would normally put in standing committee.

The great majority of those amendments presently withdrawn because of the Minister's explanation or undertaking to look again would not need to be put again because the Minister would have answered those questions in that vein during the first stage; or because the Minister at this second stage would put forward amendments to meet the suggestions made, thus enabling this second stage in part to function as a report stage. Indeed it is obvious that since this proposal adds a new stage to the procedure, there would have to be closer control by the chairman of the committee on both stages to ensure that business was done within the available time. If this control were exercised it should be possible to ensure that the two stages together took no longer than the present single stage.

Let Richard Crossman have the last word.[5]

Tuesday, July 5th

In the morning I went to the Standing Committee on the Local Government Bill. Fortunately for me, Geoffrey Rippon, who has taken Boyd-Carpenter's place in leading the Opposition, is idle as hell. He would be prepared to pair with me for every single sitting and leave the work to Temple, the Chester MP, who is a kind of professional representative of the local government associations. My job is to go there whenever the Whips feel that my presence would move the Committee on a bit faster. Oh dear, the whole procedure of a Standing Committee is insane. What is the sense of starting at the beginning and working line by line through each clause when in many cases there is no one there who understands what they mean? If we had a Select Committee at which I could be cross-examined on the main policy and the Committee could get down to discussing the controversial issues, that would be far more constructive. Under the present system there is no genuine committee work, just formal speech-making mostly from written briefs. All the Opposition can do is to read aloud the briefs they get from the city or county treasurers and I then read back to them the brief I get from my Department. Talk about Parliamentary reform. This is an area where it is really needed.

6 Private Members' Legislation

PETER G. RICHARDS

The common criticism of the House of Commons as a legislature is that it merely records and legitimizes the wishes of the party in power. Party loyalty controls the votes, if not always the voices, of Members, so the wish of the Cabinet always prevails. This view, of course, is an over-simplification. Ministers are frequently persuaded to have second thoughts through back-bench pressure and by representations from various other quarters.[1] But it is still true that, for the greater part of the legislative programme, Members are reacting to government proposals. However, a part of the legislation that comes before Parliament is still sponsored by individual Members and Peers.

This private initiative is restricted by the Standing Order which forbids government expenditure other than on the recommendation of the Crown. So the central purpose of a back-bench bill must not be to spend the taxpayers' money. (New categories of local authority expenditure are permitted.) If it implies incidentally some minor amount of state spending, the appropriate resolution signifying permission to proceed with the measure will be moved by a Minister in Committee of the Whole House. This procedure is a valuable safeguard against abuses as it eliminates the possibility that Members might promote legislation in an attempt to obtain financial benefits for their constituents or other sectional interests.

Back-benchers in the Commons have three separate methods available to them for sponsoring bills. Twelve Fridays in each session are allocated for private Members' bills: priority on these days is determined initially by a ballot. Good fortune in the ballot is normally a prerequisite of success for a Member who hopes to steer a measure on to the statute book. The two other procedures offer little prospect of time for discussion and, therefore, of ultimate enactment, unless the proposals are exceptionally uncontroversial.

Under Standing Order No. 37 a Member may present a bill without obtaining leave from the House and the bill is read a first time. Bills introduced in this way are termed unballoted bills. They receive no further consideration unless one of three things takes place: an unopposed second reading is allowed – the Government provides time for debate – or all balloted bills down for discussion on any Friday are disposed of before the end of the sitting. The second and third possibilities are highly unlikely. A Member who hopes to get an unopposed second Reading will bring forward his bill at the close of the main debate on a Friday, but the attempt will fail if any other Member shouts the single word 'Object'. It is, therefore, essential to conciliate all interested Members, including the department(s) concerned, before such a bill can succeed.[2]

Another means whereby private Members may initiate legislation, the Ten minute Rule, was revived in November 1950 through a Government defeat on the issue by 235 votes to 229.[3] Under this procedure (Standing Order No. 13) one bill may be introduced at the end of Question Time each Tuesday and Wednesday with a short speech not exceeding ten minutes. A single speech of similar length may also be made in opposition, and then the motion for leave to introduce the bill is put. If the bill is unopposed, or is successful in a division, it is available for further consideration in the same way as the unballoted bills described in the previous paragraph. The right to use the Ten minute Rule is distributed on a first-come first-served basis[4] and it introduces an attractive element of flexibility into the parliamentary timetable. If there is a division, no Whips are on. If a bill cuts across the lines of party controversy, both sides may be hopelessly divided. A good attendance is assured because the discussion takes place normally within half an hour of the end of Question Time. Here is an admirable opportunity to command the attention of the House with no need to win a place in a ballot. A better audience is available than for an adjournment motion, both in terms of the attendance of Members and in terms of coverage by the mass media.

Two quite separate purposes may be served by the Ten minute Rule. The short speech that it permits a Member to make may succeed in satisfying any opponents to his measure and may smooth the path towards an unopposed second Reading. Alternatively, it permits a Member to make a demonstration on some more controversial topic in the hope that the interest and support aroused by the brief introduction may improve the chances of legislative action in a subsequent Session. The abolition of capital punishment and theatre censorship and the change in the law on homosexuality were all assisted by preliminary ventilation under this procedure.

The one serious hope for the back-bencher who wishes to promote important legislation is the ballot. Yet the obstacles in his path are formidable. The number of bills brought in under the ballot depends on the time available for them. In the 1966 Parliament with 16 Fridays available, 27 bills were introduced: since 1970 with only 12 Fridays available, 20 bills have been introduced. Around 400 Members enter the draw.

Members successful in the ballot present their bills in dummy form on the fifth Wednesday of Session. The three-week gap between ballot and presentation allows time to decide how to use the opportunity. At this stage nothing more than a short title for the bill is required but a sponsor must ensure that his bill is printed seven to ten days before the day fixed for second Reading. Not to allow reasonable time to study the text of a bill provides a legitimate source of complaint. The time needed for drafting and preliminary consultations may affect the choice of date for second Reading.

Drafting of legislation is a highly specialized art only understood fully by the limited group of official parliamentary draftsmen. Except when ministers are sympathetic, official assistance is not available to a back-bencher. So sponsors need help. They may obtain it from the House of Commons' Clerks in the Public Bill Office who, through experience, acquire something of the art. Help may come from other Members with legal training or from an interest group who are pressing for a particular change in the law. Since 1971 Members who obtain one of the first ten places in the ballot have been able to claim a small allowance to pay for drafting assistance for their bills.

Members are allowed to choose a second Reading Friday in the order of their precedence in the ballot. Three or four bills fall due to be considered on each of these days: if the debate on the first bill occupies the whole of the time available, the other bills due to be discussed on that day go to the end of the queue and will almost certainly die for the lack of time. Alternatively, the time left for the second (or third) bill may be too brief for any reasonable discussion of it to take place, and no decision will be reached. Probably about six out of the twenty bills get no attention at all. It is possible that the debate on the first bill on a Friday will be un-necessarily prolonged in order to obstruct the passage of another and highly controversial bill due for examination the same day. Members who draw a higher number than six try to choose a Friday when the preceding bill(s) seems so un-controversial as to require a short debate. It is also good tactics, *ceteris paribus*, to choose an earlier Friday rather than a later one so that a bill will have a higher place in the queue of measures waiting for consideration by Standing Com-mittee.

A further problem is to keep the House in session. On Fridays the call of constituencies and the weekend encourage Members to be absent from Westminster. A Member introducing a bill must do his own 'whipping' to keep his supporters present. When a bill is supported by a majority of Members present it is still sometimes difficult to obtain a decision on the second Reading, for opponents will try and avoid a vote. If no decision is reached by four o'clock, the bill is 'talked out' and it is improbable that time will be available for further consideration. The sponsor of the bill can claim to move that 'the question be now put', but the Speaker may refuse the motion if he is of the opinion that the bill has not been adequately discussed: in practice, the Speaker will always permit a division on the first bill of the day when it has been debated for five hours. So the first six

Members drawn in the ballot are guaranteed a vote on the second Reading of their bills. Even when the closure motion is accepted by the Chair and is carried by a majority, it still needs one hundred Members in support to be successful: in May 1974 a Conservative attempt to amend the electoral law failed when the closure motion was carried by 65 votes to 2.[5] So a contentious measure, even with the advantage of a high place in the ballot, still needs the presence of 100 supporters if it is to proceed. Divisions other than those seeking a closure require forty Members to participate for a decision to be made: when the total vote is below forty the question is left unresolved and the House passes immediately to next business. The Farriers Registration Bill gained a majority of 30 to nil in favour of its second Reading but this was still insufficient.[6] This particular Friday, 24 January 1975, was exceptional in that the Commons dealt with six private Members' bills, five of which gained a second Reading. When the agenda consists of back-bench bills there is an attractive element of unpredictability about parliamentary behaviour.

The Standing Committee which examines the detail of a private Member's bill is composed as far as possible of Members who have showed an interest in the measure. If the bill is carried by a majority vote at second Reading, then the Committee should reflect the balance of opinion in the House. Normally the sponsor can be sure that the Committee will favour the principles of his bill, but it does not follow that the majority of Members will favour each separate clause. There may be difficulty in selecting a Committee to reflect fairly the opinion of the House as expressed in the vote on second Reading. Members who vote in favour of a bill may do so for different reasons. The majority supporting the 1975 Abortion (Amendment) Bill sponsored by James White (Lab., Glasgow, Pollok) were divided between those who objected to abortion on principle, those who favoured abortion in some cases but felt that the existing law was too liberal, and those who objected to private medicine. If a bill is contentious it is probable that its opponents will put up a determined fight by tabling a large number of amendments. No guillotine or timetable motion is available to aid a private Member's bill.

Thus a determined filibuster can kill a controversial measure, e.g. the successful campaign by Sir Cyril Black (Con., Wimbledon, 1950–70) against the 1968 Sunday Entertainments Bill. Very occasionally a bill is referred to a select committee and not a standing committee. A select committee invites evidence from witnesses on the subject matter of a bill before making its report to the House. This offers an opportunity for a wider public to express its views but this procedure is almost certain to ensure that the bill is not passed, at least in the current session, as the hearing of evidence uses up so much time. White's Abortion Bill was the most recent measure to be treated in this way.

After a bill has emerged from the committee stage it goes to the Report Stage in the Chamber. Here time is even more at a premium since only six Fridays are available for the Report Stage and third Reading of all private Members' bills. If a bill passes safely through Report, then success at the third Reading should be assured. However, no bill that meets severe opposition can survive the Report Stage unless the government agrees to make extra time available. The Wilson administration accepted this should be done when a substantial body of parliamentary opinion is shown to be in favour of a change in the law. Time can be obtained by allowing the House to have additional or extended sittings so the progress of Government business is not affected. Two devices are available. The House can continue to sit after the normal 10 p.m. closure – if necessary all night. Alternatively a limited morning session could be held. Both these techniques were needed to pass the Divorce Reform Act 1969 sponsored by Alec Jones (Lab., Rhondda West). In 1970 the new Conservative Government intimated that it would do nothing to assist private Members' legislation: however, when in 1972 a bill to authorize vasectomy operations under the National Health Service introduced by Philip Whitehead (Lab., Derby North) stood to fail because of a procedural technicality at the very last stage of its parliamentary progress, ministers made extra time available to allow the bill to pass.

The final hurdle is the House of Lords. More than once the Upper House wrecked attempts to abolish capital punishment. Yet since the advent of life peers the atmosphere has changed considerably. None of the controversial private Members' bills passed between 1965 and 1970 were impeded by their Lordships. Bills to reform the law on homosexuality and abortion passed the Lords before the Commons.

Successful private Members' bills fall into three categories. Some are measures of social regulation usually of a minor nature; some are designed to amend existing law in areas where its operation has been unexpected or inconvenient; a few deal with contentious issues and raise questions for which the government prefers to evade prime responsibility. A particular bill may, of course, fall into more than one of these groups. It is the third category which commands most public attention. During the 1966–70 Parliament private Members' bills became a major feature of the work of the legislature and new laws were passed relating to contraception, homosexuality, abortion, divorce, and theatre censorship.[7] The tradition of private Members' time is that there is no party constraint on attendance or voting: the Whips are 'off'. However, if a backbench measure is basically unacceptable to ministers, if it represents a challenge to government policy, then either it will be defeated in the division lobbies or it will expire through lack of Parliamentary time. Proposals which would involve a substantial increase in government expenditure are unsuitable for private Members' bills: the government must accept full responsibility for the direction of the national economy and, therefore, for the total of public expenditure and the allocation of priorities within that total.

A Member who wins a place in the ballot must first decide on the subject for his bill. He may already have a project for reform which he is keen to introduce. Most Members are not so well prepared. So they have a choice – either to go to official sources for a bill or to take up an idea from another Member or a pressure group. The Government Whips' Office can provide minor items of projected legislation which government departments would like to have passed but which cannot obtain adequate priority in the ministerial programme of legislation. A Member who adopts such a bill is quite likely to get it passed for he will enjoy official support and assistance. Another possibility is the recommendations of a report from the Law Commission for which no Parliamentary time has been found. Anyone lucky enough to win a high place in the ballot will be besieged by other Members and by pressure groups urging that this good fortune be used to assist their cause.

Especially when a bill is adopted from an unofficial source a substantial amount of negotiation may be required with government departments and other interested organizations if the measure is to reach the Statute Book. An extract from the speech of Mr King (Con., Bridgwater) moving the second Reading of his Mobile Homes Bill in February 1975 indicates the nature of the process:

> I am also grateful for the consultations that have taken place outside the House with the National Caravan Council, the National Federation of Site Operators and the National Mobile Home Residents' Association . . . We have also had discussions with the Association of County Councils, the Association of Metropolitan Authorities and the Association of District Councils. I hope that the House will feel that we have made every attempt to take into account the various points of view that are relevant to the bill.
>
> I have appreciated greatly the extremely constructive and helpful discussions I have had with the Minister's officials. I know his kind blessing. Undoubtedly that has been of great value in getting the bill right . . . The discussions we have had and the help which has been given in complicated matters by the Government Department concerned have been in the best tradition of private Members' bills.[8]

Some Members are very active in supporting, or perhaps opposing, private Members' bills. In recent years Leo Abse (Lab., Pontypool) has been the outstanding Member in this regard. His main interests have been family law and sexual behaviour, topics which readily attract publicity. *Private Member*,[9] his autobiography, contains much fascinating detail about the preliminary negotiations that surround back-bench legislation. Abse relates how in 1970 Lord Hailsham, the Conservative Lord Chancellor, decided that the newly elected young Winston Churchill (Con., Stretford) should have the opportunity of introducing a bill to implement recommendations of the Law Commission which would extend the rights to widows to claim compensation for the demise of their husbands. Arthur Probert (Lab., Aberdare) also wished to introduce the bill, which was of particular concern to his constituency. Probert had a higher place in the ballot than Churchill so that if both bills were presented, priority would be given to Probert. To try to persuade Probert to withdraw the Lord Chancellor intimated that he would be given no help in the preparation of what had to be a complex measure. Hailsham's motive was to provide a good start for the political career of a young man with a famous name. Probert, supported by Abse, refused to be bullied and it was made clear to the Lord Chancellor that the Labour Members from South Wales would produce a measure without official help. Thereupon Churchill and Hailsham gave way.[10]

While the vast majority of Government bills reach the Statute Book, the mortality among private Members' bills is high. The table below records their fate since 1970.

Private Members' and Peers' Bills considered by the Commons

	1970–4 Parliament		1974 Session		1974–5 Session	
	Enacted	Failed	Enacted	Failed	Enacted	Failed
Ballot Bills	22	58	4	6	9	10
Other Bills	23	218	3	27	1	66
Totals	45	276	7	33	10	76

It will be seen that almost half the bills introduced under the ballot do survive. The figures for the 1970–4 Parliament are affected by the cutting short of the 1973–4 session to hold a general election with the result that no ballot bill succeeded in this session. When this is taken into account the fairer assessment for the whole Parliament is 22 Acts out of 60 Bills. Of course the fate of bills depends upon their content. If Members use their luck in the ballot to produce controversial or complex measures, then most of their projects will wither.

Bills that are hotly opposed may well be defeated or fail for lack of time. An item that consumes many hours in committee or in the Chamber, even if it is ultimately accepted, may well destroy the chances of other generally popular bills which have a lower place in the draw. The tendency in more recent years has been for a higher proportion of balloted bills to succeed than in the pre-1939 period. Back-benchers are using their opportunities with greater care and realism.

The remaining categories – unballoted bills, Ten minute Rule bills and measures introduced by individual peers which are passed down from the Lords – have no chance of success unless they are non-controversial or are supported by the government. There has been one recent exception to this rule. The Sunday Theatres Act 1972 to permit performances on Sunday was a private Peers' Bill which surprisingly obtained a second Reading 'on the nod' (i.e. without debate) and joined the queue of bills awaiting attention in standing committee. Then the Member in charge of the bill, Hugh Jenkins (Lab., Putney) moved at 4 p.m. on a Friday that the Committee stage be taken immediately in the Chamber. No time was available for debate but no one present objected so the remaining stages were achieved automatically and the bill went forward for the Royal Assent.[11] This represented a remarkable contrast to the experience of the Sunday Entertainments Bill in 1968 when a long campaign by Members supporting the views of the Lord's Day Observance Society managed to destroy the measure by protracting debate at the Committee stage.

Some topics constantly recur in private Members' time. Sunday observance is (or was) one example. Still unresolved are the arguments about hare coursing and divorce in Scotland. The Divorce Reform Act 1969 did not extend north of the Border and regular attempts have been made since 1970 to end this anomaly. A substantial majority of Scottish Members appear to favour a change in the law but there has been a determined minority group which upholds the *status quo*. The procedural difficulties in the way of this reform are almost insuperable. On Friday afternoons English and Welsh Members feel that they have other things to do rather than stay at Westminster to intervene in the domestic affairs of Scotland. They may think that Scottish Members should be left to deal with this problem on their own. But it is still necessary to have 100 supporters in the Chamber to secure the closure and so force a vote at 4 p.m.: in January 1971 the Divorce (Scotland) Bill was destroyed when the closure motion failed with a vote of 71 to 15 in favour.[12] As there are only 71 Scottish Members this reform cannot be achieved unless either more non-Scottish Members intervene or its opposition fades away. An alternative would be to amend Standing Orders so that a smaller attendance is required to force the closure on business relating solely to Scotland.

Is it desirable that back-benchers should play a part in the initiation of legislation? Opinions on this issue have changed over the years. There is now far more support for back-bench activity than in the pre-war period.

The Select Committee on Procedure which sat in the 1930–1 Session heard criticism of private Members' bills from adherents of the two major parties. Conservatives wish to restrict the range of state activity. Wider opportunities to promote legislation are likely to increase government intervention in social and economic affairs. It is a traditional Tory cry that there is too much legislation. So Mr Winston Churchill told the Procedure Committee that it should be made difficult 'for all sorts of happy thoughts to be carried on to the statute book'.[13] Labour was unenthusiastic for quite different reasons. In the 1920s Labour Members who won a place in the ballot often used it to promote some item of party policy. Inevitably their bills were defeated. So it is unsurprising that the Labour Chief Whip told the Committee that the time spent on private Members' bills was 'very largely wasted'.[14] The Labour view was that legislation would play a vital role in building a more equal and a more just society. Clearly the necessary Acts would not be passed until Labour had a Parliamentary majority. When this majority was achieved the appropriate measures would be introduced with the full authority of a Labour Government. Private

Members' legislation, even items introduced by Labour Members, was likely to get in the way of the programme of legislation presented by ministers.

For the first three years the post-war Attlee Government operated the theory that back-bench measures could not assist with a socialist reconstruction of society. Democratic centralism was in the ascendant; pluralism was out of fashion. So the Attlee Government insisted on continuing the wartime custom of refusing to find space for back-bench bills in the Parliamentary programme. In 1948 the energy of ministers was flagging and they bowed to pressure from all parts of the House to find time for bills introduced under the ballot. Since then the need to operate the ballot system had not been seriously questioned. Sir Ivor Jennings' verdict would be widely accepted: 'The fact that much Government legislation is either vote-catching or of a departmental character renders desirable the provision of time for other measures.'[15]

Conservative criticism of private Members' bills developed briefly between 1967 and 1970. This was a response to a series of important measures which raised basic moral questions – contraception, abortion, homosexuality, theatre censorship, and divorce. While these measures had all-party support, the majority of Conservative Members were opposed to most of them. This produced an inevitable reaction. If a system produces unpalatable results, there is a tendency to cry 'Foul' and to claim that the system is unsatisfactory and should be altered.[16]

There were two major complaints about the use of private Members' bills to deal with substantial moral issues. One was that the measures were rushed; that inadequate thought had been given to all their implications. This again is a standard tactical response by those who oppose change. If revision can be delayed, the desire for it may fade away. In fact, all the moral questions raised by private Members' bills in the 1966–70 Parliament had been the subject of extended public discussion. With one major exception they had been the subject of some form of official enquiry in the recent past.

The other objection was more fundamental. Traditionalists tried to argue that the Commons had no mandate to pass legislation on moral issues. At the 1966 General Election Members had not explained to the voters what they felt about homosexuality, abortion, divorce, etc. So they could not claim to represent public opinion on these matters and so should not legislate upon them. It is undoubtedly true that politicians do not discuss moral questions at election times. The religious affiliations of candidates are scarcely felt to be a decent topic of conversation since such discussion could lead to allegations of religious discrimination or intolerance. The major political parties have a class basis. The electors are invited to attend to economic questions: the dominant issue is whether the Government had done well or ill in promoting material welfare. If items of moral controversy are not to appear on the parliamentary agenda until they have been debated at election time, then reform can never take place.

In any case, the mandate argument is essentially anti-parliamentary and, therefore, anti-conservative with a small 'c'. If Members cannot legislate until they have a mandate, it follows that they should and must legislate when they have a mandate. Legitimation of legislation moves from Parliament to the electors. Members should do as they are bid and surrender all discretion. Thus the mandate theory is ultimately totally destructive of Parliamentary institutions. It is also based on the nonsensical proposition that an elector agrees with every opinion set out in a candidate's election address. The theory of the mandate was developed by Conservatives early in the twentieth century in an attempt to defend the veto powers of the House of Lords, but there is now fairly wide Conservative acceptance that the doctrine can become a double-edged sword. Indeed, the criticisms of private Members' procedure have died away since 1970. They were limited and tactical.

The essence of the argument in favour of private Members' legislation is that the Government should not monopolize the right to propose reform. The priorities of politicians, even those elected to high office, are not necessarily those of the man in the street. Ministers are inhibited by the environment within which they have to work. They avoid some topics because they are awkward. Anything which can lead to deep divisions within a party tends to be pushed to one side. Where powerful interest groups are involved, ministers may wish to persuade through negotiation rather than coerce through legislation. Then, if the persuasion fails, the issue can drag on and on.

Moral questions that excite the churches are precisely the type of matters that it is convenient to avoid. Here the party Whips cannot impose discipline. There may be trouble in some constituencies. Loyalties can be strained. Votes may be lost. So it is safer to concentrate on problems than can be made to fit more easily within the contours of party orthodoxy. The Wolfenden Committee reported that homosexual acts committed in private by consenting adults should cease to be criminal. This was in 1957.[17] No Government action was taken, for the subject was too delicate. Ten years later the recommendation was put into effect through back-bench initiative. Throughout the 1960s there was a steadily increasing acceptance of the idea that divorce should be based not on the concept of matrimonial offence but on evidence of the breakdown of marriage. Again, there was no response from ministers and a back-bench bill was needed to effect the reform. Indeed it could be said that a convention has developed that some matters of conscience are now most appropriately dealt with through the action of back-benchers.

Unsuccessful bills can still be of value. They may push ministers into taking more positive action than would otherwise have been forthcoming. These considerations apply especially where protracted negotiations have taken place between pressure groups and government departments. Thus on the second Reading of Philip Whitehead's Police Acts (Amendment) Bill 1973 to reform procedure for handling complaints against the police, the Home Secretary announced that he accepted the principle of introducing an independent element into the proceedings.[18] Presented with this assurance of future progress, the sponsor withdrew his bill. Similarly, the campaign against smoking has been assisted by back-bench bills. The Tobacco (Health Hazards) Bill 1970 introduced by Sir Gerald Nabarro[19] and a series of measures promoted by Laurie Pavitt (Lab., Brent, South) were all aimed at restricting advertising or otherwise warning the public of the dangers of smoking. These bills have strengthened the hand of ministers in discussions with tobacco interests. It may well be argued that the Government have moved very slowly on smoking but, without this back-bench pressure, even less might have been achieved.

Every Session sees a number of minor but useful Acts passed through private Members' procedure which could not find a place in the Government programme. Apart from the question of the content and influence of private Members' bills, they also have an effect on the morale and the image of Parliament. They provide an additional dimension of freedom for Members. They offer an extra outlet for energy. On Fridays the House may be released from the normal routine of reacting to the ideas of ministers. The Whips can be relegated to the sidelines. As noted above, the unexpected may happen. The House of Commons becomes a legislature in a truer sense. If a controversial issue is debated, the level of public interest will be high. Pressure groups will be aroused. There will be some effect on Members' postbags.[20] The public are far more sensitive to capital punishment and abortion than they are to issues linked to the reorganization of industry. Granted that back-benchers use their opportunities with imagination, then private Members' time increases the probability that the Commons will debate questions that actively concern the electors. And if a Member occasionally suffers criticism in his constituency because of his activities on a Friday, this is good for the health and vigour of the representative process.

There remains the question of how far the government should be prepared to assist the passage of private Members' bills. It would be a great help if the official parliamentary draftsmen could be used to prepare the detailed wording of measures introduced through the ballot. At present this is not possible because of pressure of other work at a critical period of the Parliamentary Session. It was shown above that no back-bench bill which is bitterly opposed by a determined minority of Members can pass unless additional time is provided for it. A controversial bill with a good place in the

ballot can gain a second Reading but it can then be delayed
by extensive discussion of a mass of amendments. Should
the Committee stage last too long, some or all of the Fridays
allocated for Report stage and third Reading of private
Members' bills will have passed. Another barrage of amendments on Report will ensure that time runs out unless the
Parliamentary agenda is made more flexible.

When a bill reaches the Report stage, it is evident that it
commands substantial support. Should it be killed by the
clock? There can be an argument over whether the government should find time for such bills to be further considered.
But this is to put the question in a misleading context. It is
not necessary, or perhaps desirable, that ministers should
sacrifice any part of their share of parliamentary time. The
issue is rather whether Parliament should continue sitting
after other business has been completed in order to continue
debate on particular items of private Members' legislation.
Surely this is a matter for the Commons themselves to decide.
If the Members who support a bill are sufficiently numerous
to defeat their opponents and are sufficiently keen to stay up
all night, why should they be prevented? It is reasonable to
suggest that the sponsor of a bill delayed at the Report stage
should be able to move that a particular sitting be extended
so that his measure can be further considered. This motion
could then be the subject of a free vote. Of course, it would
be intolerable if such an arrangement meant that the House
sat up all night every night. Nothing of the kind would
happen because the free opinion of Members would prevent
it. There are only one or two private Members' bills each
year which arouse enough passion to persuade Members to
abandon their beds.

7 The House of Commons and Public Expenditure

ANN ROBINSON

It has long been supposed that the House of Commons holds 'the power of the purse' over governments. Some writers have even gone so far as to suggest that the power which the House has over the granting of funds to the Government provides the basis of its supremacy.[1] The theory is that governments spend the taxpayers' money, but they can only do so with the consent of the House of Commons. If the House should refuse to grant supply to a government, that government would be placed in a position where it would not be able to govern and so would have to resign. Under this theory the power to grant or withhold supply is the ultimate sanction which the House wields over government. Indeed, if a government found itself defeated on even one or two items of expenditure, it would probably interpret this as a vote of no confidence in its policies and as a call for its resignation.

In the twentieth century, however, this theory has never been put to the practical test. The House of Commons has never tried to invoke the ultimate sanction over government. Nor has it, in recent times, refused to grant individual items of supply – unlike the Canadian House of Commons where the defeat of several estimates in 1974 led to a general election. Nor does the House of Commons have, like the United States Congress, the ability to alter details of spending plans laid before it. Estimates presented to the United States Congress by the President are rarely passed as they stand, since they are often substantially modified as a result of their passage through Congress. The estimates presented to the House of Commons may only be accepted or rejected *in toto*. They cannot be altered.[2] This is in sharp contrast to other legislation, and indeed is even in contrast to the legislation authorizing taxation, i.e. the Finance Bill. The House frequently makes significant amendments to Finance bills, so government's plans for taxation do appear to be subject to real detailed scrutiny, alteration, and control by MPs.[3] The fact that the House now has no part to play in the detailed control of the government's estimates for spending is recognized by recent changes in procedure. The myth of examination of the estimates in the 29 days allotted to the consideration of supply has now been totally abandoned. The 29 Supply Days still exist, but the estimates no longer form the basis of debate. In the practical sense, therefore, the House has no 'power of the purse'. It cannot alter the details of spending estimates and it has not for a long time exercised its powers to reject them. Members have apparently decided that they do not wish to hold tight the purse strings of government. They simply, and apparently blindly, follow the party Whips when asked to vote the passage of supply.

If MPs wished to revive their power of control over expenditure, they would be faced with immense practical problems. It would be extremely difficult to devise appropriate procedures for the task. The primary difficulty now preventing detailed control of the government's spending plans is that public expenditure has become so large. In 1976 it was about 60 per cent of the Gross National Product. How, one wonders, could 635 Members of very different interests, backgrounds, training and aptitude for figures, be able to exert detailed scrutiny over more than half the entire British economy? MPs have, moreover, many other functions to perform besides that of consideration of the government's spending plans. Full-scale examination of public expenditure is thus ruled out on the grounds of its scale and on the grounds of Members' abilities, resources and inclinations. Another practical difficulty, which would face members of the House were they to try to revive detailed control over public expenditure, is that much of government's spending today is undertaken, not by central government departments for which ministers are responsible and answerable to Parliament, but by local authorities, nationalized industries and other, quasi-governmental bodies. Local authorities alone accounted for about one third of all public expenditure in 1976. Whereas the House of Commons could in theory exert detailed control over the central government departments, it has not developed any machinery to allow it to exert detailed scrutiny and control over the estimates of spending from local authorities and other quasi-governmental bodies. Brand new procedures and a more ample provision of time would be required to extend the scope of Parliamentary control. It is not just the sheer size of government spending which renders it hard to control, but the very diversity of spending bodies and the looseness of the relationship of these bodies with Parliament.

The House of Commons itself exacerbates the problem of control by the manner in which it constantly passes new legislation committing the government to further spending. Members do have opportunities to debate the financial implications of new legislation, but each piece of legislation is taken on its own and there is no machinery to co-ordinate the expenditure effects of various new Acts. Many of the items on which legislation has been passed in recent years commit the government to spend money over long periods or, in the case of much social-security legislation, indefinitely. By its own actions, therefore, the House creates a situation in which, had it a wish to revert to a more detailed form of control over public expenditure, it would find it had very little room for manœuvre. So much of the expenditure is in the form of 'relatively uncontrollable' long-term commitments that, even if the House did have the ability to tinker with estimates, such changes as it could make would be marginal.[4]

As well as the practical difficulties of establishing adequate and appropriate procedures to allow for control of expenditure by the House, there are other difficulties stemming from the unwillingness of MPs to act as watchdogs. If Members were to exert any detailed control over expenditure, they would have to be interested in finding economy and value for money and be prepared to work hard at discovering how much the government spends, what it spends its funds on, and how it monitors them. Some MPs lack this interest altogether and feel it is none of their job to provide a detailed control over spending. This loss of interest in control is probably due to changes in the general attitudes of members of the House. In the nineteenth century many MPs felt they had a duty to ensure economy in government and see that it did not spend more money than was absolutely necessary. This is revealed in the terms of reference of Select Committees set up in the nineteenth century to consider public expenditure. The Select Committee set up in 1807 had the following terms of reference:

> To examine and consider what regulations and checks have been established in order to control the several branches of Public Expenditure in Great Britain and Ireland, and how far the same have been effective, and what further measures can be adopted for reducing any part of the said expenditure or diminishing the amount of Salaries and Emoluments without detriment to the Public Service.[5]

A similar sentiment, namely, that the House should have the ultimate ability to oversee details of expenditure in the interests of economy, was behind the establishment in 1861 by Gladstone of the Public Accounts Committee. Whether in practice the House of Commons was ever, even in the nineteenth century when public expenditure was a smaller proportion of a smaller Gross National Product, able to exercise much detailed control is open to doubt. Some commentators have wondered whether all nineteenth-century MPs wanted to play the role of economy seekers.[6] By the turn of the century there was probably a mixture of attitudes among Members, some being savers and some spenders. Attitudes of Members changed fundamentally following the advent of the 'collectivist' era of politics. There was no longer the same urge to ensure that the House had proper procedures for detailed control, and the uses which Members made of established financial procedures altered. By the late 1960s the mood had changed to the extent that Members used the opportunities available for debate on public expenditure to consider general matters of 'policy', and to ask the government to increase spending on individual items or functions, rather than to press for economies.

Although the House no longer makes any overt political use of its 'power of the purse', this is not to say that Members have no interest in public expenditure or that the subject is never debated. There are many occasions when MPs may express their views on expenditure. They can debate the financial implications of new legislation before the House, use the 29 Supply Days, raise expenditure matters in adjournment debates and on private Members' motions, and question ministers. Added to these procedures time has been allotted since 1970 for debate on the Public Expenditure White Paper, which shows the course of public expenditure over the coming five years. So far as more detailed scrutiny and examination are concerned, the only opportunities are provided by Select Committees. *Post hoc* control is provided by the Public Accounts Committee, which receives the accounts of Departmental spending from the Comptroller and Auditor General. Scrutiny of plans for future spending is undertaken by the Expenditure Committee, which in 1970 replaced the Estimates Committee. Members serving on other Select Committees such as that on the Nationalized Industries may also sometimes be able to discuss the expenditure implications of their area of investigation.

The main opportunity for Members to debate expenditure comes in the 29 Supply Days available each Session. These are still called Supply Days even though most debates are on motions quite unrelated to financial estimates. The debates take place on a variety of motions devised by the Opposition to allow it to criticize the Government. In the session 1975-6, for example, one Supply Day debate took place on a motion to reduce the salary of the Secretary of State for Industry by £1000. This permitted debate on the motor industry and specifically on the Government's financial support for Chrysler. By chance the motion was carried and the Government had, the following week, to introduce another motion to reinstate the salary of the Minister concerned. This example shows that, even if the opposition does win a vote on a Supply Day, it is not really exerting the traditional 'power of the purse' since the vote is not on an actual estimate. Therefore the government will not consider the loss of such a vote as a call for its resignation.

The topics chosen by the Opposition for debate on Supply

Days cover a wide range of subjects. Some of these have an obvious connection with public expenditure and invite Members to debate in terms of spending, but other subjects have no obvious connection. The number of Supply Day debates with little obvious connection with expenditure was very noticeable in the 1975-6 session. This was partly due to a heavy timetable in a session in which a Government with the slenderest of majorities tried to push a full programme of legislation, some of it very controversial, through the House. In such circumstances several Supply Days had to be used by the Opposition to raise debates on subjects for which the Government might itself have given time in a less crowded session. For example, the Government allowed only one day for debate of the Public Expenditure White Paper in March 1976 instead of the more normal two. The second day had to be taken from the Opposition's time in Supply Days. In the session 1975-6 subjects debated on other Supply Days included the European Community (Development), Foreign Affairs (East-West Relations), and Northern Ireland Security. None of these had any noticeable connection with public expenditure and members did not refer to expenditure in the debates. In some other debates not obviously connected with expenditure MPs nevertheless did take the opportunity to raise the question of spending. In the debate on the fishing industry which was mainly concerned with the 'Cod War', several Members suggested to the Government that subsidies should be paid to the fishing industry. And the debate on Personal Taxation on 22 March 1976 turned out to be on the relationship between taxation and public expenditure.[7]

Some of the topics debated on Supply Days do deal specifically with areas of expenditure policy. In the 1975-6 session, for example, debates were held on the Royal Air Force (which dealt almost exclusively with the effects on operations in that service of recent expenditure cuts), on the Royal Navy (where the effects of expenditure cuts were also the major focus of debate), on local government, on the motor industry, on Reports of the Public Accounts Committee, and on Reports of the Expenditure Committee.

Supply debates are used by Members to reflect concerns

among the public at large. They use these occasions to convey to the government what kinds of expenditure the people want and how much they are prepared to pay for. Because debates are used in this way they perform the function of a 'political pressure gauge', and their contents tell us much about the attitudes of the public and of Members to public spending. In the 1960s a general view that shortcomings in society could and should be remedied by collective (public) spending had its effect upon the sort of things that Members said in these debates. The general impression gained from reading Supply debates of the 1960s is that MPs used their opportunities to press claims upon the government for higher spending on individual projects and local causes. The claims were related to particular political events and circumstances, or to constituency interests. These debates allowed Members to display to their constituents that they were taking care of their interests and pressing their demands. When unemployment rose in the 1960s there were more Supply debates in which Members called for greater spending on industry and on aid to hard-hit areas. Debates on housing, education and health were all full of demands for increased spending on the total function and on individual local projects. The one exception to this pattern came in the debates on defence, in which a group of left-wing MPs committed to cuts in defence expenditure demanded reductions. One argument used by this group was that more could be spent on social services if defence spending were cut. On the whole, though, Supply debates in the 1960s provided a platform for the presentation of unco-ordinated and unrelated demands for higher spending. The unco-ordinated nature of these debates was heightened by the way in which Members failed to sit through entire debates listening to all points of view but simply made their entrance, stated their case, and left the Chamber as soon as decently possible after their speeches. The Chamber was rarely full for Supply debates, and rather than real interchanges of ideas they became a series of statements and requests.

Other opportunities for debate in the whole House are used in similar ways to the Supply debates. Short adjournment debates are sometimes used to comment upon 'general policy' but more often to make claims for higher spending on individual and local items. Examples from the 1975–6 session included a debate on the Open University (Northern Ireland) which took the form of a request to the Government to make funds available for Northern Ireland students to obtain assistance towards costs of attending summer schools on the mainland. Other debates in that session made requests of a similar order asking for increased spending on matters of local concern.

Members successful in the ballot for debates on private Members' motions may also, if they wish, raise matters of public expenditure. Such occasions may provide an opportunity for the Opposition to criticize the general spending policy of the government. An example of this type of debate took place on 9 April 1976 on local government finance. The motion before the House was:

> That this House acknowledges the growing public concern at the level of spending by local government and the simultaneous deterioration in the value of the ratepayers' money; calls upon Her Majesty's Government to resist further legislation which imposes extra financial burdens on local government; and urges early implementation of cash limits and new methods of financing local government following the Layfield Committee's report.[8]

In the debate Conservatives suggested that local authorities should be brought into the annual spending review at an early stage. They were concerned with whether 'value for money' was being obtained in local government and whether better services could be provided at lower cost. This debate gives the impression that some Members are beginning to look once more for economy in government. But a number of Labour MPs took the opportunity to express the view that people in their constituencies were still demanding increased spending.[9]

In the mid-1970s there does seem to have been a quite noticeable change in the general tone of debates concerned with public expenditure. Demands for spending to be increased on specific items had not entirely disappeared, but they were less frequent and had become somewhat muted.

There was more comment on, and criticism of, the government's general approach toward spending and more talk about 'value for money'. The main exception to this change of attitude came from the left wing of the Labour Party which continued to demand increased spending. There are many reasons for the changed mood of the mid-1970s. The most important is the apparent inability of governments to control spending. From 1961 considerable efforts have been made by governments to design more rational methods for planning expenditure levels and priorities. In 1961 the Public Expenditure Survey Committee (PESC) was set up to produce each year for the Cabinet a five-year projection of public expenditure. Since 1970 many departments have made fundamental re-examinations of their functions through the system of Policy Analysis and Review (PAR). The Treasury has greatly expanded its facilities for collecting and processing information about the present and future state of the economy. But the government has not devised any new machinery to monitor and control actual spending. The Treasury still maintains the traditional power to vet departmental estimates, but as spending has expanded, this method of control has weakened. It has not been able to develop any satisfactory machinery for control of the rapidly growing spending by bodies outside the central government departments. The result is that while successive Cabinets have made decisions about future patterns of expenditure, the actual outturn in terms of money spent has always proved higher. By 1976 the discrepancy between planned and actual expenditure was so serious that neither government nor the House of Commons could fail to notice it.[10] The Government in 1976 instituted a system of 'cash limits' on spending authorities and the House of Commons began to look more critically at the Government's own methods of planning and controlling spending.

Both Government and MPs had by now noticed a connection between public expenditure and taxation which, hitherto, they had largely ignored. The Government's recognition of this problem is set out in the opening passage of the 1976 White Paper which states:

In the last three years public expenditure has grown by nearly 20 per cent in volume while output has risen by less than 2 per cent . . . The tax burden has also greatly increased . . . The increase in the tax burden has fallen heavily on low wage earners. Those earning less than the average contribute over a quarter of the income tax yield.[11]

Members were being pressured in a new way by constituents who were concerned at the level of income tax. They found constituents arriving at their 'surgeries' waving pay slips and demanding to know why, out of a relatively low wage, deductions for tax and national insurance were so high. This had its effect on the attitudes of MPs, who always seek to represent constituents' interests. Members may now have to point out to those who demand increased spending on some cause that their particular project may only be promoted at the cost of some other, perhaps equally deserving cause. Many Members have discovered that public expenditure may only be able to grow above present levels if the economy also grows. In such circumstances Members, receiving conflicting messages from their constituents, are bound to look at public spending in a new light.

Another reason for the change in attitude in the mid-1970s, as revealed in debates, was that a Conservative Party formed the major portion of the Opposition. In spite of its own past record as a generous spender, it was by now firmly committed to control of, and reductions in, the level of public expenditure. And it was supported in this stand by the Liberal Party.

Whatever the reasons for it, there can be no doubt that the debates of the House in the Session 1975–6 do reveal changes in the attitudes of Members toward expenditure. Curiously enough there is an exception to this pattern. In the 1960s, when heavy demands were made for increases in spending, defence stood out because a group of Members called for cuts in spending on that function. In the retrenching attitude of the seventies we find a Conservative Opposition calling generally for cuts but containing a section of its membership that stoutly argues that spending on defence should actually be increased. On all other functions of government considerable concern has been expressed at the failure of governments both to contain the levels of spending within reasonable bounds and to devise means for ensuring that actual spending conforms to the Cabinet's plans.

It is clear from the above analysis that debates fail to provide any positive check over the government but do provide part of the political background against which the government must make its expenditure decisions. In the 1960s when the Cabinet constantly acquiesced in ministers' requests for permission to overspend, the Government did not feel restrained by the House of Commons. MPs thought and spoke about expenditure almost exclusively in terms of requests for higher spending. A profligate Government was therefore bolstered up by a free-spending attitude in the Commons. The Government in the mid-1970s found a different background to its decisions. Members of the Opposition parties were not the only ones demanding that public expenditure be controlled and restrained – though they were the loudest calling for actual cuts. MPs from the Government side were also less insistent in their demands, since they too had to face constituents whose pay packets were eroded as much by taxation as by inflation.

Though MPs succeed in giving the Government a general impression of attitudes towards spending, they need to do more than this if they are properly to represent the national interest. Present procedures of the House do not help them. The problem is that debates are normally arranged on single, specific subjects which encourage Members to think about expenditure atomistically. They are not asked to think about relative allocations between competing functions, or about differing means of achieving desired goals. Only rarely has there been a motion before the House bringing forth Members' views on the effects which spending on a particular function might have on other functions, on the total level of expenditure or on taxation. In the absence of suitable procedures for broad discussion, a rather distorted image of national needs is likely to emerge from speeches in the House of Commons.

The Commons began to sense in the late 1960s that it

required opportunities for broader discussion. The Procedure Committee set up in 1968 to study the control of Public Expenditure recommended that regular debates be held on the Public Expenditure White Papers. High hopes were held out for these new debates and it was suggested that they might become more important than the Budget debate and so provide 'the highlight of the Parliamentary year'. The experience of the first five years of debates on Expenditure White Papers has, however, proved disappointing. Debates have been poorly attended and there have been few speeches of high standard. In part this has been due to the behaviour of successive governments which proved unable to present the White Papers to the House regularly each November (as they were supposed to). Elections, financial crises, and pressure for changes in previously agreed spending plans have held up publication in most years. The White Paper due in November 1975 did not appear till March 1976, only seven months before the next White Paper of November 1976 was due. During the seven months between March and November changes were made to the 1975 White Paper. Members can never be sure that a White Paper means what it says.

Members were unenthusiastic about White Paper debates in the early years for other reasons. The document, in spite of improvements in presentation over the years, did not tell Members much about the policies behind the figures. Unless he was already an expert in a policy area, a Member could not tell whether the figures for that function of government were too high, too low, or just about right. There was little background information about policies. No 'costed options' were presented. The assiduous Member who really wanted to know what lay behind the figures had to consult the writings of independent bodies which have recently begun to analyse the Expenditure White Papers.[12] Then there was the further reason that few MPs were interested in the priorities for Public Expenditure which they were invited to consider in White Paper debates. They were more concerned in representing the interests of their constituents than in the matter of allocation and rational choice. Finally, MPs seem to have realized that White Papers bear little relationship to the amounts of money that governments actually will spend in future years. Each successive government promised one pattern of spending and in the event produced a different and always higher one. In such circumstances Members have not really felt that anything they may say in a debate about the wider issues will have much influence over a government which goes ahead with its spending regardless.

The changed economic situation which faced the government and nation by 1976 meant that the debate on the Expenditure White Paper presented to Parliament in March of that year was different from previous White Paper debates. There was a new sense of interest and urgency, so that the debate exhibited some of the characteristics which those who had first called for these debates had hoped to find. Attendance was not particularly high; like many other debates in the crowded Session of 1975–6 it suffered from pressures of other business, especially committees, which syphon off Members from the Chamber. Nevertheless this debate contained references to the need to think carefully and rationally when planning and monitoring public expenditure. Many MPs referred to the fact that higher spending on one item may mean lower spending on another. There was a recognition that the Government's (and taxpayers') pocket is not bottomless. Edmund Dell, summing up for the Government, said:

> It has been a very fine debate. One might say that it has been the only real debate we have yet had on a Public Expenditure White Paper.[13]

Members were forced in this debate to think as never before about priorities and allocations because as Mr Dell pointed out:

> We have come to the point where we cannot persuade people of the need to pay 50p out of every additional pound that they earn, or perhaps eventually more.[14]

The greatest procedural deficiency inhibiting MPs from getting fully to grips with the wider questions of expenditure is that expenditure and taxation are considered separately by the government and are therefore presented separately to the House for its consideration. In the 1976 White Paper debate Mr Tony Newton said:

It is clear that we can judge the White Paper properly only
when we have the Budget figures.[15]

But when the Budget debate took place a month later, MPs
seemed largely to have forgotten the White Paper. This is
not surprising if one looks at the contents of the Budget statement forming the basis for the Budget debate. The Budget
statement is largely about taxation. Tax proposals are presented in some detail. The statement concerns itself with
management of the economy, since taxation is used for this
purpose.[16] It is not about the relationship between income
and expenditure, between taxation and government spending.
As a result Members make general speeches about the
economy or tend to fix on trivial or minor points of changes
in taxation, e.g. changes in VAT or taxes on whisky.

There has been some criticism of the present practice of
presenting the House with separate statements about income
and expenditure. Mr Michael English, Chairman of the
General Sub-Committee of the Expenditure Committee, has
said:

Britain is unique . . . in considering expenditure separately
from taxation.[17]

Sir Alec Cairncross has argued in evidence to the Expenditure Committee that one should consider taxation with
expenditure because this would enforce a sense of reality upon
the people considering either. Others, while making the same
point, have recommended changes in the procedures of the
House.[18] Of course, the first step to reform of procedure lies
with the government. A proper Budget showing both expenditure and income would be better basis for debate. The bifur-
cation of tax and expenditure both by government and in the
procedures of the House has serious consequences. If government plans are devised without consideration of the means to
pay for them, this is a recipe for living beyond one's means
and for failure to invest in the right projects when income is
buoyant. Members of the Commons receive simultaneous
demands from their constituents for higher spending and
lower taxation. Under existing procedure these demands reach
the government separately, and no one is encouraged to see
that the two are related.

All of the procedures for debate in the House allow Members to express opinions, but they do not allow them to obtain information from the government or to subject the government to cross-examination. Though the majority of Members are not interested in the details of spending, there are a few who are. They can question ministers in Question Time, but analysis of the answers to Parliamentary questions on expenditure matters during the early 1970s reveals that this device is of extremely limited use for the purpose of extracting information. Sometimes the answer to a question is a complete blank, sometimes evasive. When on 29 April Mr Norman Lamont asked what percentage of the GNP the Public Sector Borrowing Requirement was for 1976–7, Mr Barnett replied that for 1975–6 it had been about $11\frac{1}{4}$ per cent and that for 1976–7 it would be 'lower'![19] When Mr Giles Radice asked the Chief Secretary to the Treasury for figures on the PSBR on 4 May 1976, the Chief Secretary said that a reply would be given 'as soon as possible'.[20]

If Members really want to get hard information about public spending, they would do better to use the opportunities presented to them by membership of Select Committees. Since 1861 the House has had a Public Accounts Committee (PAC) which receives from the office of the Comptroller and Auditor General the accounts of government departments and of some other bodies which spend public funds such as the universities. These accounts have been examined in detail by the 600 or so staff of the Comptroller's office to see whether the money was actually spent as Parliament had authorized. The accounts are sent to the PAC, which picks out a number of subjects for detailed investigation. Work on the PAC is popular among MPs and its chairman is a prominent Opposition Member. But its influence is limited by time and by the small size of its membership. Moreover, its investigations only take place after the money has been spent. In too many cases its strictures are like shutting the door after the horse has bolted. The power of the Public Accounts Committee is commonly held to lie in its ability to call civil servants to answer for their errors. Fear of having to appear before the committee is supposed to keep civil servants on their toes.

This theory is a bit worn in the 1970s. In the past fifteen years civil servants have been living in a situation where over-spending is the rule rather than the exception and where the scope of spending is so great that errors of judgement are bound sometimes to occur. Once a project has started, little can be done to stop it, regardless of how inefficient it is. The Swansea Licensing Bureau has become a symbol of the way in which government departments and agencies may over-spend without fear of punishment if they are caught out. The PAC may have complained that the delays, lack of prepara-tory work, and the inexperience of those concerned meant that this bureau cost £13·5 million more than was intended and that running costs are higher with staff at 50 per cent higher than forecast.[21] But a rap on the knuckles from the PAC does not put the clock back. The Swansea Licensing Bureau continues to operate in its costly way.

It is difficult for members of the PAC to focus their atten-tion on large-scale examples of overspending or inefficiencies, so they often pick out trivial examples of bureaucratic blunder. For this reason few other MPs are attracted to the reports of the Public Accounts Committee. It is difficult to see how the majority of Members of the House could be inspired to debate, for example, the latest revelations con-cerning the Inchilan Bridge which costs £18,000 per annum to maintain yet which has yielded a revenue of only 80p in the past three years.[22] This may be an amusing example of bureaucratic inefficiency, but it has not the type of political appeal to draw MPs away from other activities and into the Chamber for a debate.

A significant procedural innovation of the 1970s was the establishment of the Expenditure Committee. The Expendi-ture Committee has wider terms of reference than the Esti-mates Committee which it replaced in 1970. The Estimates Committee could only consider the annual departmental Esti-mates, but the Expenditure Committee can look at all govern-ment spending and the five-year forward projections as set out in the White Paper. Its terms of reference also allow it to examine the methods by which the government plans and controls spending. Those who recommended the establishment of this new committee hoped that the procedure would provide MPs with more appropriate opportunities to scrutinize expenditure in some detail; that it would present, through its reports, a flow of information to encourage more informed debate on the floor of the House; and that it might go some way towards redressing the balance of power between government and the House of Commons.

After five years it is now possible to make a preliminary assessment of how the new procedure has been used. The committee started slowly, then was interrupted during the 1973–4 Session by two general elections. However, it has now produced a considerable number of reports. No one should imagine that the Expenditure Committee is a monolithic structure, for it is in practice six committees. In 1975–6 these were the six sub-committees called General, Defence and External Affairs, Trade and Industry, Education and Arts, Social Services, and Environment. Each sub-committee enjoys a considerable degree of autonomy in its choice of subjects for enquiry. As a consequence each has developed its own style and manner of working. There is now little attempt to co-ordinate the work of the six. Early plans for co-ordination were soon dashed when it became apparent that the sub-committee chairmen each wished to move in their own chosen directions. The terms of reference have therefore been interpreted in the widest possible way. Subjects of Expenditure Committee enquiries include technical appraisals of the way in which the government draws up its annual Expenditure White Paper and of the assumptions behind that exercise,[23] examination of spending on particular functions of government,[24] and the operations of individual departments.[25] There have been a few enquiries into specific decisions of government spending.[26] The terms of reference have indeed been so elastic that one sub-committee has been able to make an investigation into a matter of political interest that has little to do with public expenditure.[27]

The apparent freedom of action which the committee enjoys masks the fact that it works within constraints imposed by the government and by its own membership. This means that it has a number of hurdles to overcome if it is to exercise any influence. The government's constraints are both overt and subtle. The government can determine membership of committees, see that chairmen of known views are appointed, and remove troublesome Members or promote them to junior office. Once the committee is set up, it has to decide on the subject of its enquiry. The Expenditure Committee has developed its own authority in this sphere and has attained a good deal of freedom to open whatever question it wants. It may still, however, find that some subjects attract greater co-operation from the government than do others.

Once a Sub-Committee has chosen its subject, its next problem is to search for information. In many cases the Government is the main source of information available.[28] This is particularly true of the General Sub-Committee, which gets most of its evidence from the Treasury, and of the Defence and External Affairs Sub-Committee, which has really only one source of information, the Ministry of Defence. The Expenditure Committee has acquired the authority to call both ministers and civil servants to give evidence, but the Government has sometimes prevented it from hearing particular witnesses. In 1975 when the Trade and Industry Sub-Committee examined the Chrysler decision, it was not able to hear evidence from Mr Harold Lever, who had been given special duties in the matter. The Prime Minister refused to let him appear on the grounds that the committee could only call ministers to give evidence on their departmental responsibilities – and Mr Lever as Chancellor of the Duchy of Lancaster had no departmental responsibilities. Even when the sub-committees have the witnesses before them, they still have to extract the information that they want. This is not always easy, for the relationship between a committee composed of non-expert MPs and witnesses who are skilled at their jobs is an asymmetrical one. Government witnesses will reveal only that which they intend to reveal, unless some committee member works very hard to acquaint himself with the subject, and is moreover skilled at cross-examination.

However successful the sub-committees are in extracting information from the government and from spending bodies, they face the problem finally of ensuring that any recommendations they make are read, digested, and acted upon by the government. The government is not obliged to take any notice of their reports and very often ignores them for as long as possible. In 1976 there were two reports for which departmental observations had still not been produced after two years. Generally the government takes from six months to a year to issue its departmental observations. The contents of these, which are usually produced as White Papers, show that the government has adopted various strategies to deal with committee recommendations.[29] It has accepted some recommendations and rejected others. In many cases it has made general remarks without committing itself to any positive action. Members of the Expenditure Committee are not, however, always looking for instant action from the government side. They realize that they cannot control the government in any detailed or specific way but that they may nonetheless be able to have some influence, perhaps in the long term, over the way in which the government makes spending decisions. The channels through which this influence is exerted are not always obvious. Sub-committees choose some subjects knowing that all they are likely to achieve is an addition to knowledge and an improvement in the standard of public debate. When reports of the Expenditure Committee are debated on the floor of the House, few, except members of the committee, bother to attend. But other Members do take notice of those committee reports which contain information on their own particular interests, and do make use of it on relevant occasions. There are few bouquets thrown by MPs to the Expenditure Committee as a body, but many tributes made to its work on specific subjects.

The second major constraint on the work of the Expenditure Committee comes from the Members themselves. If the committee is to have any influence on the government, it needs a stable, hardworking and expert membership. The recent decision to appoint the committee for a whole Parliament rather than choose one anew for each Session allows for greater continuity in its work. But there is still too much movement of Members on and off to ensure that each individual is an active participant. Furthermore, few Members are willing to devote the necessary effort to make full use of their time on the committee, since they have many other tasks to perform. Constituency work is an increasing burden, and so long as governments persist in introducing heavy legislative programmes many Members will be required to service other committees as well. It is not possible for anyone to become an effective participant in Select Committee proceedings if he is dodging about the committee corridor. MPs could probably make more successful use of the Expenditure Committee if they had more assistance to help them sift through memoranda and papers. The House has no 'counter-bureaucracy' to match the expertise of government. Members find it hard to acquire information with the present facilities of the House. It is significant that the US Congress, which is already so well served with research assistance, has found it necessary to establish a Congressional Budget Office to help it reassert the 'power of the purse'. Even if all preconditions for an effective Expenditure Committee were fulfilled, how much influence would it have on government? In the British tradition, whether it is appropriate in the 1970s or not, the government governs and the House of Commons supports it. Perhaps no government in Britain wants the House to become a more effective watchdog over expenditure.

8 Questions in the House

SIR NORMAN CHESTER

In the late eighteenth and early nineteenth centuries, Questions were very few and were mainly concerned with the business of the House or the government intentions in respect of legislation. By the time of the Reformed Parliament the right to Members to ask Questions of ministers or other Members was clearly recognized. Nevertheless, the first edition of Erskine May's *Parliamentary Practice*, published in 1844, and the next eight editions treat Questions to ministers not as a procedure in its own right but as an exception to the general rules of debate, i.e. that Members could not address the House except to debate a motion. During the remainder of the century there were two important developments. On the one hand, the rules of procedure governing the form and content of Questions and their place in the proceedings of the House were worked out. On the other, the steady increase in the number of Questions asked began to raise problems for the other business of the House.

The Increasing Use of Questions

The number of Questions grew rapidly in the second half of the nineteenth century – from two or three hundred in 1850 to 4000–5000 a year in the 1890s. Members also started to ask 'subsidiary' or supplementary Questions. The Irish Members used the device a great deal as part of their harassing and time-consuming tactics. But the major reasons were the growth of governmental powers and the restrictions being placed on other devices available to back-benchers.

Had Questions been taken at the end of each day's sitting the growth in the amount of time needed for their answer would have caused less concern. But they came just before Public Business which could not commence until the last

Question on the Paper had been answered. Quite apart from the legitimate use of the device, it was also used to delay the onset and reduce the time available for government measures. Opposed Private Business and Adjournment Motions were also in the same position. Therefore though in 1900 the House usually met at 3 p.m. on four days (with a short afternoon sitting on Wednesdays) Public Business might not be reached until 5.30–6 p.m., or even later, because of those earlier items of business which had precedence. Mr Balfour therefore decided to introduce major changes. Balfour's aim was to secure pre-eminence and certainty for Public Business, much of which, by this time, was government-arranged business. Apart from those 'of an urgent nature relating to the order of business', he proposed that Questions were to be answered between 7.15–8 p.m. and any not then answered would be dealt with at midnight. Moreover Members were to be given the choice of an oral or a written answer. In this way Balfour hoped to reserve 'the kernel of the day' for Government Business and prevent any other business interfering with it. He also hoped to reduce the number of Questions needing answer in the House mainly by way of the new device of a written answer but also because the late evening would be a less popular time for Members, if only because their Questions would be less likely to attract newspaper publicity. The changes he proposed were part of a whole series of proposals.

However, like present-day reformers he met opposition. In particular there was strong support for Question Time to continue to come at the beginning, rather than much later in the day's proceedings. Balfour would only agree to this providing Public Business was given a fixed and certain time for its commencement. It was agreed therefore that the House should meet at 2 p.m. and that after certain business, e.g. prayers, had been taken, Question Time should start at 2.15 and continue until 2.55 p.m. when Questions of an urgent character of which private notice had been given and Questions relating to the business of the House could be asked. The Government could therefore count on Public Business beginning at 3 p.m. on the great majority of days.

Thus for the first time a limit was placed on the amount of the time of the House that would be available for oral answers. The 40 minutes of Mr Balfour was increased in 1906 by Mr Campbell-Bannerman. Instead of Questions starting at a fixed time they were to start immediately after Prayers (about 5 minutes) and certain other business, e.g. Unopposed Private Business, if any, was out of the way. It could amount to as much as 55 minutes and never be less than 45 minutes. Thus the term 'the Question Hour' came to be used. But it was a 45–55 minute not a 60-minute hour.

The change from an unlimited to a limited period came to have increasingly warping effects on the use of Questions as a Parliamentary device. As a result it now works very differently than it did in say 1900 and is a much less effective weapon for the back-bencher.

Mr Balfour's 40 minutes, in so far as it had a statistical justification, was based on the experience that 60 to 65 Questions could be answered in about 40 minutes and this number, plus the new device of the written answer, were sufficient, he thought, 'to bring to book even the wickedest and most flagitious Government'.

Until the First World War the time allowed was usually sufficient to enable all starred Questions to be given the oral answer to which they were entitled. This was so notwithstanding a steady increase in the average daily number of starred Questions from 38 a sitting in 1904, to 72 in 1907 and 88 in 1913. For several years after the war, however, the number rose above 100 a sitting. Perhaps more significant was the growth in the practice of asking supplementaries, a practice which Mr Balfour had, without success, tried to curb in his original reform proposals. In 1908 42 per cent of the oral answers were followed by a supplementary, rising to 51 per cent in 1918, to 62 per cent in 1928, to 70 per cent in 1938–9, until it became rare for there not to be at least one supplementary to each Question.

The House was faced, therefore, with the old problem of the quart and the pint pot. As no government and apparently few Members were ready to increase the size of the pot the problem of how to deal with the overspill became increasingly difficult. The history of Question Time since 1902 is the history of increasing restrictions placed on the use of the starred Question.

The Rota System

Limiting the time allowed for the oral answer of Questions obviously opened up the prospect that when the time limit was reached some Questions on the Paper would remain unanswered. Two possible solutions were canvassed at the time of the Balfour 'reforms'. One was that answers to any outstanding Questions should be given at the end of the day. This was not popular either with ministers or Members. The other was that the order of Questions should be arranged so that those which seemed to be of the greatest general interest should be reached earliest. Thus by definition any Questions left unanswered because they were at the bottom of the list would be unimportant. Mr Balfour suggested that Mr Speaker would lay down general principles which would guide the Clerks at the Table. It was not acceptable in 1902 and has never since proved acceptable because it is considered impractical to give the Clerks such discretion. The increased time made available in 1906 deferred the problem a few years though there were already occasional grumbles.

Until 1902 Questions were answered roughly in the order they had reached the Table. Only Questions to the Prime Minister had a special place – last on each day's list.[2] Thus the first, fifth, eighth and twenty-third Questions might be addressed to say the Home Secretary with Questions to other ministers equally scattered throughout the list. As part of the 1902 changes Questions to the same minister started to be grouped. At first the order in which ministers, other than the Prime Minister, appeared was accidental but by 1906 it was arranged that Questions to the Foreign Secretary would come first on Tuesday and Thursdays and Irish Questions should come first on some days and last on others.

Whilst the great bulk of Questions on the Paper continued to receive an oral answer the order in which ministers appeared was largely a matter of convenience. But after

1918 as an increasing proportion of Questions failed to be reached, ministers low down in the order were almost certain not to have to answer Questions that day. By 1929 a list headed 'Order of Questions' was printed. By then some departments had begun to be placed in rotating order, being fourth on, say, Tuesday of one week, third on the same day of the following week, and so by the fourth week were at the top of the list. The Parliamentary doldrums of the 1930s allowed the system to work reasonably well. But after the war the situation became more and more difficult – the number of starred Questions increased and the capacity of Question Time to provide replies decreased.

Nowadays, the Order of Questions (or rota) is an essential element in the procedure of the House even though there is no reference to it in Standing Orders.[8] It is fixed by the government after consultation through the usual channels and covers the period between the end of one Recess and the expected beginning of the next. It gives for each day the order in which the ministers for four or five departments will answer orally questions addressed to them. To illustrate the process, let us look at the rota covering the fourteen weeks from Monday 12 January to Thursday 15 April 1976. On the first day, six departments were listed: Energy, Overseas Development, Wales, Industry, Prices and Consumer Protection and Trade. On the second, there were four: Defence, Employment, Social Services and Education and Science, and on the third only three: Environment, Scotland and Foreign and Commonwealth affairs. On the following Monday, Welsh affairs were at the top and Energy did not come first again until five weeks later, i.e. Monday 16 February. The turn of departments regularly listed on Tuesdays and Thursdays came round rather more frequently but this was offset by the fact that the time available for their Questions ended at 3.15 p.m., when the Prime Minister came on automatically. Environment appeared at the top every third Thursday but this is a vast department and there were always more Questions on the Paper than the several ministers concerned had time to answer.

To prevent them being crowded out, a new arrangement

has been introduced for some of the smaller departments. It follows the treatment accorded to the Prime Minister by bringing on their Questions automatically not later than a stated time. Thus, during that rota, Questions to the Minister for Overseas Development came on not later than 3.15 p.m. at three sittings; to the Minister for the Civil Service at not later than 3.10 p.m. at three sittings followed by Questions to the Lord President of the Council not later than 3.20 p.m. A refinement of this device was that when the Foreign Office was top of the list Questions about the European Community came on not later than 3.10 p.m.

The rota does not, however, guarantee the Member an oral answer even if the minister he is pursuing is at the top of the list. Since the establishment of very large departments it is indeed a rare occasion that the second department is reached, except where it has been given a fixed time. In the rota period just described, the first minister exhausted his Questions on only two occasions, both being in respect of Wales, and this allowed the Industry Minister, next on the list, to answer a few Questions. In contrast, the five occasions when Environment was at the top, Members put 51, 93, 73, 69 and 68 starred Questions on the Paper on this topic, of which the Ministers concerned answered only 22, 21, 24, 20 and 22 in the Chamber.

Evidence to the Select Committee on Procedure of 1964–5 showed the deterioration of Question Time in the immediate post-war years. Figures for a representative period – the week before Christmas – showed that the average number of starred Questions on the Order Paper had risen from 85 in 1937 to 128 in 1946, 124 in 1950, 148 in 1952 and 131 in 1959. In contrast, the number of such Questions answered orally declined from 61 in 1937 and 1946 to below 50, being only 41 in 1959. The reasons for the decline were in some part an increase in the number of supplementaries (20–30 per cent or so over 1937), but more specially a doubling of the length of supplementaries and of ministers' replies to them. As a result, the number of starred Questions which were not reached and therefore did not receive an answer in the Chamber greatly increased. Whereas in 1937 only an average

24 Questions a day were not answered orally, in 1946 the number had risen to 67, was 66 in 1949, 106 in 1952 and 90 in 1959. Put another way, Question Time would have had to have been at least three times as long in 1959 to give every starred Question a chance of being answered.

Since then the capacity of Question Time has fallen even further. During the fourteen weeks – Monday 12 January to 14 April 1976 – the number of Questions answered orally was around 20–22 each day, falling however as low as 15–18 on several days. The trend noted by the Select Committee of 1964–5 for supplementaries to take up more and more time has continued. On one day when only 13 Questions were answered in some 40 minutes, there were 2½ supplementaries on average. One supplementary took up 17 lines in Hansard and the ministerial reply took up 32 lines. On several occasions, the Speaker cut short a supplementary and urged Members and ministers to keep their Questions and answers short, but to little or no avail.

During the period covered by this rota there were 54 Question Times which attracted some 3400 starred Questions, an average of 63 per sitting. However, nearly 800 of these were addressed to the Prime Minister for answer on 26 occasions, an average of some 30 a sitting. If these are excluded the average per Question Time for all other ministers falls to 48, of which in practice about half received oral answers. But only 108 of the 791 starred Questions addressed to the Prime Minister on Tuesdays and Thursdays received oral answers. All those not reached in the day received answers printed in next day's Hansard, unless deferred or withdrawn by the questioner. In addition during this period there were some 11,000 unstarred Questions (some 160 a day), of which over 4800 were of the new W variety.

The inability of Question Time to ensure oral answers for all the Questions on the Paper combined with the rota has completely changed its character.

In 1901, and indeed for some years after, a Member could hand in a Question at the Table as late as 11 p.m. or 11.30 p.m. on, say, Monday for answer the next afternoon. His Question would be certain to be reached. If he did not like the answer he could come out of the Chamber, think out one or two further Questions, hand them in and be certain of the minister having to reply on the Thursday. If the minister again failed to satisfy him he could put another Question which would be reached on Friday,[4] and so on, day after day if he so wished.

Contrast the position of the Member of 1976. He has to have his Question at the Table Office before 2.30 p.m. on the Monday for it to appear on the Order Paper on the Wednesday. But the minister he wishes to question may not be among the four or so listed for answering on the Wednesday or the Thursday or indeed for several more sittings. In that case it is fruitless for the Member to put down his starred Question for such a day for he will receive only a written reply.[5] Even, however, if the minister is first on the list on the Wednesday or the Thursday he will very likely find that there are already so many Questions down for that minister that his will not be reached in the time available. He could, however, take his chance and, should his Question not be reached, go immediately to the Table Office and ask for it to be deferred to a later date (unless he did this he would be automatically given an answer printed in the next day's Hansard). Or if it were clear that his Question had no chance of being reached, he could withdraw it and subsequently put it down for the first day it looked to have a real chance, possibly two or three weeks ahead. To make certain that their Questions were reached, Members started to give notice of them a month or even six weeks ahead. Some of these were overtaken by events or became stale for other reasons. The Select Committee of 1958–9 therefore recommended that a limit of 21 days should be imposed. The recommendation was repeated by the Select Committee of 1964–5 and adopted by the House in October 1965. Since 1970 the maximum notice allowed is ten sitting days (i.e., a fortnight during the time when the House is continuously sitting).

However, let us suppose that by perseverance and foresight on the part of the Member his Question is eventually reached and he is not satisfied with the reply. Unlike the Member of 50–60 years ago he knows that if he lets this chance slip he may not reach the minister for another four or five weeks. He therefore tries to frame a supplementary on the spur of the moment. Not all Members have the quick wit and command of words to ask a single short follow-up Question immediately after hearing the minister's reply. Many take 10–15 lines of Hansard to make their point and are unlikely to be allowed to ask more than one, though perhaps Mr Speaker might allow one or two other Members to put supplementaries to the minister's reply. Thus the impossibility of a Member being able to rely on questioning a minister on successive days or within a short period drives Members to take advantage of their rare chances, makes it difficult for Mr Speaker to curb even the most rambling of supplementaries, and so reduces the capacity of Question Time which in turn means that it takes longer to answer the same number of Questions, and so extends the period during which a particular Minister is unlikely to be reached because other ministers are above him in the rota.

Altogether then, the elements of immediacy and rapid follow-up have disappeared from Question Time. Members are presumably expected to feel well done by if by good management or chance some of their starred Questions are reached and receive an oral answer.

At one time one of the attractions of the starred Question was that an answer could be obtained more quickly than it could for an unstarred Question – for there was no obligation on departments to answer the latter on a specified day or even to answer it quickly. In contrast, starred Questions had to be answered on the day for which they were put down for even if the minister to whom it was addressed was not reached the answer would have to be printed in the Hansard covering that day's proceedings. The Select Committee on Procedure of 1946 thought that if Members could be assured of a written answer within a reasonable period they would make more use of unstarred Questions and so relieve the pressure on oral Questions. The Government thereupon undertook to try and answer such Questions within seven days and this was reduced to three days in 1960, but this was a target rather than a firm commitment.

In 1972, following a recommendation of the Select Committee on Parliamentary Questions, a new form of unstarred Question was introduced. Where a Member particularly wants a written answer on a named day he may indicate this by marking his Question with the letter W and the specified date, providing he has given the same minimum amount of notice as is required for an oral answer, namely two sitting days. The committee expressed the hope that ministers would endeavour to provide answers for other unstarred Questions within a working week of their being tabled, and in any case provide a holding answer within that period.

If one were to be shown a list of, say, 100 recent Questions and ask which would be likely to be starred and which left without the asterisk any answer would be mainly guesswork. There are no obvious criteria, no obvious differences between the two kinds. Thus on 18 June 1969, Mr Gardner asked the President of the Board of Trade 'how many prosecutions have been initiated since the Trade Descriptions Act came into force' and Mr Speed asked the Minister of Transport 'what action he is taking to improve the accident record on the A45 road between the Coventry and Birmingham city boundaries'. The former, which demanded a numerical answer, was put down for and received an oral answer and attracted two supplementaries, whereas the latter was unstarred.

There are various reasons why Members deliberately choose one form rather than the other. Questions for oral answer require the Member to be in his place on the day when his Question is called, for nobody else is allowed to ask it for him. He may have other business, or not be a regular attender at that time in the House, or he may not want to commit himself to be present on a particular day some time ahead. There tend to be fewer starred Questions down for answer on Mondays, when many Members are returning from their constituencies. Second, though two Questions both ask for information, e.g. about the number of civil servants employed by a department, in one case the Member may want to use the factual answer as the basis for what he thinks will be a telling supplementary, whereas in the other case he genuinely only wants information, e.g. for a speech or an article he may be writing.

One consideration is the glamour and publicity of Question Time. It comes right at the beginning of the daily business, the Chamber is much fuller than for most of the rest of the day and it is a convenient time for the Press reporters, some answers even being early enough to appear in the evening papers. There is something for everybody at Question Time – a minister may shine or be caught out and 40 or 50 Members have a chance of getting on their feet and uttering a few words in the Chamber, a rare event for most of them. It is a treasured British institution, loved by the public and Members and well reported by the Press. The fact that most of the information could have been obtained by way of written answer, that few Members are particularly brilliant at asking supplementaries and that few ministers are caught napping by them still makes it a special occasion. Above all it is not given over to lengthy front-bench speeches, it is largely a back-benchers' affair, and Ministers are there to answer to even the newest and humblest Member of the House.

For many years the glamour of Question Time caused the unstarred Question to be overlooked and its importance underestimated. For fifty years after the Balfour reforms the increasing difficulty of obtaining oral answers did not result in a corresponding increase in Questions needing only a written answer. Between 1902 and 1913 their daily number was 17 to 24 and 15 to 21 in the 1950s. Since then, however, the daily average has greatly increased, being 31 in 1962–3, 46 in 1964–5, 77 in 1967–8 and in 1974 rose to 133. The number is now higher. There were 354 Questions for written answer on the Order Paper for 9 February 1976.

The growth in the number of unstarred Questions in the last few years is only a partial reflection of the difficulties Members have in getting an oral answer to a starred Question. There is also the limit on the numbers which can be put down – a limit which does not apply to unstarred Questions. The unstarred Question can also be used to create an impact. It is possible, for example, for a Member to give notice of, say, 30, 50 or even more unstarred Questions each asking for information about an aspect of the same issue. Thus on 14 July 1969 Mr Ernest Marples put down 68 unstarred Questions to eight ministers asking for information about the procurement arrangements in their departments. The political impact of this kind of questioning is potentially quite great – on Members, who see the mass of similar Questions first on the paper and next when they are answered, and on ministers and civil servants who have to provide the answers.

In passing it is worth noting that the unstarred Question reflects the relationship between the House of Commons and the governmental machine. Members obviously need all kinds of information in order that they can perform their functions. Some of it is fairly readily available to them in statistical and other reports, but even so may require time to dig out. They can write to the minister for the information but their relations with civil servants is such as to discourage their ringing up or calling on the official concerned. To put a Question on the paper is the formal procedure for acquiring information from the civil service. It is a simple method for the Member and it keeps the Member and the civil service away from each other.

Ministerial Responsibility

Two features of Questions and Question Time need underlining. First, they are a very important element in the doctrine of individual ministerial responsibility and second, they are one of the last procedural devices at the complete disposal of the back-bencher.

According to the 19th edition of Erskine May (1976), 'Questions addressed to ministers should relate to the public affairs with which they are officially connected, to proceedings pending in Parliament, or to matters of administration for which they are responsible' – a definition which has hardly changed since 1893. The simplest and clearest form of ministerial answerability arises from the official actions of ministers and their departments. Nowadays the great bulk of departmental powers are set out in Acts of Parliament in which a particular minister is given the authority to perform certain functions – such as to build trunk roads or to appoint the members of the National Coal Board.

Questions enable a minister on whom Parliament has conferred a particular power to be asked why he has exercised it in such and such a way, how he is exercising it or whether he will exercise it in a particular case or manner. It follows that if a minister does not possess a particular power he cannot be questioned about it. He cannot, for example, be asked why the National Coal Board has dismissed a particular mine manager or closed a particular pit, for these are powers vested not in the minister but in the Board. Similarly, where powers are vested in local authorities a minister cannot be made answerable for their performance in particular instances. On the other hand, a Question to the minister about an explosion at a particular pit is perfectly in order because he has had certain responsibilities for safety in mines since long before nationalization.

This important and obviously very desirable limitation is some barrier against Members interfering in everything that happens in the country – the appointment by a university of Dr X to its Chair of Politics, the shape of the package of a detergent or the thousands and thousands of decisions which bodies and individuals can take without the approval or interference of Whitehall. At the same time, the device enables the ordinary Member of Parliament to hold a particular minister accountable – that is answerable – for all the functions and powers vested in him by Parliament.

In recent years the ever-increasing range of departmental powers combined with an apparent desire of Members of both major parties to discuss anything that currently interests them, have perhaps made it easier to find ways round the strict interpretations of ministerial responsibility. Thus the Member who cannot ask questions about the day-to-day actions of the National Coal Board may try to link his point to the minister's powers to issue a general direction or to approve schemes of capital development or even to collect statistics. Or he may try to bring his Question under some such broad heading as the government's responsibility for full

C.I.S. – F

employment, or incomes policy, or social welfare. Nevertheless, the rule that the minister to whom the Question is
addressed must either have acted or have the power to act
both limits the range of Questions and pinpoints the responsibility of a particular minister. Questions which are mis-
directed, i.e. addressed to a minister who has not the
statutory authority, are transferred to the minister who has.

The fact that the Questions addressed to each minister are
grouped or bunched adds emphasis to this aspect. The whole
or a major part of the Question 'hour' may be taken up by
one minister, or since the advent of very large departments,
by the two or three ministers responsible for that department.
He may answer 20 or so original Questions and even more
supplementaries, 40 or so Members taking part in a fairly full
Chamber.

Thus a large number of his own supporters will see how
he performs, whether he appears to be on top of his job and
gives an air of confidence, and what his attitude is to this or
that facet of the work of his department. It is also the part
of the day's proceedings which is likely to get a greater share
of Press publicity than all except major speeches. Unless the
minister has a bill to pilot through the House or is a main
front-bench speaker Question Time will be the main occasion
when, as the minister responsible for a particular area of
government activity, he confronts the House. Moreover, Members particularly interested in, say, Defence, Scotland or the
Social Services will make a special effort to attend Question
Time when these departments are at the top of the list. Even
though they may not have a Question on the Paper, those of
other Members may be of interest to them and also they may
get a chance to ask a supplementary.

It must also be remembered that a minister personally
handles very few of the day-to-day decisions which are taken
by his civil servants in his name. These decisions are, of
course, made in a way which the official thinks conforms to
ministerial policy. A Question about one of these decisions
brings the case on to the minister's desk. The decision may
have been taken at quite a low level in the department. It now
is looked at by the senior members of the department, even

the Permanent Secretary as well as the Minister and one or more Parliamentary Secretaries. The PQ file (each Question is normally given its own file) will normally contain not only a draft answer but also any relevant facts. The minister has no excuse for not going into the case and satisfying himself that the departmental decision was correct and conformed to his policy. When he examines it he may be surprised, even shocked, and make a different decision or clarify or redefine the policy to be followed in future. This is the internal reality of the public answerability of the minister. Members' correspondence asking a minister about constituency cases have a similar internal effect: they bring day-to-day decisions to the notice of the top level of a department, and so do unstarred Questions. But the fact that the minister has to give his answer in a full House and to be prepared for one or two supplementaries should cause him to give greater personal consideration to cases raised by starred Questions.

A major reason for the growth of the public corporation form of public management has been the desire to avoid day-to-day matters of administration becoming subject to Questions and other forms of Parliamentary scrutiny. The process is sometimes described as taking the service or function 'out of politics'. The vesting of the function in a statutory Board precludes the minister being asked about its day-to-day exercise.

One recent development illustrates the close relationship between Questions and ministerial responsibility and the manner in which procedure can be adapted to the changing needs of Members. Though his constitutional influence has greatly increased the Prime Minister still has very few statutory powers. If, therefore, Members try and put down questions to him about, say, inflation, wages policy, unemployment or some issue of foreign policy, these will almost certainly be transferred by the staff at No. 10 for answer by the minister with the appropriate powers. Thus, broadly speaking, only questions dealing with the general machinery of government, the content of speeches made by Cabinet Ministers and the Prime Minister's actions are admissible. But Members now feel that the Prime Minister is much more the source of policy and much more powerful than any of his ministers. So they have found a way round the rules. They have developed a curiosity about the personal activities of the Prime Minister – what are his main engagements on the day in question; has he ever visited or thought of visiting, or been invited to visit Iceland, Glasgow, South Wales and so on. Nowadays more starred Questions are put down to the Prime Minister than to any other minister, and the great bulk of them are of this kind. On hearing the Prime Minister's answer, the Member asks a supplementary which had he tried to put it on the Order Paper would have been refused or transferred to the appropriate departmental minister. He might ask why the Prime Minister has not arranged to discuss unemployment with the TUC, prices with the CBI, or the plight of the Grimsby trawlermen with the Prime Minister of Iceland, and so on. On occasion the time available – 3.15 p.m. to 3.30 p.m. every Tuesday and Thursday – provides a kind of bear-baiting session with the Prime Minister as the bear. Usually, only four or five of the twenty or so Questions are answered in the fifteen minutes, the very generally phrased supplementaries often encouraging lengthy and general answers. Many would say it was hardly the most productive fifteen minutes in the daily life of Members. Others would stress the significance of the House being able to question the Prime Minister for thirty minutes each week on a wide range of issues.

A Back-bencher's Weapon

A hundred years ago back-benchers had a wide variety of procedural opportunities at their free disposal uncontrolled by what have since come to be known as the 'usual channels', that is the Whips acting mainly for their respective front benches. A Member could, for example, still move the adjournment of the House either before or during Public Business if he wished to raise an issue. Many of these opportunities disappeared or were restricted in the 1880s when the Irish used them to obstruct other business and so call attention to the wrongs of Ireland. Then, as party discipline became stronger and the government began to dominate the business and timetable of the House, the opportunities under the complete control of the back-bencher became even fewer.

Questions, however, have been an exception. They are not controlled by the Whips nor are they a front-bench device. True the changes in 1902 limited the time available for oral answer and as we have seen this was later to impose a severe limitation on the numbers that could otherwise have been answered orally. But the time remained at the complete disposal of the ordinary Member. Suggestions that there should be some kind of control to separate important or general Questions from the rest and give them priority were always strongly opposed. It would have restricted the freedom of each Member and subordinated his wish to the wishes of the majority, which if accepted would eventually bring Question Time under the control of the usual channels. Equally significant, starred Questions are not normally put down by leading front-benchers. The Leader and the Deputy Leader of the Opposition seldom ask them except by Private Notice for matters of major current significance. Since the development of 'shadow ministers' it is now more usual for Opposition front-benchers to put down Questions. But even now the vast bulk of Questions are put down by the ordinary back-benchers on both sides of the House, many of whom will never reach even junior ministerial office nor even aspire to it. The supplementaries may be taken up by active and ambitious Opposition Members of the junior shadow minister level – but only after the original questioner has had an opportunity to ask his supplementary.

In so far as the purpose is to seek information there is obviously no reason why Questions should be confined to Opposition back-benchers, for government back-benchers have no special sources of information. In so far as Questions are asked to embarrass a minister, however, they are more likely to attract Opposition Members. In actual practice, government supporters, particularly when Labour is in power, always ask a substantial number of Questions, many of the harassing kind. This again emphasizes the back-bencher character of the device.

It must be borne in mind that the opportunities to speak in the House are very limited, particularly for a back-bencher. He may very occasionally 'catch the Speaker's eye' and be able to speak in a debate. He will get a greater chance in the committee stage of a bill if he is a member of the standing committee. Neither of these infrequent opportunities offer him much freedom to raise an issue of his own choosing. He may try his luck in applying or balloting for an Adjournment motion – but he is unlikely to get more than one of these a year. In contrast he can even now, without needing anybody's permission or approval, put down his quota of starred Questions and an unlimited number of unstarred Questions which, providing they do not transgress the rules of the House, will have to appear on the Order Paper for the minister to answer either in person or by printed answer. If the Question he asks is about an issue of importance to his constituency, it and the minister's answer are likely to get publicity in the local Press. Members may correspond with ministers about particular issues and may get satisfaction in that way. But the Question and answer, particularly those dealt with in the House, may mean welcome publicity to the Member and may cause the minister to ponder his reply more carefully.

Problems of Question Time

Members regularly complain about the working of Question Time. Between 1959–75 it was dealt with in six Reports of Select Committees. Several courses of action have been considered. First, as we have already seen, there is the attempt to relieve the pressure on Question Time by making written answers more attractive, i.e. by guaranteeing that they receive quick answers. Second, there is the continuous attempt by the Speaker to restrain the length of supplementaries and ministerial replies to them. It is, however, a losing battle in the long run. It depends on the good sense and abstinence of Members, for it is difficult for the Speaker to keep intervening. He cannot tell how long a supplementary is going to be until he has heard a good part of it, and if he calls the

Member to order he may take up more time than in allowing him to proceed. Moreover, it has to be remembered that the Member may have waited three or four weeks to reach the minister, the point of the Question may be of major importance to him and his constituents and this may be one of the few occasions when he has a chance to speak in the Chamber.

Third, there have been various proposals for increasing the time available. One such proposal is to have a Question Time on Fridays. This has been rejected by several select committees on the grounds that it would be of little value to Members with constituencies far from London and would interfere with the work of Ministers with official responsibilities outside London. It has to be remembered that the House is rather thinly attended on Friday and in any case the sitting normally ends about 4.30 p.m. However, the Select Committee of 1971–2 recommended as an experiment that Questions should be taken on Fridays from 10 a.m. to 11 a.m. The aim would be to provide an extra opportunity to question those ministers currently attracting the most starred Questions. Not more than two departments would appear on the rota and these occasions were to be additional to the existing opportunities to ask Questions about those departments. This proposal received little support. On the whole Members are not very interested in any suggestions that do not provide the atmosphere and full attendance characteristic of Question Times at present. They are not attracted by proposals such as that by the late Sir Edward Fellowes, then Clerk of the House, that starred Questions could be put down for answer in one of three Grand Committees on the mornings of Mondays and Wednesdays. Yet attempts to increase the length of Question Time do not get much support. Thus in 1965 a Select Committee rejected a proposal that the present 55 minutes, i.e. 1 hour less Prayers, should be extended to a full hour. Even the 55 minutes can be eroded by Private Business and Motions for Writs.[6] The Select Committees of 1966–7 and 1969–70 recommended that extra time be made available by the House meeting at 2.15 p.m. or 2.20 p.m., instead of at 2.30 p.m. Nothing came of these proposals, the objections being that standing committees could be meeting until 1 p.m. and that there were many official lunch engagements.

The alternative would be to extend the time available by delaying the onset of Public Business. But suggestions of this kind run into even more powerful opposition. For one thing they raise the big issue of the purpose of the change. Is it to ensure that all starred Questions receive an oral answer or only that rather more do so than at present? It is generally accepted that the former is not a practical possibility. At the current rate of answering in relation to numbers on the Paper, it would take up to a further two hours. But inevitably, if Question Time were extended to two and a half or three hours, the number of starred Questions would increase. The difficulty, indeed impossibility, of reaching a particular minister causes many Members not to bother to star their Question or even to ask it. This is a major reason why the numbers being currently asked are only half the number in the 1950s, notwithstanding the steady growth in governmental responsibilities in the past 20–30 years. More significant, even as it is, the House finds there is little enough time for major debates, the legislative stages taken in the Chamber and other elements that make up Public Business. On four days a week the House normally meets for eight hours, of which one hour is largely devoted to Questions. There would be no real support for extending the latter to two or three hours and so reducing the time available for Public Business to five or six hours.

If on the other hand the aim is only to secure a few more oral answers, there is a tendency to doubt whether the trouble is worth the while. The Government and to a large extent the Opposition front bench are not enthusiastic supporters of Question Time, certainly if any change means even half an hour or so less available for Public Business. The back-benchers, who make the greatest use of the time, are by no means homogeneous. At one extreme there is the Member who puts down only half a dozen starred Questions a year – at the other is the small number of Members who take advantage of the whole of their 'allowance' – 100 or so during the normal Parliamentary year. The former are in the great majority and they are inclined to feel that enough time would be available for them to receive oral answers if the persistent questioners did not put so many Questions on the Paper. Whenever Select Committees consider the issue they are usually given statistics illustrating this point. Thus the Select Committee of 1971–2 were told that in 1971 while 496 Members made use of starred Questions, 46 Members tabled 47·8 per cent of the total.

On the whole, Members are tolerant even of those who make persistent use of Question Time. Most of them see it as a device to be used occasionally, for example, when correspondence with a minister about an issue of great importance to his constituents, or to some interest he has at heart, has failed to secure a satisfactory outcome. But to ensure that only Questions of this type and seriousness were allowed on the Paper would require a degree of control from which all Members shrink. Hence the uneasy situation that though all is not well with Question Time, Members are prepared to make do with it. They will complain about the difficulty of reaching ministers, about lengthy supplementaries and ministerial replies, but any solutions proposed always appear worse than the present situation.

Thus we come naturally to the only proposal which has received general support. If the size or capacity of the pint-pot cannot be increased, then efforts must be made to reduce the quart. In other words, limits must be put on the number of starred Questions which may be asked. After Balfour's changes in 1902 there was a gentleman's understanding that a Member would not put down more than eight starred Questions for answer on any one day. In February 1919, with the big increase in total numbers, the maximum was reduced to four, and in February 1920 to three. In February 1960 it was reduced to two per day. The Select Committee of 1964–5 recommended no change in the daily maximum, but an overall limit of eight a month. This recommendation was successfully and rather less stringently reiterated by the Select Committee of 1971–2. As a result, Members may not table more than eight Questions for oral answer in the period of ten sitting days ahead and not more than two of these may be tabled for answer on any day and only one to any one minister on that day.

This new rule has undoubtedly reduced the numbers on the Paper. Nevertheless, there is still a substantial gap on many days between the number put down and the number receiving oral answer. This led me to make a drastic proposal to the Select Committee on Parliamentary Questions of 1971–2. I suggested that the House should start by reaching agreement on the reasonable number of Questions for which each Member ought to receive an answer from ministers in the Chamber if he or she is to fulfil their obligations, as Members. Assuming that neither ministers nor members of the Shadow Cabinet received a quota, that would leave some 500 Members. If 15 was the agreed number per Member that would mean time would have to be found for some 7500 Questions, 10,000 if 20 were the agreed quota. As some Members would not use all their quota the total would be less – say, 5000–7000. Many years ago, when ministerial powers were very much less, the House found time to handle that number of starred Questions. Should it, I asked, not be ready to do so now? If the demands could be more nearly equated with the capacity, then the whole system would work differently, ministers would be reached much more frequently and the rota would not put the proceedings in a strait-jacket. As I expected, the Select Committee did not favour the idea. One reason they gave was that 'Questions would become so sparse that the rota would no longer work as it does, in providing an opportunity to hold one minister to account for the bulk of Question Time'. Apparently they put this feature of the rota above the advantage of getting speedier replies. They also pointed out that the effect on Members who choose to make regular use of oral Questions would be severe. There were also no doubt other good objections. Nevertheless, their limited recommendation was a good example of the unwillingness of the House to face the issues involved in its procedures and the changing demands made upon them.

The situation may be summed up as follows. Since 1900 the functions and powers of ministers have multiplied probably twenty or thirty fold. It follows that the number of reasons why Members should wish to interrogate ministers must also have greatly increased. If Parliament were keeping pace with the growth in the Executive one would expect an increasing number of Questions being answered by ministers in the Chamber. Instead of which the number has steadily declined. In the twenties and early thirties some 60 Questions received oral answers each day; this had fallen to 40 a day by the fifties and is now nearer 20 a day. Given the usual length of a Parliamentary Session, covering some 120 Question Times, this means a fall in total from some 7000 to some 2400. With this decline has come increasingly the lottery element. If there are 60 Questions down for answer and only 20 are reached, there is only a one in three chance, and luck can play a part, e.g. by the order in which the printer puts the notices sent to him on the Notice Paper.

Having said that, it still is possible, justifiably, to claim that Question Time remains a special occasion. To the back-benchers who by luck or good management are called upon to put their Questions, there is the opportunity to probe the intelligence and honesty of senior ministers, even the Prime Minister. It is an occasion which all Members may enjoy and benefit from. There is likely to be something for everyone without having to listen to long speeches or read hundreds of pages of Hansard. If your Question is not reached, then at least there is the vicarious thrill of having participated in the occasion. And anyhow an hour is probably enough, for the making of Questions is without end.

There are two developments that might greatly alter this picture. The first would be devolution. Assuming either that the appropriate ministers were answerable to the regional assemblies or that these new bodies had powers of their own, Questions about the domestic affairs of these areas would presumably no longer be a matter for the Parliament at Westminster. This can be seen by the disappearance of the large number of Questions about Irish domestic affairs when the independent state of Eire was created and Northern Ireland was given its own Parliament. Now that the powers of the latter are suspended it becomes once again admissible to put down Questions about housing and schools in, say, Belfast. The extent to which the Order Paper would be relieved would clearly depend on the character and extent of the powers transferred from Whitehall ministers to the regional bodies. It is interesting to note that of the 56 Question Times covered by the rota for January–April 1976, no less than 12 were taken up mainly by Questions about Northern Ireland, Scotland and Wales.

The second would be a much greater use of specialized committees. Excluding the persistent questioners, whose questions are likely to be concerned with a great variety of matters, most Questions reflect the current preoccupations, specialisms, and constituency interests of the Member asking them. They may all be about the aircraft industry, atomic energy, social security or prices. If there were to be set up a series of Select Committees covering the whole range of governmental activity, presumably Members would serve on the committees which most interested them. This would give them the opportunity to obtain information more fully and under better follow-up arrangements than exist at Question Time. One would thus expect specialized committees to be an alternative to Questions and so relieve the pressure on that device.

It by no means follows that this would prove to be the case. For one thing it is most unlikely that a few Questions and answers out of the many thousands during the course of the proceedings of a Select Committee would ever attract the immediate publicity received by the single question printed on the paper, answered in the House and with the printed answer also readily available to ministers and Members. Moreover, Select Committees' proceedings are generally devoted to one theme at a time and the Members may want to deal urgently with quite a different theme. Finally each Select Committee will contain only a dozen or so members and even if these are the enthusiasts for the subject there may still remain a lot of Members of the House, including many of the persistent questioners who, not being on the appropriate committee, will still have to get their information through starred or unstarred Questions.

The fact is that Question Time and specialized committees would be performing different functions. The primary purpose of the latter is to enable a small group of Members to study a governmental activity in some depth mainly so as to be better informed but also to improve the House's control over Departments. There would still be a substantial function left for Questions to perform – the raising of the individual case, the personal or group campaign to stimulate action or to change ministerial policy, the testing of the minister's actions in a full Chamber.

At some time in the future the House will have to think afresh about the real purpose of the Question Hour. At the moment discussion still centres on getting as many Questions answered as possible. Select Committees recommend stricter control of supplementaries and Speakers try to restrict their number and length. But what is the point of a starred Question if supplementaries cannot be asked? How does it then differ from an unstarred Question? Surely the difference does not really lie in the minister having to read out an answer in public. Are supplementaries being restricted merely in order to enable more of the original Questions to be answered orally or because experience shows that an average of, say, $1\frac{1}{2}$ or 2 supplementaries a Question is sufficient to satisfy the proper curiosity of Members and that anything beyond that would be idle and wasteful? If there are many Questions which could be dealt with more satisfactorily by the asking of five to seven supplementaries, what are the relative merits, so far as the effective use of Parliamentary time is concerned, of trying to rush through 30 or so original Questions as against dealing with, say, 10 really effectively?

The difficulty of finding a solution satisfactory to all Members lies in the character of the device. Many Members believe that a lot of starred Questions could just as well be left without the asterisk. They know of no way of preventing what they regard as the misuse of Question Time other than by methods of control which would alter its character and limit its value to all back-benchers. Failing a satisfactory method for ensuring that only Questions warranting the use of the limited time available can find their way on the Paper, Members are likely to continue to accept each Question being treated alike.

9 Select Committees as Tools of Parliamentary Reform: Some Further Reflections

NEVIL JOHNSON

The past six or seven years have seen a continuing expansion in the investigative activities of House of Commons select committees. Bearing in mind the fact that the Parliamentary reform proposals of the years 1965 to 1969 were characterized by a strong commitment to the development and diversification of select committee enquiry, it would appear that at least superficially much has been achieved in recent years to satisfy the claims of those who saw in select committees dedicated to administrative and policy scrutiny the best hope of restoring Parliamentary influence over the executive and of providing a definition of the role of back-benchers adequate to the needs of the contemporary situation. It is true that the tentative thrust in the direction of an evolution marked by specialist or subject committees on the one hand and departmental scrutiny committees on the other soon petered out: that particular pattern was nipped in the bud with the disappearance between 1969 and 1971 of such departmental committees as Education and Science, Scottish Affairs, and Agriculture. Nevertheless there has been a steady growth in the number of select committees and of their sub-committees. In the sessions from 1972–3 to 1975–6 the total number of operating units, i.e. committees and sub-committees, was 38, 28, 31, 40 and 38 per session. Of these on average just over half have been committees of executive scrutiny such as this essay is chiefly concerned with as opposed to domestic, procedural or special purpose select committees. At the same time the range of the committees' investigative interests has widened and the quantity of reports and evidence produced has increased enormously.

It is against this background – which will be set out in rather more detail below – that we must try to evaluate what the achievement of select committees has been, and in particular consider whether the progress made has removed the basis for the scepticism about the effectiveness of select committees as tools of Parliamentary reform which I expressed six years ago.[1] The conclusion reached then had two main elements. First, it was argued that the plea for select committee development overlooked the significant separation which exists between what goes on (or can go on) in essentially non-partisan investigative bodies and what both the government and Members do on the floor of the House. For the government the main concern on the floor is to get legislation through and to maintain its political reputation; for Members it is to engage in often highly partisan debate and to press their particular concerns, sometimes on behalf of constituents, sometimes on behalf of particular organizations, interests or causes with which they are associated. Overarching the activity and interests on the floor of the House is the competition between Government and Opposition. As a result of these conditions it was argued that the work of select committees 'must always have a certain academic quality, removing them from the day to day press of business'.[2] This implies that much of the output of select committees will and can have no direct effect: at best it has a therapeutic value, though it may often be uncertain to whose advantage this is – Members, ministers, civil servants, the staff of nationalized industries or the public at large? The second point was that the reform movement as a whole, and select committee development in particular, underlined a dilemma for the House of Commons. Here it was faced by a relentless growth in governmental functions, in the complexity of public policy issues, and in the impact on individuals of public action. It was natural in such a situation to seek means of redressing the balance, of enabling the House of Commons to keep up with the changing context in which its Members hoped to exercise their traditional rights and functions. But was it likely that this would be achieved through the growth of select committees? The danger was that the House (and the

Government for that matter) wanted to have reform at no political cost. Despite the changes in party representation of 1974 there has in practice been no significant shift away from the traditional view of the House as the place where great issues are fought out, nor has the structure of the parties in Parliament and the confrontation of Government and Opposition yet been substantially modified. But for reform to be effective in the sense of altering relations between Government and Parliament, it seemed to be necessary to challenge accepted views both of how the House should operate and of party alignments within it. Only in this way could the House as an institution hope to exert a major influence on the conduct of governments. Select committees seemed to be a way of avoiding the awkward dilemma lying at the heart of the Parliamentary reform argument, or at the least of softening its impact.

In what follows we shall look again at these questions in the light of what has taken place in the last few years. After discussing in broad outline the evolution of select committees since about 1970 I shall consider whether these earlier judgements still hold good, or whether we can now conclude that the reform dilemma has been overcome and that the new, expanded pattern of select committees has established for them a satisfactory and stable role and by so doing contributed to significant changes in institutional relationships, particularly in respect of those between Government and Parliament.

Of the expansion of select committee work in the period since 1970 there can be no doubt. The quantitative growth is in fact intimidating. Since its establishment early in 1971 as successor to the Estimates Committee the Expenditure Committee alone has produced reports and evidence which occupy about four feet of library shelf space. The select committees on Nationalized Industries, Science and Technology, and Race Relations and Immigration continue to produce long reports, backed up by compendious volumes of oral evidence and written memoranda. The committees on the Parliamentary Commissioner for Administration, on Public Accounts, on Overseas Development and on Statutory

Instruments have been somewhat more restrained in the amount of material published, though this is not to imply that they have been less active. More recently the Select Committee on European Secondary Legislation, etc. has added to the flow of reports (though abstaining generally from the customary publication of extensive supporting evidence). Finally, there have been a number of *ad hoc* select committees, related chiefly to legislative proposals and possibilities, which have too in some cases issued very substantial documentation.

So extensive has the material produced by select committees become that even in respect of a short time span it is no longer practicable to offer anything like a detailed appreciation of its contents, range, quality and significance. If we want to consider select committees as a whole there is now no escape from an impressionistic treatment: it is then to be hoped that from time to time the findings of research in depth into particular select committees will confirm, correct or refute the conclusions suggested by a general appreciation such as is offered here.

The quantitative growth immediately suggests a number of consequences and effects. First, it is clear that the proportion of Members engaged in select committee work is now high. In the 1974 session 219 served on committees, and in 1974–5 the figure was 291, not far short of half of the total membership of the House.[3] Yet this does not really represent a significant change from the position already reached in 1969–70 when 254 served on select committees. The real contrast is with the period before 1964 when there were far fewer committees to take Members away from the Chamber. The implication is that the Chamber is now less well attended, at any rate for much of the time, and that select committee growth, along with the increasing burdens imposed by standing committees, has contributed to this. As is well known, there is no reliable means of measuring attendance on the floor of the House. But there does appear to be widespread agreement that it has dwindled: the forms remain, but the priority accorded to the floor has diminished in the perceptions of many Members.

Of rather more obvious significance are the effects of select committee growth on the government and on those required to provide evidence. Undoubtedly the time demand on ministers has grown as a result of the desire of many committees to take evidence from them. But this should not be exaggerated as far as ministers go. In the period 1970–4, for example, fourteen ministers appeared before select committees, a figure which suggests that no major burden was being imposed. Nevertheless, the need for the politicians to be aware of select committees, of their interests and demands, has increased, and they can no longer (subject to a few exceptions like Public Accounts) be regarded as essentially the place where civil servants interact with Parliamentarians. *Pari passu*, however, the burden on officials and departments has risen, both to appear for oral evidence-taking and to provide supporting papers. In the period just mentioned well over three hundred civil servants had to attend select committees, a figure which totally leaves out of account those engaged behind the scenes in preparing material.[4] There seems little doubt that select committees – and most notably the Expenditure Committee and its Sub-committees – are fairly unrestrained in the demands they make on departments and that in turn the latter still show a remarkable readiness to give priority to the preparation of material to be laid before their inquisitors. Indeed, it is hard to suppress the thought that select committees rarely contemplate what might be the relationship between the administrative costs incurred by and the political-administrative benefit to be imputed to their enquiries.

More striking, however, than the rising demand on officials' time and energies is the increase in the burden placed on people outside the central government machine. These include officials of public corporations (for the Nationalized Industries Committee chiefly, but for Science and Technology too), of local authorities (notably for Race Relations and Immigration) and of a wide range of organized interests (clearly so in the case of the Sub-committees of the Expenditure Committee dealing with economic, industrial and employment questions, and of Race Relations too). In addition, the desire to have 'expert' advice has stimulated the search for 'professional' witnesses – academics, the staff of research bodies, representatives of the world of management consultancy, etc. Clearly these trends must in some degree have widened the public awareness of select committees. Equally they suggest a certain shift in the style and thrust of select committee work towards the Royal Commission technique of wide-ranging enquiry. We shall come back to this point later.

So far we have considered quantitative growth in general terms and in relation to its implications for those who provide the basis in fact and opinion for it to take place. It is necessary now to say rather more about the structural characteristics of select committee evolution. The most obvious point is that there has been no systematic plan or scheme underlying this.[5] In so far as conceptual distinctions were earlier made, these were chiefly in terms of the subject/specialist-departmental division. But that was hardly tenable when in vogue, and was soon allowed to fade away, though there are still echoes of the distinction in the relationship between the Race Relations and Immigration Committee and the Home Office, between the Defence and External Affairs Sub-committee of the Expenditure Committee and the Ministry of Defence, and between the Overseas Development Committee and the Ministry for Overseas Development. These three all show signs of a departmental attachment, though by no means an exclusive one.[6] Similarly, of all select committees Science and Technology is the nearest to subject specialization. The distinction between 'subject' and 'departmental' committee is clearly, however, of little use now. But what can we put in its place? The difficulty in the way of a satisfactory answer to this question is that no matter what classification procedure is used, the majority of select committees have some features which warrant their being put under every heading chosen. Administrative scrutiny merges into the analysis of policy; financial scrutiny throws up both administrative and policy issues; many committees can, if they wish, make proposals for legislation; even concentration on the individual grievance leads to administrative methods and then on to policy. In short, select committees are characterized by their diversity, their unpredictable shifts of emphasis, and the manner in which they combine several roles according to taste and opportunity.

There is really no mode of classification which is precise and allows us to divide the committees up into distinct groups. There is a loose distinction between those for administrative scrutiny or *contrôle*, those for the investigation of how policy is being implemented, and those for enquiry and proposal. Similarly there is some distinction between those which are in principle dedicated to financial supervision, those which deal with particular administrative procedures and decisions and those which examine how policy is being put into effect. But the distinctions remain messy and full of exceptions,[7] so much so that there is some temptation to distinguish simply between narrow gauge select committees (i.e. PAC, PCA, Statutory Instruments, European Secondary Legislation, etc.) and broad gauge (all the rest).

There are, however, a number of characteristics which we can usefully bear in mind when trying to distinguish committees one from the other. First, do they have anything to go on? Do they operate on the basis of reports or proposals put to them, usually prepared by special staff agencies or by the Government (which includes for this purpose the Commission of the European Community)? The Public Accounts Committee, the Committee on the Parliamentary Commissioner for Administration, the European Secondary Legislation, etc. Committee, and the Statutory Instruments Committee meet such conditions. That they enquire on the basis of specific papers and investigations is reflected in the form of their reports and in the character of their proceedings. They deal in reasonably precise questions, they report often in a rather judicial style, usually with firm recommendations on often narrow points, and their contacts are chiefly with officials of the central administration.

Second, there are committees charged with a very broad field of interest and activity to oversee, with the terms of reference loosely defined and open-ended. The Committees on Expenditure, Nationalized Industries and Science and Technology are the leading members of this category. Then there are Overseas Development and Race Relations and Immigration which have restricted fields to survey, but with a very loose remit. All these 'broad gauge' committees tend to choose topics for enquiry which reflect contemporary perceptions of interest, are much influenced by the presence of committed committee members with their own ideas, and often take shape in accordance with the flow of evidence and the impact made by witnesses. Recommendations tend in consequence to be diffuse and wide-ranging.

Third, there is the factor of relatively specialized interest and knowledge amongst members. This has probably been most marked on the Science and Technology Committee, on the General Sub-committee, the Employment and Social Services Sub-committee, and the Defence and External Affairs Sub-committee of the Expenditure Committee, and perhaps on the Overseas Development Committee. But it is necessary to be very careful when attributing specialized knowledge and concern to committees: nearly all can show members of whom this is true, while equally there are hardly any without a substantial proportion of generalists.

Fourth, there is the dimension of political commitment and pressure group attachment. Undoubtedly the work of some committees has been more marked by party political argument than used to be normal in select committees, and, still more significant, some have become rather closely identified with client groups. The Employment and Social Services Sub-committee of the Expenditure Committee has shown signs of strong party divisions,[8] while as far as client connections go, the Science and Technology Committee, the Race Relations and Immigration Committee and the Overseas Development Committee have tended to develop these. Likewise the Defence Sub-committee of Expenditure has built up close ties with its official clients in the Defence Ministry.

Fifth, there is the factor which I will call 'direction of attention'. This may be inwards to the methods of administration, similarly inwards to some form of policy evaluation in particular functional sectors of government action, outwards to quasi-autonomous agencies like the public corporations, or outwards to other subsidiary levels of the government structure, to private associations and voluntary action groups. The Public Accounts and Parliamentary Commissioner for Administration Committees are predominantly 'internal methods' oriented; the Expenditure Committee offers the clearest examples of functional interests (though still relatively discontinuous and unspecialized, except in the case of Defence); Nationalized Industries has a vast semi-autonomous sector of public enterprise to survey; Race Relations and Immigration spends much of its time talking with people in local government and in private bodies, in fact with all those agencies below the level of the central departments which are involved in the handling of race relations. It might be noted too that on some occasions *ad hoc* select committees charged with something in the way of pre-legislative policy formulation have ranged very widely in their search for evidence. For them too it has seemed important to reach out beyond the central administration and to widen the scope of consultation and their sources of advice.

It is, however, no good pretending that there can be satisfactory conclusions to a classification exercise. In their terms of reference composition, methods of work, findings, and the disposition to proceed opportunistically select committees reflect the characteristics of the parent body. Their members see the committees as fulfilling many functions, not all at the same time, but individually and severally according to what seems practicable, politically rewarding or of urgent interest. Thus, we find that the Expenditure Committee quickly got on to the condition of the motor industry in 1975, Overseas Development picked on the oil crisis and its implications for British aid policies in 1973–4, the European Secondary Legislation, etc., Committee has repeatedly highlighted proposals from Brussels which appear to touch some political nerve-end, no matter what their intrinsic significance might be, and even the Parliamentary Commissioner for Administration Committee has been reluctant to abandon its interest in securing access to the PCA for civil servants raising complaints in respect of their position in the service. These are all examples of issues which, rightly or wrongly, have claimed the attention of some committee members. They have then in some cases been actively pursued despite the fact that they could hardly be said to fit into a planned work programme. It is, of course, true that a touch of opportunism may enable a committee to achieve a more immediate political impact than would be possible if it sticks to a regular and planned cycle of work. But equally, events move quickly and what seems urgent at one moment in time may have lost all interest by the time a report is published. Alternatively, the crucial decisions may already have been made, so that the committee finds itself composing an epitaph.

It is worth turning now to a few aspects of method, procedure and operations. Most committees still proceed predominantly by discursive discussion. They secure papers (sometimes rather tenuously related to the topic in hand) and they then present questions to witnesses. The merits of this basic method seem rarely to be considered, still less challenged. Yet it remains a diffuse, time-consuming, expensive procedure.[9] It is also one which tends to put obstacles in the way of the coherent pursuit of an issue (since only few members have the skills of a judge or of counsel), and it establishes a formal framework within which the unfolding of a genuine argument and the exchange of ideas are made difficult to achieve. In summary, there is here no sign of a departure from procedural conservatism. It is worth noting too that public hearings and the summoning of witnesses from more varied fields have made no real difference in this respect.

Then there is the question of administrative support, both in the preparation of the enquiry and in the drafting of reports. In this matter it is necessary to draw certain distinctions. There are at least three categories of special assistance in addition to the normal support from the Clerk's Department. There have been a few appointments to permanent adviser posts, usually of civil servants nearing retirement who can then stay on to sixty-five. Such people are integrated into the Clerk's Department and for the most part have been experienced generalists with a special knowledge of a relevant section of administrative activity, e.g. public expenditure control. Then there are certain semi-permanent advisers such as the two members of the Exchequer and Audit Department seconded to help the Defence Sub-committee of the Expenditure Committee in its study of defence expenditure, and more recently a civil servant seconded to aid the 1975–6 Select Committee on Abortion, in the examination of the memoranda sent to it. Finally, there are temporary advisers of different kinds. Some have been specialists brought in from universities or other research institutions. In a few cases such people have advised a committee for two or more sessions, thus gaining an opportunity to inject a certain continuity of direction and interest into the committee's approach to its field of enquiry. Mr Wynne Godley, temporary adviser for some years to the General Sub-committee of the Expenditure Committee, exemplified this. In other cases the advisers have been chosen only for one particular topic, of which they are held to have specialized knowledge. The recruitment of this type of temporary adviser has not been easy: committees often find it hard to determine exactly their needs. For the academic such work is interesting, but often a distraction from his principal professional activity, and there remains some ambiguity and uncertainty in the role of such advisers.

The main burden of servicing committees does, however, still fall on the shoulders of the clerks working in the Clerk's Department. And they remain essentially general administrators, skilled in knitting together the diverse strands of information and opinion which come before the committees, and in producing drafts which have some prospect of expressing a latent consensus. In the case of some committees there is, of course, the substantial support and preparatory work of proper administrative agencies, notably the Comptroller and Auditor General and the Parliamentary Commission for Administration. Analogous to these offices but much more modest in scale, are the Speaker's Counsel who service the European Secondary Legislation, etc. Committee and the Statutory Instruments Committee.

The conclusion to be drawn on supporting services for committees is that they are characterized by diversity of type and scale. There is a justification for this, which is that select committees vary greatly themselves: even amongst the sub-committees of a single committee like Expenditure there are different approaches to the question whether specialist advice is needed and, if so, from what kind of people.[10] While there can be no doubt that the appointment of supplementary advisers has helped the committees to handle the increasing volume of material put before them, it is, as a rule, hard to detect any basic changes in style and presentation which have appeared in the reports as a result of these staffing developments. It might be held that the General Sub-committee of the Expenditure Committee acquired a rather unusual degree of technical sophistication fairly quickly which owed something to the quality of the advice it secured (though undoubtedly the presence of members with strong methodological interests in public expenditure forecasting and control also played a part in this achievement). But even this case does not reveal marked differences from the character and quality of the reports of other committees which have made less use of special advisers. Additionally it should be noted that too much reliance on technically qualified advisers increases the risks of committees producing reports which few of their members really understand. This in turn may reduce the impact on the House itself.

The relatively high degree of stability in methods of work and style of reporting owes much to the working habits of select committees and to their necessary dependence on the guidance of those senior members and permanent officials of the House who know well the procedures of the place and can judge shrewdly its expectations. Select committees have remained in operation relatively discontinuous bodies. Attendance is irregular, members suffer from many distractions, and there has in several committees been a fairly high turnover in the membership.[11] Thus enquiries are nearly always exposed to the risks of discursiveness, lack of awareness of what the objectives are, and the temptations which arise from the knowledge that the committees are not decision-making but advice-proffering bodies. The effect of such circumstances can be seen from the verbatim record of proceedings, and often from the written memoranda too: sometimes what is said or written fails to focus on clearly defined issues and appears to be more in the nature of an attempt to throw something into the pot in the hope of keeping the discussion going. It is on the clerks that the committees must chiefly rely for an attempt to extract from what are often very unsystematic proceedings both an account of a problem and recommendations which will satisfy quite different addresses. There is the Government which ideally should be persuaded to act in some respect, but which it is sensible not to provoke by proposals seen as hopelessly unrealistic, or by demands in the course of an enquiry which are embarrassing or overburdensome. There are the permanent officials who share most of the predilections of the Government they serve, and on whose co-operation the work of most committees depends appreciably. There is the House of Commons itself, to whom all reports are formally addressed. Its attention is fickle and its interest is more likely to be caught by politically contentious items than by serious and detailed analysis, whether of particular cases or of whole policy areas. There is increasingly an audience of associated interests which look in the first place for signs of support for the objectives they seek. And finally there is a vague and indefinable public opinion to which many committees aspire to reach out in the hope of stimulating a climate of opinion favourable to the recommendations made.[12] To suit simultaneously the needs of these different addressees of committee findings is a very difficult task. The committees and their staffs have to try to remain sensitive to the expectations of the various addressees, even though it may not often be possible to satisfy all of them and at the same time take full account of the competing assessments within a committee of what is important. It is hardly surprising that the outcome is often a report which is elegant in exposition, but sometimes rather loosely related to the evidence on which it is said to rest and revealing those signs of compromise which enable ministers and officials to interpret it according to their own judgement of what is opportune and desirable.

There are other aspects of the operation of select committees which tend to show how resistant the House of Commons has remained to significant changes in the habits of its

Members, in their expectations and in the understanding of their functions. We have already underlined the way in which the current pattern of committees has evolved without any deliberate plan or carefully thought out objectives. The Expenditure Committee succeeded the Estimates Committee early in 1971, and is distinguished from its predecessor chiefly by somewhat broader terms of reference which explicitly allow it to examine the policies underlying expenditure. Despite this change it has for the most part shown restraint in issuing challenges on policy. Part of the work of the Expenditure Committee gains a limited coherence from the annual appearance of five-year Public Expenditure White Papers, though these have on some occasions been delayed, are still defective on the resources side of the equation, and have been seriously modified in their implementation by economic difficulties. Working through six Sub-Committees, five of which operate within very broad functional sectors, the Committee has been eclectic in its choice of topics. It has recently shown some tendency to react to current circumstances and to take up issues of immediate practical importance on which decisions have just been taken or are impending. In 1974–5, for example, it issued reports on The Public Expenditure Implications of the April 1975 Budget (9th Report, HC 474), on Cash Limit Control of Public Expenditure (12th Report, HC 535), on the Motor Vehicle Industry (14th Report, HC 617), and on the Redevelopment of London Docklands (5th Report, HC 348). But only in the defence field and in relation to the Treasury's role in expenditure control and economic management has there been a fairly high degree of specialization. In other functional areas the Sub-Committees have selected topics in a manner not very different from that of the Estimates Sub-Committees. Members have taken up topics which interested them or which had received some public attention. There has accordingly been little evidence of a desire to cover particular sectors of government activity systematically, nor to stick closely to 'value for money' questions. The total output of the committee has been large. For example, nine Reports were issued in 1971–2 and fourteen in 1974–5. In the latter Session topics covered included Central

Management of the Services, Defence Review Proposals, Redevelopment of London Docklands, British Forces Germany, Diplomatic Manpower and Property Overseas, Public Expenditure Implications of the April 1975 Budget, Charity Commissioners and their Accountability, Children and Young Persons Act 1969, Cash Limit Control of Public Expenditure, New Towns, and the Motor Vehicle Industry. The last two alone were accompanied by seven volumes of evidence.

The Race Relations and Immigration Committee has in theory a specific field to oversee and rather tightly-drawn terms of reference. But this has not prevented it from ranging widely over such topics as relations between the police and the immigrant population, education and employment opportunities for immigrants, and housing. This Committee has distinguished itself by travelling a great deal within the UK, taking evidence from local authorities and a large number of immigrant organizations. Its disposition to interrogate local government personnel has occasionally provoked criticism. Given the political sensitivity of the immigration issues it is likely that this Committee will endure, signifying as it does a special Parliamentary concern for the problems of race relations.

The Overseas Development Committee has ranged widely too, though it is hard to avoid the conclusion that the supply of topics in relation to which a British Government can take action is strictly limited in this field. Science and Technology remains the best example of a subject Committee, and one which achieves a fairly high level of specialization. Though a small committee of fifteen members it has managed to operate through several Sub-committees and to issue at least three reports a year. It is one of the few select committees which has tried to develop a policy of following up its reports. This policy was even laid down formally in a letter from its chairman to the Prime Minister in 1972 in which he made known the Committee's 'intention to call from time to time for progress reports from Ministers on the action taken following our reports'.[13] The Committee also complained of delays in securing departmental comments, though there is little to show that the normal gap of nine months to a year between a report and the Government's observations was significantly reduced.

The Nationalized Industries Committee faces a growing problem. The sector for which it is responsible has been expanding, and inevitably the frequency with which it can examine a major publicly-owned industry has declined. In relation to its task the Committee is small, having in 1974-5 only fifteen members, as against eighteen in 1969-70. It has operated generally through two and more recently three sub-committees and this may have overstrained its limited resources. Though it has used specialist advisers it continues to lack anything in the nature of a staff trained in industrial performance evaluation. Given the extent and complexity of the field to be covered as well as its modest resources it is doubtful whether the Committee can now achieve the impact which it undoubtedly had in the sixties when it produced a series of notable Reports on several of the major nationalized industries, as well as the 1968 across-the-board analysis of ministerial powers. What is more, the Committee has to operate in a context in which on the one hand the industries are in principle expected to operate with the maximum autonomy, while on the other the Government remains deeply concerned that they should respect its economic policy require-ments and adapt themselves to whatever policies for the co-ordination of investment programmes, prices and incomes have been adopted. How far a single, relatively small Com-mons committee can now insert itself effectively into such a complex situation is highly speculative.[14]

Though a discussion of further examples must be omitted, enough has been cited to justify the conclusion that it is possible to talk of systematic patterns of enquiry only in relation to those committees which have a prepared agenda, constituted by the reports or proposals put to them. There are in the first place the Public Accounts Committee and the Committee on the Parliamentary Commissioner for Administration. The Statutory Instruments Committee, now working for much of the time jointly with the corresponding Lords Committee, scrutinizes delegated legislation in much the same manner as its predecessor did from 1944 onwards, and reports in the same compressed and formal manner. Though the European Secondary Legislation, etc. Committee, appointed first in 1974 to scrutinize proposals from the European Community's agencies was initially beset by internal political tensions arising from the hostility of some members to the very principle of Community membership, it too has reported in a similar style, concentrating on drawing the attention of the House to instruments or proposed measures which it regards as meriting debate. And like the Statutory Instruments Committee it is backed up by legally qualified advisers.[15] Thus, in respect of all these committees there is a predictable output, fairly consistent in form and content, and related closely to the matters put before them. In so far as we can properly talk of committees of *contrôle* in the continental sense of that word, these come nearest to such a characterization.

It is, however, the other committees with their more open-ended remits which on the whole have gained more public attention and been the objects of rather more academic research. In the light of the experience of the past five years or so, it is perhaps reasonable to regard them as approximating more and more to the Royal Commission or Committee of Enquiry model. They range widely, they seek to consult affected interests, they draw on informed opinion and occasionally they commission research. In reporting, their preference is for opening up a subject, throwing out ideas, contributing to public knowledge of government policies, of social and economic problems and of such developments as are thought to be in the offing. It is not surprising that in relation to such activity it remains impossible to assess with assurance the influence actually exerted by select committees. Indeed, those in this 'broad gauge' category can hardly be said to aspire regularly to a precise and identifiable influence, despite the fact that their reports do often contain recommendations which could in principle lead to specific decisions different from those taken or in prospect. Instead, they hope to contribute to the environment of opinion within which policy evolves and to remind those with executive responsibilities that there are interests and opinions in Parliament

and outside which should be taken into account. It is hard
to discern in this respect any radical departure from the
traditions which were evolving in the twenty years after
1945.

One of the major demands of many Parliamentary reformers a decade ago was for more specialization by Members. This has not been achieved in any systematic way,
though far more signs of it are to be found now than seven
or eight years ago. Given that there is no pattern of permanent committees, defined by reference either to subject or
functional area or to the allocation of departmental responsibilities, the organizational basis for specialization does, however, remain tenuous. Within the Expenditure Committee
specialization is more nominal than real, despite its functional
sub-committees, though some elements of it are to be found,
especially in the Defence Sub-committee. The nearest to a
specialized committee is Science and Technology which also
has had in most years a very low rate of turnover in membership. On the other hand it has to be remembered that the
number of Members wanting to join select committees usually
exceeds the number of places available : here at least are
signs of a desire to pursue particular interests, even though
this often fails to develop into a sustained subject specialization.

Turnover is a factor which usually militates against
specialization.[16] In many committees it has been quite high,
for example Public Accounts, Nationalized Industries and
even the General Sub-committee of the Expenditure Committee. In contrast the Parliamentary Commissioner for
Administration Committee shows quite high stability; so does
the Defence and External Affairs Sub-committee of the
Expenditure Committee. Naturally, turnover does not express
merely the mutability of Members' interests. It is affected by
the decisions of the electors, by commitments in Government
and Opposition, by other demands within the House, and by
personal factors. But it is hard to avoid the conclusion that
high turnover is nevertheless an expression of the continuing
aversion to consistent specialization as well as being a reflection of the fact that select committees offer no significant

political rewards. Men still do not rise to the top in politics, nor even to key positions of influence, through the select committee structure.

The preceding remarks point to another continuing feature of select committees. This is that they remain essentially committees of back-benchers, symbolizing the distinction within the House between private Members and those who are in office, expecting office or fiercely competing for office. If the return of select committee members is examined, certain features stand out immediately. It nearly always contains the names of a few elder statesmen, people who have held office and for one reason or another have no further aspirations in that direction. Then there are some – not a very numerous group – who are well known for their strong opinions on particular matters. Often such people are regarded by party Whips as being rather unsound and even troublesome. But on select committees they can voice their commitments in a way which causes little embarrassment to the party leaders. Then there is a large group, the rest in effect, who with the aid of careful investigation might be broken down into two sub-groups. There are those who do not seek office, but feel the need for some role in Parliament other than that of constituency ombudsman or listener in the Chamber and standing committees. More often than not, select committees are effectively carried along by such Members, many of whom give long service to the committees of their choice. The other sub-group would consist of new Members who cannot immediately aspire to office, real or shadow, but who want to acquire an experience which may later prove useful in their political careers.

What is clear from this crude classification of Members is that in political terms select committees are not and cannot be places where much power resides. They represent predominantly those in the House who do not have much scope for determining what is done. To an extent not found in any Parliament of non-British provenance the committee structure[17] reveals a dearth of clues to the manner in which major decisions are made – or unmade. This has always been so in this century and there is no reason to believe that the past five years or so have seen any major shifts in a new direction. Nor does the treatment of reports by the House undermine this judgement. There continues to be a disjunction in timing and usually in focus of interest between what Select Committees are doing and the cycle of House of Commons business. Debates on reports remain infrequent,[18] are attended chiefly by those who had a hand in the report under discussion, and are fitted somewhat arbitrarily into the nooks and crannies of the Parliamentary timetable.

These comments on the weight of select committee membership as a whole should not, however, obscure two points, both of continuing importance. One is that select committees do work in a substantially autonomous way, though guided (like departmental committees of enquiry) by sensitive secretaries and by the hints of those witnesses who really count. The independence of select committees correlates with the restraint they are expected to show in their findings, with the relative political weakness of their members, and with the non-partisan outlook which convention often (though not always) imposes on their proceedings. Under these conditions neither the Government nor the party Whips have any cause to intervene in the operations of select committees.[19] The advantage still gained from the independence of select committees is that at their best they can and do achieve a high level of impartiality and objectivity: their findings can command respect and stand the test of time as sources of reliable information and balanced analysis. The other point is that in the conditions of a sharp separation between political activity and service in public administration membership of select committees constitutes one of the few methods by which Members of Parliament can gain some detailed knowledge of administrative processes and problems. If there is a useful non-partisan explanatory dialogue in the British system of government between elected representatives who are not office-holders and those charged with the formulation and implementation of policies, then it is still most likely to be found in the proceedings of select committees of the House of Commons.[20] Whether this particular dialogue has now been supplemented by another with those organized interests who are affected by or joined in the making of government decisions must remain at present doubtful, though there are signs of it emerging in some fields, for example in the links between the Science and Technology Committee and parts of the scientific community. Certainly select committees have enormously widened the range of witnesses on whom they call. But inevitably such contacts as arise in this way are discontinuous, and it is hardly possible to overlook the fact that at least one major force now bearing heavily on government action – the trade-union movement – has had but tenuous links with select committees.[21]

This essay began by referring to an earlier judgement of some of the weaknesses in that case for Parliamentary reform which saw in a build-up of select committee enquiry the key to a more effective role for Parliament *vis-à-vis* Government. In one version the argument presented select committees as a device for reasserting Parliamentary control over the executive even though no major change in procedures and powers was envisaged; in another and more cautious version it saw select committees in the first place as generators of advice and information, influential because their findings would compel respect by reason of their detachment from the commitments of day-to-day decision-making and partisan politics. It is doubtful whether the stronger version of the case for select committees would anywhere now command support: it was always implausible and it has been rendered the more so by the experiences of the past five years which have simultane-ously concentrated even more responsibility on governments and greatly increased the dependence of government on the goodwill and co-operation of powerful organized groups in the society. It was the more qualified version of the case for select committees against which nonetheless the criticism was brought that it had an academic quality, while at the same time obscuring the conditions which need to be met if any Parliamentary reform is to change the position of the House of Commons and its Members significantly.

It is hardly to be questioned that the increased effort put in by select committees and by their various agents and witnesses, resulting in so large a quantity of evidence and recommendation, has had but a modest impact on the course of public policy, on patterns of expenditure, and on levels of spending. But though public decisions are rarely shaped decisively by select committee pressure, their work has a continuing influence on the ways in which officials behave and conduct business, and on the climate of opinion affecting the problems examined by committees. This effect is achieved most obviously by those committees which are backed up by agents invested with considerable powers of investigation and scrutiny, notably Public Accounts and the Parliamentary Commissioner for Administration Committees. In such cases the select committee adds authority to the findings of its agents. As for the broader, less specific investigative work of the majority of select committees, this has retained much of that quality of detachment from actual decision-making of which it showed many signs in the earlier phase of the Parliamentary reform movement. The sheer quantity of material now produced suggests that this must be so. How many people, even within the small arena of national politics, really pay much attention to what is said in select committee reports? Does not the reluctance of Government and Opposition, not to speak of the House itself, to make room for debates on reports bear witness to the belief that after all they are not so important? Are there not signs that governments even welcome the tendency of committees to ape commissions of enquiry, some of which produce venerable storehouses of information but have little impact on the decisions which have to be made?

The relegation of select committees to the sidelines can be deduced from other conditions and habits too. The work of the House is still confined within the overarching conventions of the adversary relationships between Government and Opposition, despite such challenges as the results of the 1974 elections may have posed to these conventions. This in itself imposes a substantial degree of bipartisanship on committees, for only by avoiding party confrontation can they hope to operate amicably and to produce results which stand some chance of commanding attention across party divisions in the House and within Whitehall. This assumes, of course, that they do not choose merely to represent faithfully the views of the majority party, for if they do that, then either they risk losing their critical function, or may be tempted to voice opinions which reflect only a minority opinion within the Government majority and *a fortiori* are unlikely to find favour with the executive. Though in recent years there have been instances of party confrontation inside select committees, in general the tradition of seeking a bipartisan consensus has been maintained. Given the present functions and powers of select committees their prospects of exerting a modest influence remain brightest if they stick to this approach.[22]

This leads us into the question whether the recent development of select committees offers grounds for believing that the reform dilemma can be overcome by further progress in this direction. Basically, there are two Parliamentary models which can be discerned in the experience of nearly all liberal democracies. One is that which sees the legislature as primarily a place for public debate, for presenting a challenge to a government and for sustaining a government. This presupposes reasonably coherent parties and the presence of a majority party. We will call it the 'majority' model. The other is a 'bargaining' model, brought into existence by the persistence of several parties, none of which regularly has an absolute majority, or by the presence of parties which are internally divided. The bargaining model is compatible with and encouraged by an institutional structure marked by a separation of powers, but can operate perfectly well in a purely Parliamentary system of government. Under the conditions of the majority model the legislature as an institution tends to be weak, being necessarily dominated by the government which commands a single party majority and hopes for re-election. This weakness may be counteracted by the prestige and authority of the Parliamentary institutions as such, and this was for long enough an important factor in Britain. However, the ever-widening scope of public powers, accompanied by the growing dependence of governments on interests external to Parliament, has worked in the other direction, leaving Parliament unable to make effective use of the authority which in theory it still possesses. Under the bargaining model the legislature, and more particularly the parties in it, tend to have extensive opportunities for influencing governmental decisions, though their power is often of a negative kind: action can be stopped, but the legislature may itself have little capacity for positive initiatives. This model does not offer any guarantee of reducing the external pressures from organized interests, though it may offer the prospect of building them into the legislative process in a way which buttresses the Parliamentary role, and it may also impose limitations on the ability of governments to act without first assuring themselves of fairly wide Parliamentary support.

These models can be found exemplified in varying degrees in different countries. The House of Commons has for the whole of this century, and perhaps ever since 1868, conformed to the majority model. But the doctrine underlying its claims to authority obstinately suggests the possibility of its securing the kind of influence only available under the second model, since it is only that model which would offer a real prospect of decisively qualifying the discretion of governments (i.e. party leaders) to do what they believe their responsibility requires. Between 1970 and 1974 neither the overall party situation nor the evolution of procedures in the House of Commons provided any grounds for believing that the majority model was exposed to a serious challenge, though without doubt it was becoming more and more obvious that the Government could not make effective those very extensive claims to authority which underpin the Executive in Britain. In parallel the ability of the House of Commons to influence events was bound to decline too. The two elections of 1974 placed serious question-marks over the two-party constellation, resulting in a situation in which minority or near-minority government became inescapable. Yet the striking fact is that this modification of one of the basic conditions of the majority model has not so far brought about any substantial change in the working of that model. The Government still behaves *as if* it had a normal majority, the House still maintains for the most part the traditional adversary relationship, and there have been few signs of the behaviour typical of a bargaining situation. Though occasionally in 1974 and again in 1976 the Government has found difficulty in securing passage of its legislative proposals, it has behaved as if this were abnormal, a serious challenge to what the conventions require.

· It is within this context that the activity of select committees must now be set. At first sight it might be thought that since 1974 party relationships favour them. But in fact they have remained constrained by conditions which have prevailed for a long time. They have no decisions to take, only the power to report;[23] this they do to a House which continues to express the majority model; and they have remained firmly embedded within the procedures and working habits which have since the Second World War shaped the internal evolution of select committees. In addition it has to be remembered that members of the two major rival parties still completely dominate the select committees: for many reasons, which cannot be discussed here, the forty or so members of the smaller parties devote little time to select committees and have but meagre access to them.

Thus we must conclude that the expanded activity of select committees has brought little genuine change in the manner in which Parliament operates and in the relations between it and the Executive. The bargaining model could be adopted only if both the institutional concepts governing Parliament's role and the structure of parties were modified far more radically than has so far happened. In particular it seems questionable whether the underlying principles determining the character of select committee activity can, in their present form, allow to such sub-units of the House a definable share in decision-making. I have in mind here the normal exclusion of select committees from the consideration of legislation, for it is in this field that the power to say 'yea' or 'nay' is necessarily vested in Parliament.

This reference to the exclusion of select committees from legislation must, however, be modestly qualified in the light of the experience of the past six years. On three occasions select committees have been set up to enquire into and report on matters likely to be the subject of legislative proposals –

Corporation Tax in 1970–1, Tax-Credit in 1972–3, and Wealth Tax in 1974–5. Only the first case was followed by government legislative action, while the others remain simply pointers for the future. In addition, there was established in 1974–5 a Select Committee on Violence in Marriage (later changed to Family) which to some extent followed on from a Select Committee on the Abortion Amendment Bill (also 1974–5), though membership was quite different. The Violence in the Family Select Committee may produce legislative proposals, though it was not specifically asked to do so and technically had in this respect no different status from that of other select committees. While it cannot yet be said that these experiments herald a serious attempt to link select committees more closely with the preparation of bills, they do indicate that there are some potentialities in 'pre-legislation' committees which may be worth more attention. Apart from this tentative move towards allowing *ad hoc* select committees to consider proposals for legislative action, there have also been two examples of referring public bills already introduced to select committees, the Anti-Discrimination Bill in 1972 and the Abortion Amendment Bill in 1975. It is true that both were bills of a traditionally 'non-party' kind, and indeed taxation methods such as have just been referred to also have technical aspects which can be lifted out of the party controversy.[24] These points underline the strength of the feeling that if select committees are to be brought into legislation, then it ought still to be in relation to matters which do not immediately evoke party conflict or strike at the Government's claim to pursue the implementation of its programme.

So far the moves in the direction just outlined have been cautious. Nor could they become more ambitious without some reappraisal of the manpower resources available to the House and of how they are used. Members cannot hope to sustain the existing select committees, as well as a range of pre-legislative and perhaps even legislative select committees. Yet if there is a way forward via select committee methods to substantial changes in the manner in which the House works, and as a consequence to some reversal of its dependence on government and the constraints of the two-party competition, it is most likely to be found in relation to the preparation and passage of legislation. Here there are even opportunities for the present 'broad gauge' select committees to get into the field of legislative proposals without change in their terms of reference. The Race Relations and Immigration Committee did precisely this in 1975 with its report on the Organization of Race Relations Administration, one which had considerable influence on subsequent government legislation. In contrast a further extension of the current types of scrutiny of administration and policy will almost certainly pay diminishing returns in an increasingly complex governmental environment. This conclusion gains some support from the experience of the past five years.

The period which has been cursorily reviewed here has been marked by a consolidation of the reform model which gained support between 1965 and 1969. It does not appear that the House has been able to escape from the dilemma posed earlier: it has, on the whole, continued to seek quantitative reform without qualitative change. Yet perhaps there are now signs of a development in respect of the handling of legislation which might open the way to some reappraisal of the role of at least some select committees. This in turn could create the procedural environment in which, should further changes in the pattern of party relationships occur, the House of Commons as an institution might be better placed to act as an effective counterweight to the Executive than it has been able to become through the widening of its purely investigative rights.

10 Parliament and the European Community[1]

DAVID COOMBES

The European Community is designed to be something more than an international organization: its rules and institutions, though based on international treaties, have direct authority within the member states; and it enjoys various means of forming and executing common policies and even of extending the area of legitimate Community activity. Acceding to the Community, therefore, was a definitive constitutional act and has profound significance for all our political institutions, including Parliament.[2]

Also important for British politics is the fact that many of the principles and procedures of the Community are derived from systems of government which are unlike our own in significant ways. Although the British constitution is not directly affected by accession in matters not covered by the treaties, we have to acknowledge that British government may be influenced indirectly by the adoption of Community forms and methods. This is especially interesting since some influential writers and politicians have compared aspects of British government unfavourably with other European countries.

However, so far the Community has evolved in an inchoate and unpredictable way. Behind this lies the post-war history of attempts and failures at European unity, which has not made as much a mark in British politics as it has in the original member states, so that the ambiguity and uncertainty which characterize the Community are not well understood in this country. The immediate impact of accession has been exaggerated. We have been confused by the 'Community Method', which pursues its bold ambition of European unity by gradually integrating limited and severely practical aspects of modern government. This helps to explain the impression that the Community gives of interference and fastidiousness by public officials. On the other hand it has been difficult for us to enter into the co-operative and pioneering spirit on which the survival of the Community has depended, and on which its future growth is largely based. The consequences of membership have also been distorted in Britain by the divisive political reaction to the act of accession, much of it caused as much by internal political circumstances as by the consequences of membership. The reaction of Parliament, as of other political institutions, has tended to be both defensive, reacting strongly to the negative constitutional effects, and conservative, showing reluctance to adopt unfamiliar principles and methods. Far more concern was expressed here than in any of the founding member states about the disturbances membership was expected to cause in the customs and status of Parliament, and this aspect overshadowed other likely consequences of membership.

However, in two particular respects the focus on the effects on Parliament should be welcomed. First, because it marked recognition that Community law and policy should be treated as domestic rather than foreign affairs. Community law has to be observed, and if necessary enforced, in this country to the same extent as the ordinary law, and the duty of applying and enforcing Community law rests on national public authorities. Most aspects of social and economic administration are liable to come within the Community sphere. Up to now it is only agriculture, coal and steel and international trade which are predominantly Community matters, but the Community has an important part in decisions about inland transportation, commercial and trading law, taxation, the law of employment, and social security, industrial, commercial and professional standards and qualifications, environmental questions, energy policy, monetary policy and policy for economic development and management of the economy. Membership of the Community requires that we accept an existing body of Community law and policy in relation to these and other matters. It also means that future measures taken in this country must conform with Community law and policy, as well as that a number of changes will be made in future at a Community level.

Secondly, the British reaction has helped to draw attention to the consequences of the Community's new legal order for representative institutions. The authority of Community acts rests essentially on their derivation from the treaties and on the ultimate jurisdiction of the Community's Court of Justice. To give such importance to a legal basis of authority is of course more usual in the continental European tradition than in our own, so that it is not surprising that it has been harder for us to accept it. The national governments have a predominant role in the making of Community law and policy, being represented on the main decision-making body which is the Council. They are also responsible for appointing the Commission, which has its own authority to initiate measures for possible later enactment, to mediate among the governments' representatives on the Council, to see that provisions of the treaties are properly interpreted and enforced, and to enact measures of its own. National parliaments, however, are given no role in the enactment of Community measures, except that when the Community acts by means of *directives* the member states are bound only 'as to the result to be achieved', and 'the national authorities' (which may of course include Parliament) are left the choice of form and methods.[3] The national parliaments are involved in practice in major constitutional changes such as amendment of the treaties, since the treaties provide that such steps need ratification by the member states in accordance 'with their respective constitutional requirements'.[4] The national parliaments are mentioned specifically only as the bodies responsible for designating the members of the European Parliament.[5] In the original member states it was largely supposed that the functions of parliamentary influence and control would be vested gradually in the European Parliament, but that body has not so far obtained more than consultative powers in relation to the making of Community law and policy. It can force the resignation of the Commission by passing a motion of censure and has come to play an increasing role in budgetary decisions now that the Community has access to its own sources of income. But the Parliament's powers are still very compensating for the national parliaments at a Community level.

However, the acceptability of what the Community proposes and does depends in practice as much on the approval of its member states' governments as on the independent legal authority of its institutions. In spite of the strict independence of the 'supra-national' institutions, especially of the Commission and the Court of Justice, most important legal acts of the Community, together with most of its major policy decisions, are made only with the express approval of the representatives of the national governments. It is here that the role of national parliaments can be crucial. Although there is nothing in the treaties to say this, it is nevertheless obvious that ministers participating in the Community will be very reluctant to agree to things when they cannot carry their national parliaments with them. It is also practical politics in the Community that governments cannot be forced into accepting any major decision again their will. It was correctly realized in Britain that Parliament's ability to influence ministers before decisions were taken at a Community level would be vital to its power over Community affairs, and that in turn Parliament would need access to timely information about what matters were likely to be decided. The fact that most Community decisions are based on proposals previously formulated and published by the Commission provides an opportunity for Parliamentary intervention before the decision-taking stage. Showing and seizing the advantage of this opportunity proved to be of great political importance for those who wished to get British accession accepted in spite of the fundamental diminution of Parliament's formal authority which membership entails.

Procedures for Community 'secondary legislation'

Since the main challenge to Parliament was seen as the Community's independent authority to enact measures having the force of legislation in this country, it is not surprising that in devising procedures for intervention in Community affairs Parliament has sought mainly legislative powers.

The European Communities Act, which made the necessary legal provision in this country for British accession, contained no special provision for Parliamentary intervention (as did, for example, the corresponding legislation in West Germany). However, verbal undertakings were given when the Act came before Parliament as a bill in 1972 that the Government would ensure that Parliament received information at an early stage about proposals emanating from the Commission (these are published anyway in the Community's *Official Journal*) and that time would be found for questions and debate on Community affairs. It was also claimed that the British Government would enjoy a right of 'veto' in the Council that would give Parliament an indirect ultimate sanction over Commission proposals.

Since it was by means of the Act that the changes in British law required by membership were made, the Government's argument was that the formal status of Parliament had not really been affected by accession. An analogy was drawn, and has been followed since, between the Community's law-making powers and the powers delegated to ministers in the United Kingdom to make 'secondary legislation'. The trouble with this analogy is that the enactments of the Community can be much broader in scope, and politically important in content, than delegated legislation made by ministers in Britain. There was concerted pressure, and not only by opponents of British membership, for the establishment of special means to ensure that Parliament's right of prior approval of major legislative acts should somehow be retained for acts made at a Community level.

This was reflected in the report of a Select Committee appointed by the Commons, and chaired by Sir John Foster, to recommend procedures for dealing with 'European Community Secondary Legislation'. The Committee, which included some prominent 'anti-marketeers', recognized that, while new and special procedures were necessary, the primary needs were: to be informed about the consequences of Commission proposals, and to be able to reach and express conclusions before the Council came to a decision. The Committee's main recommendation was that 'a new and different' type of Parliamentary committee should be established to sift draft Community measures, to report to the House on their legal and political importance, and to make recommendations for their further consideration by the House as a whole.[6]

In May 1974 a 'Committee on European Secondary Legislation' was appointed and this 'Scrutiny Committee' has now become an essential part of the Commons' procedure for dealing with Community enactments. It consists of sixteen members and is appointed for the duration of a Parliament. It has the usual powers of a select committee: to send for persons, papers and records; to sit when the House is adjourned; to adjourn from place to place; to make reports to the House including its minutes of evidence; and to appoint sub-committees. It may also appoint expert advisers for particular enquiries, and is assisted, in addition to its clerks, by a legal adviser and by four civil servants especially seconded to it. However, its functions are unlike those of a select committee. Its reports classify Commission documents into categories according to their legal and political importance and on this basis recommend some documents for debate in the House as a whole.[7] At first its reports simply contained a classification, but they now normally contain some explanation of the recommendations made, including a summary of the nature of the document concerned. The Committee is assisted in its task by explanatory memoranda issued by the government department concerned for each document (and signed by the relevant minister).[8]

The House of Lords took a rather different approach, although it too has set up a committee to sift proposals of the Commission.[9] The Lords' 'Select Committee of the European Communities', set up at the same time as the Commons' Scrutiny Committee, behaves much more like a normal select committee, enquiring by means of oral and written evidence and reporting to the House with conclusions and recommendations on matters of substance.[10] It has worked through sub-committees, a practice which the Commons' Committee has only recently begun to adopt in a modified form, and these are specialized for the main subjects of Community business. It has also made ample use of its right to appoint expert advisers, again unlike the Commons' Committee. It has taken in public and published oral evidence from departmental representatives and also from a variety of bodies outside Parliament (in particular, interested private organizations like the CBI and the trade unions) while the Commons' Committee usually takes oral evidence only from ministers. Peers who are not members of the Committee may attend its sub-committees, and in this way it has been able to draw on a wide range of experience and knowledge, including that of peers who are members of the delegation to the European Parliament.[11]

The Commons' 'Scrutiny Committee', on the other hand, is essentially a political filter, with the task of testing the degree of controversy likely to be caused by a proposed Community enactment. After experiencing great difficulties in its initial months in keeping up with the flow of Community documents (about 4000 a year), mainly owing to the backlog of measures growing during the delay between accession and its appointment, it now maintains a regular supply of weekly reports which provide the basis on which the Commons decides whether or not to debate proposed Community acts. What matters in the Commons' procedure is the follow-up of the Committee's recommendation that a draft act should be debated, whereas the reports of the Lords' Committee, although they can be, and sometimes are, debated, can be taken as an expression of opinion and sources of detailed information in their own right. In this, Parliament has expressed its traditional attitudes, first, that joint procedures by both Houses are avoided, and secondly, that opinions on matters of major political importance must be confined to the floor of the Commons rather than in committee.

The procedure for considering Community 'secondary legislation' on the floor of the House has been a persistent cause of dissatisfaction, and not only the Scrutiny Committee itself,[12] but also a Select Committee on Procedure,[13] have recommended changes. A major debate on the question was held on 3 November 1975 when a number of grievances were ventilated and certain improvements offered by the Government.[14]

There are essentially three causes of discontent with procedure for dealing with Community legal acts: the nature of the Community's own procedures; the Commons' own shortage of time; and the form of debate adopted in the Commons.

I have already explained that much of the politically important 'secondary legislation' is made by the Council, acting usually on a proposal of the Commission. The Council is essentially a venue for negotiation among representatives of national governments, with the Commission playing the role of arbiter, and a number of difficulties for national parliaments flow from this. The most fundamental difficulty of all is that ministers in the Council are empowered (and are expected) to make decisions collectively in their own right, without any necessary formal prior consultation of national parliaments. As I have said, in practice it would be unusual and unwise for a minister of any member state to agree to a decision without having first ensured that it could be broadly accepted by his national parliament, or by the organized interests directly affected in his country. Moreover, the member states' governments work on the understanding that unanimous agreement will be sought before a decision is made on any matter affecting a vital national interest of one or more of the states. It is quite common for ministers to delay decisions, or even to postpone matters indefinitely, on the grounds that unanimity is not possible on a matter considered to be of vital national interest, which can be interpreted as insuperable Parliamentary opposition.[15] It is particularly important for Parliament, therefore, that the Government has undertaken to withhold its agreement in the Council to any proposed measure on which the Scrutiny Committee has not had time to report, or which the House as a whole has not had time to debate when the Committee has recommended further consideration.[16] This undertaking goes further than strict Community procedure allows. Moreover, the member states' governments have recently agreed to relax the requirement of unanimity and to try to carry out the treaty provisions for majority voting in the Council. All the same it is unlikely that either the Scrutiny Committee or the House as a whole will be by-passed very often only because the delay between the Commission's initial proposal and the Council's decision has been too short. Once a proposal has been first made by the Commission there are normally a number of occasions for the governments to make objections before a final decision, ranging from preparatory working parties of national officials to full meetings of the Council.[17]

In practice, the Community's procedure is nothing like as summary or clandestine as many British observers predicted it would be. (Indeed it could well be argued that it is too cumbersome and slow, and too sensitive to special interests – a point to which I shall return.) However, Parliament has had difficulties with the uncertainty of the Council's agenda, and with the way in which proposals can be amended or replaced following preliminary negotiation by ministers and their officials, often on many different occasions, before a decision is finally made. One controversial recent example was a decision of the Council to dispose of the Community's surplus of skimmed milk powder by making its use compulsory in feeding animals, a decision which was taken as part of a 'package deal' enabling the Community's annual price review for agriculture to be agreed in April 1976. This decision was based on a proposal which the House had already disapproved but which the Commission had subsequently amended. However, the Council's decision was made before the House had considered the amended proposal. Subsequently both the decision itself, and the action of the British Minister of Agriculture in agreeing to it before the Commons had debated it, have been strongly criticized.[18]

Both the Scrutiny Committee and the Procedure Committee have suggested improvements in procedure to help to avoid this sort of difficulty. First, it has been suggested that the government should make available supplementary explanatory memoranda on any draft measure which is substantially amended, and that the Scrutiny Committee should take a second look at such measures. This proposal was accepted by the Leader of the House, subject to the Community's rules of confidentiality, for 'proposals which involve major policy developments'.[19] Secondly, and the Scrutiny Committee now seems to feel that this is the major outstanding problem, it is maintained that there is too great a delay between the reports of the Scrutiny Committee and the holding of a debate. As a result, debates are often held shortly before the Council meeting in which final decisions are to be made, and so after the member states have already reacted to the proposed measure and amendments have been made. The Scrutiny Committee proposed a change of Standing Orders to impose a time-limit on the delay between its recommendation for further consideration and debate in the House.[20]

The fact is, of course, that the Commons are short of time already; there is particular difficulty in finding time for matters other than the government's own legislative programme or debates on major domestic issues. The Scrutiny Committee commented in a recent Special Report that, although as many draft Community acts still awaited debate from the previous twelve months as had received it, the government had kept to its undertaking to get measures debated before a Council decision.[21] It saw the problem of delay between its reports and the subsequent debates as far more serious. Nevertheless the Procedure Committee also voiced dissatisfaction that debates on Community measures come at a late hour (usually at ten o'clock) and are subject to a time-limit (usually of one and a half hours).[22] Following in part a recommendation of the Procedure Committee the government can now send draft measures which do not raise questions of policy to standing committees using the same procedure as that for statutory instruments requiring affirmative resolution of the House.[23]

Many Members have also expressed dissatisfaction with the form of debates held to give further consideration to Community 'secondary legislation' because they are unable to vote for or against a particular draft measure, and vote only on a motion to 'take note' of the document concerned. However, the 'take note' procedure has now become accepted practice, and it is possible to move and vote on amendments expressing disapproval of the contents of Commission proposals.[24]

The form of debate is itself limited by the nature of the Community's procedures. The Commission, from which the draft measure comes, is not answerable to any national parliament or to any other national body. Nor for that matter is the Council, in which draft measures are amended and enacted. Parliament's approval or disapproval does not affect the legality of a Community enactment.

However, this could give Parliament greater freedom in debating and voting on the content of Commission proposals than it has in other matters, if it is accepted that in so doing it is merely expressing an opinion, and binding neither the Community institutions nor British ministers. Thus it has been suggested that back-benchers could be given a greater share of the time devoted to Community business. There have in fact been increasing opportunities to move amendments expressing disapproval of proposals. What the Commons are really doing when considering Commission documents as Community 'secondary legislation' is seeking to express general opinions on the documents concerned that ministers can then take into account during deliberation and decision in the Council. In this respect the filtering role of the Scrutiny Committee has been both essential and unique, for, as long as government can provide for debates before decisions are made, it enables back-benchers to influence the timetable of the House so that they can be heard at a pre-legislative stage.

Where the Commons' procedure has been resistant to change, however, is in finding means of saving time on the floor of the House. The arrangements for submitting measures to standing committees have been strongly criticized. A time limit of two and a half hours is also applied to the standing committees and only minor issues can be submitted. The committees are empowered only to report that documents have been considered and not to debate substantive motions. In practice Members with special interest or knowledge in Community affairs have not found it easy to get appointed to standing committees dealing with their subject. The Chairman of the Scrutiny Committee has described the present standing committee procedure as an 'emasculated operation', while the Government justifies its reticence by the familiar argument that only the House itself can approve or disapprove policy matters. Suggestions for a special Standing Committee on Community 'secondary legislation' have been rejected on these grounds.[25]

There has also been resistance to the idea that Community business should be treated by select committees with investigatory powers. It has been suggested that membership of the Community makes a system of specialized committees covering all aspects of government policy even more necessary. Whatever the merits of such ideas, they would not answer the Commons' demand for a means of expressing opinions on those proposals for Community enactments which raise important political or legal issues for this country. The present procedure may seem cumbersome and time-wasting, and in other national parliaments existing procedures (such as sifting of measures by the parliament's president or bureau and treatment in specialized committees) may have probably been more satisfactory. The fact is that in Britain membership of the Community, and in particular its effects on Parliament, have been matters of the greatest political controversy.[26] This, combined with the traditional reluctance of the Commons to delegate business to committees, explains, if it may not entirely justify, the present procedure. It is also worth noting how in Community business Commons and Lords have adopted – whether consciously or not – an interesting division of labour. The Lords' Committee on European Communities does provide through its sub-committees what amounts to a series of specialized committees dealing with the various aspects of Community law and policy, while the Commons are more concerned with voicing political controversy by debate on the floor. This division of labour might be regarded as appropriate to the differences in functions of the two chambers.

Other Methods of Parliamentary Intervention

The basic problem of adapting Commons' procedure to interventions in Community 'secondary legislation' seems to be that, although it has the same force as law made by Parliament, Community law is not made in a way which is truly comparable with previous British legislative procedure. Holding out the possibility of incorporating it in the legislative procedures of Parliament has caused confusion, false expectation and awkward gaps in procedure. The development of the scrutiny procedures has proved to be successful in the ways we have just seen, but there are some problems which defy adjustment.

I have remarked that Members have sometimes been frustrated by their inability to bind ministers before decisions are made in the Council, and by their lack of power to accept or reject draft enactments. Whether they would use this power if they had it is, of course, another matter, and we know that the Commons' role in general legislation is not all it is supposed to be. Where Community business is concerned, Parliament has to accept certain special limitations. It cannot always be informed in advance of proposals to amend draft Community measures, and cannot always be guaranteed an opportunity to express a view in advance of decision by the Council (as the 'skimmed milk powder' case illustrates). This is because the part played by ministers in the making of Community enactments is essentially that of negotiating with ministers of other member states in a forum which is legally separate from Parliament. For the same reason Parliament cannot even ensure that its views will be taken into account by British ministers, and has difficulty in finding out what British ministers actually do in the Council.

All this is another way of saying that Community acts result from a procedure of their own, in which national parliaments have no formal or explicit part. This fact was probably played down by supporters of British membership for fear of exacerbating the argument about sovereignty. However, it is crucial, especially for the Community's efficiency and future development (matters which are now of direct interest to us as members), to realize that the Community is not like other international organizations where national governments may simply veto decisions which they do not like or where the obligations imposed by membership are fixed and determinate.[27] The Community has a momentum of its own and has its own constitutional legitimacy.

Nothing illustrates this last point better than the role of

the Court of Justice as the ultimate, supreme authority on the enforcement of Community law. This in turn gives special importance to the role of the Commission, not only in giving expression to the common interest of the Community in its proposals and recommendations, but also in interpreting it, by among other things exercising powers of decision. Although most of the enactments made by the Commission on its own authority are of detailed day-to-day significance, it is the source of many decisions of social and economic importance, affecting national law and practice in regional and industrial development, competition among enterprises, and many aspects of agriculture including price-fixing. It also negotiates trade agreements with other international organizations, and makes expenditure from the Community's funds. These powers are not, and cannot be, encompassed by the scrutiny procedure of Parliament.

Another sense in which it is too restrictive to concentrate on the Council's legislative powers is that many decisions affecting the future policy of the Community, indeed often the most important ones, do not take the form of official enactments and may not come either from the Commission or the Council. Thus both Commission and Council are accustomed to issue statements of policy or sets of proposals in the form of opinions, recommendations, study documents, reports of specially nominated working parties and (in the case of the Council) communiqués or resolutions of meetings. A number of vital matters can be dealt with in this way, particularly the co-ordination of economic policies, relations with non-Community countries, and the powers and structure of the Community institutions. Especially important in the Community's future development are the meetings of heads of government, which now take place on a regular basis as the 'European Council'. The member states also now seek to co-ordinate their foreign policies by regular meetings of foreign ministers and officials.

Ministers make statements to the House before and sometimes after a Council meeting at which important matters are to be discussed, and this can be the occasion for Members to express grievances or to question the minister. In addition the government makes a regular six-monthly report on Community affairs which can be debated. Parliamentary Questions may be put to the departmental minister concerned on particular aspects of Community business, and general European Questions are allotted twenty minutes every three weeks.

However, these means have not proved very useful so far for following up earlier Commons debates or reports on Commission proposals and ministers are not of course responsible for the views or acts of the Commission, although they can give information about these as about other actions of the Community institutions. When decisions of the Commission have resulted in controversy, as when 200,000 tons of surplus butter were sold to the Soviet Union in 1973, Members have used Questions, ministerial statements and debate (for example, on the adjournment) to express disapproval.[28] The enactments made by the Commission itself are usually made in consultation with committees of national officials, and may be referred by them to the Council for revision. These enactments, however, are not sent to the Scrutiny Committee in draft form, and it would be a considerable additional burden even if the government were to make available the documents which come before the various committees which control the Commission's independent powers of decision. To do so would anyway almost certainly be regarded as a breach of confidentiality and of Community law, since the Commission's decision takes legal effect as soon as it is published. The proceedings of other consultative bodies of officials, of Council working parties, as of the Council itself are also confidential. Decisions about Community expenditure, for example, whether made as decisions to set up funds (like the revised Social Fund or the Regional Development Fund), or as part of the Community's budgetary procedure, result from a series of shifting and private negotiations at official and ministerial level. There is also now the added complication that the European Parliament and not the ministers has the final word on some expenditure, and that it is included in the deliberations on the budget as a whole and on major proposals for expenditure.

In their different ways these are all indications of the way

Parliament in this country has to accept that joining the Community implies fundamental constitutional change. A major consequence of membership is the need to decide what sort of organization the Community should be, and how its own political institutions are to develop the checks and balances associated with parliamentary government. This is why it is so important for Parliament to have means of considering in a timely and informed way proposals emanating from the various Community organs designed to set the Community's future development, but not yet taking the form of legal enactments. The Commons' Scrutiny Committee has drawn attention to this gap in its terms of reference.[29] The stress on 'secondary legislation' in the Commons has probably contributed to this tendency to neglect the wider institutional significance of the Community.

Yet Parliament is given by the treaties vital powers over the future constitution of the Community, and could well be called upon to exercise these in the near future. Not only are there the general proposals emerging from the decision to create a European Union and contained especially in the report of the Belgian Prime Minister, Mr Tindemans, to the Council, but also the specific question of direct elections to the European Parliament. The introduction of direct elections, changes in the powers of the Community institutions, the admission of new members and other constitutional issues can be decided only after a procedure involving ratification by member states' parliaments.[30] The Lords' Select Committee on the European Community has already reported on the question of direct elections, and a special select committee on the subject has now reported in the Commons. Far too little constructive debate, however, has been held in Parliament about the consequences of developing the status and powers of parliamentary institutions at a Community level.

The European Parliament itself has tried many times to get the treaty provision for direct elections carried out, but there has always been opposition from some governments. There is now a better chance than ever of direct elections being introduced on the basis of a revised convention approved by the Parliament in January 1975 and envisaging elections in May 1978. The governments have now agreed themselves to the necessary decisions getting the convention implemented, although HM Government has reservations about the timing, and has made little progress so far towards introducing the necessary legislation here. According to the present agreement (which will have to be approved also by all the national parliaments), each member state will adopt its own system of election and draw up its own constituency boundaries on the basis of an agreed distribution of seats. The agreement provides, however, for a uniform system of election to be introduced by 1980.[31]

One of the questions yet to be resolved is whether the members of the directly elected Parliament will continue to serve concurrently in their own national parliaments. The present method, by which the Parliament consists of members of delegations from national parliaments, offers an additional means for Parliament at Westminster to influence and control Community business. It does seem that in practice the European MPs from Britain have been able to act as a link in this way, and that they have been influenced in their work in the European Parliament by proceedings at Westminster.[32] However, the advantages of the double mandate are outweighed by the enormous strain on the Members concerned, so that one reason for introducing a direct mandate is a purely practical one. Moreover, the European Parliament is presently restricted, not only by its lack of formal powers, but also by the fact that most of its members are essentially back-benchers whose main loyalty is to their national parliaments. Although the British Parliament would be obliged to work out new ways of organizing its relations with the European Parliament, introducing direct elections would so increase the status and efficiency of the European Parliament at a Community level that any loss of status or influence by the Westminster Parliament would be more than compensated. The fact which has not been fully grasped here is that the European Parliament is not some foreign institution threatening to interpose itself, but is now a British institution, and one of the means – undoubtedly the best in the long run – of conserving parliamentary government at a European level.

Conclusions

The negative effects of the Community on parliamentary influence and control must be seen in relation to the development of the Community's own institutions. Although the role of the national parliaments is fundamentally limited by the supra-national element in the Community, it is self-defeating to seek to limit Parliament's loss of powers simply by restraining the supra-national element in favour of national ministers and officials. In the first place the Community's present difficulties, which are serious enough to take away many of the advantages of membership, result above all from the inability of the national governments acting on their own to adopt a view of the common interest and put it into effect. The Community in its present form is not a lion, but a mouse, trapped by the greed and arrogance of the national governments. Secondly, governments tend to be at least as free of parliamentary influence and control in international decision-making as they are otherwise. It would be far better to recognize that an important part of government has shifted to a new level, and to make the necessary adjustments in representative institutions, than to pretend that traditional methods of international negotiation offer any safeguard to Parliament. If it is argued that parliamentary forms have been slow to develop at a Community level, the answer is that in recent years this has been largely a result of obstruction by the British government.

Some Members of course are dissatisfied with the effects on Parliament of joining the Community simply because they object to any transfer of authority from the nation state. Thus some proposals which have been made, such as that Parliament should be able to give ministers a fixed mandate before any decision is made in the Community, or that no further powers should be delegated to the Commission, imply a fundamental change in the constitution of the Community. This attitude is unrealistic, not only because the other member states are not likely to agree to such changes, but also because – to the extent that European integration is a reality – asserting the national government's power in this way is designed neither to get benefits from the Community nor to conserve parliamentary institutions.

The stress in the British reaction to membership on asserting formal powers over 'secondary legislation', and the concentration on negative constitutional effects, is partly a result of the political pressure of those who are still fundamentally doubtful about the need for change at all. However, this should not obscure the important, constructive role which the national parliament should still play in European affairs or the opportunities for doing so. The Community is governed essentially both by supra-national institutions, and by the governments of the nation states, so that, even if the supranational element emerged from its presently suppressed condition, Community decisions would continue to be just as much and as properly a matter for the British Parliament participating by means of its ministers as for a Community-level parliament and executive. This element of federalism in the Community has been extremely difficult to understand in this country, although in time we might do well to learn and adapt, both in this and other unfamiliar aspects of European government.

To make ministers aware of its views regarding Community business, Parliament now has the advantage that proposals for Community decisions appear in draft form sometimes long before a decision is actually made. By means of the Scrutiny Committee in the Commons it can be alerted to those issues which need to be debated in the House, and the Lords Committee on the European Communities provides with its subcommittees what is effectively a set of specialist committees. Moreover, since debates take place at a pre-legislative phase and the government's own programme or policy is not formally in question, members are probably more free than in dealing with normal legislation.

There are signs that the process of learning and adaptation might be already under way.[33] The experience of dealing with Community affairs might well lead in time to a different attitude towards other business, as the advantages of prelegislative scrutiny and debate get acknowledged. Already, to some extent adapting to membership of the Community has illustrated how Parliament can be obliged by its shortage of time, and need for better means of processing information, to make greater use of committees. However, the long-term consequences go far beyond the procedures of Parliament and affect the very role of Parliament in our system of government. As we wake up to the facts, for example, that some of the powers of Parliament of vital importance for the British people can be legitimately exercised away from Westminster, or that Acts of Parliament can be made subject to the superior jurisdiction of a written constitution and a court, we might realize that changes now being considered in the unity of our government or in the form of our constitution, are not so radical any more.

11 Parliament and the Redress of Grievances: the Parliamentary Commissioner in the 1970s

GEOFFREY MARSHALL

When Mr Harold Wilson's Government decided – surprisingly – in the 1960s to equip the House of Commons with an ombudsman (heavily disguised under a more decorous style and title) many things could not have been predicted. No one could have guessed on the First of April 1967 what use Members would make of their new opportunities; or how Ministers would react to criticism and inquisition by the Parliamentary Commissioner for Administration; or how many injustices by reason of maladministration would present themselves for redress. By 1970, however, the system had had time to settle down. The Commissioner's Annual Report for 1970 recorded that 651 cases had been completed and 362 rejected on jurisdictional grounds. This rejection of rather more than half the complaints submitted had become a familiar feature of the scheme. (Rejections in the previous two years and in the subsequent year were 727 out of 1181; 445 out of 790; and 295 out of 516.) These figures reflected in part the significant difficulty of deciding in many cases whether complaints revealed matters proper for consideration under the 1967 Parliamentary Commissioner Act. They may also have been affected by the advice given to Members by the first Commissioner, Sir Edmund Compton. When the Act first came into operation Members were informed that the essential material to be submitted when forwarding a complaint was simply the name and address of the complainant, the department against whose action the complaint was made, and a written statement by a complainant of the circumstances in which he claimed to have suffered injustice. The extent to which Members scrutinized cases for eligibility was expressly left to them[1] but the Commissioner encouraged Members to forward cases on the ground that the jurisdictional tests laid down in the 1967 Act could be applied by his staff and in many cases a judgement would in any event not necessarily be possible without some initial investigation into the actions of the impugned department.

The Parliamentary Setting

In retrospect it seems evident that the legislation setting up the office of the Parliamentary Commissioner evolved in a way which prevented or hindered the asking of a fundamental question – what is the place and function of the ombudsman institution in the machinery of government? (Compare the Franks Committee's question about tribunals: are they, properly considered, part of the machinery of administration or part of the machinery of justice?) The Commissioner was brought into existence as a piece of Parliamentary machinery. As Sir Edmund Compton used to emphasize, he is a *Parliamentary* Commissioner.

This concluded what might have been an open and pertinent question. Is the ombudsman function anything essentially to do with Parliament at all? The answer might have been that it is not; and that although Parliamentarians might make use of an ombudsman's services – as they might make use of the Post Office as an adjunct to their functions – the institution is essentially not a piece of Parliamentary machinery but a central part of the mechanism of administrative law and justice.

It is now too late to give this answer (even if it is the right answer). But we can perhaps draw up a profit and loss account that results from the decision to attach the Commissioner's office to Parliament rather than to set it up as an independent statutory institution.

On the profit side we could put:

1. The Parliamentary connection contributed to the initial acceptability of the office, since, with its attendant select committee, it looked like a familiar bit of the Westminster scenery.

2. The Select Committee and the Commissioner have supplemented and encouraged each other. Examples can be seen in the Committee's ability to carry further the Commissioner's dialogue with departments on such matters as the merits of administrative policies; and the Committee's role in occasionally emboldening and advising the Commissioner. He can ask the Committee for opinions on difficult points and quiz it on ways in which his functions may be developed within the 1967 Act, and even on the more delicate point of when to ignore the Act – as on the scrutiny of 'bad decisions'.

On the other side of the ledger we might put:

1. Certain awkwardnesses about the reporting of decisions, given the obligations of the Commissioner to Members of Parliament. Otherwise the analogy for publicizing the results of the Commissioner's findings could be nearer to what happens with the reports of judicial proceedings or administrative adjudications with reports made available directly and contemporaneously to the public and the Press as well as to complainants and MPs. Even so, some things said in support of the existing system of reporting primarily to Members are not very convincing. It is suggested, for example, that the Parliamentary Commissioner Act does not confer privilege for reports to the Press. (But they could be published as Parliamentary papers and protected by the 1840 Act and no doubt the 1952 Defamation Act.) It has also been argued that Members' names cannot be attached to the Commissioner's reports, because if the Press approached them to give further particulars about complaints and about the persons referred to in them, MPs might be embarrassed and find themselves in personal difficulties. (The answer to that is that there exists a useful negative monosyllable which in any such circumstances MPs ought not to be too feeble to articulate.)

2. The informal extensions and accommodations resulting from the Select Committee–Commissioner relationship, have furthered the continuance of a certain vagueness in the public mind about the nature of the ombudsman remedy. Thus when the Home Secretary, for example, proposed for police complainants an 'ombudsman-type review', it was not immediately obvious what form of review this amounted to. In its pristine

form the British version of ombudsman-type enquiry was designed as something that in terms of the legal distinction between appeal and jurisdictional review was neither one thing nor the other. In effect it was a thin type of procedural appeal allegedly covering faults in the decision process but not touching the merits of the decision itself. What has developed is a more substantial review of what might be called 'merits', exercised with restraint – or with what in some jurisdictions is called a 'margin of appreciation' for administrative judgement. The moral for complainants is clear. Even when a complaint is merely against the decision itself it should be framed in terms of an allegation of irrelevant, irrational or inconsistent reasons or considerations infecting the decision process,[2] or 'mishandling' of the complaint or failure properly to investigate the facts of the dispute or failure to take account of all the evidence or to give sufficient weight to particular considerations.[3]

3. The Parliamentary setting of the institution raised awkward questions when it was extended into local government – particularly about the need for enforcement and the avenues for submitting complaints. The Parliamentary model of using the elected person as a channel is inappropriate here but was in fact adopted. Oddly the Secretary of State told the Parliamentary Select Committee that to allow MPs to submit complaints to a local government commissioner would undermine the status and position of local councillors who would be the main channel of complaint.[4] What local councillors were and are more likely to be, of course, is the main object of complaint.

The 1967 Act: Some Problems
Perhaps we may sum up as follows some of the questions that have arisen from the working of the 1967 Act and the practices adopted under it.

Rules causing hardship
Where the Commissioner concludes that a departmental rule, though properly applied, causes hardship he may invite the

department to review it and to consider whether it is defective or whether to make an exception to it because of hardship in the particular case even if the rule is not in general defective. Sometimes, however, the Commissioner seems to have a clear view of the rule and despite individual hardship he may decide not even to invite the department to review its rule (e.g. Annual Report 1971 310 [the 'Would-be law students case']).[5]

The merits of a Departmental Review

Sometimes, however, the Commissioner does ask the department to review a decision or a rule and when they have done so reports that he is precluded by s 12 (3) from questioning the merits of *this* decision. Should not the Commissioner's dispensation (or whatever it is) to enquire into whether a decision is a 'bad' decision apply to this review decision as well as to an original disputed decision? What is the rationale for treating this decision differently?[6]

Straight or simple 'unreasonableness' as a ground for complaint

'Unreasonableness' was not an item in the 'Crossman catalogue'. But at p. 36 of the 4th Report, 1971–2,[7] there is a case in which it is held that the Department of Education after a local authority had allegedly acted unreasonably had been *wrong* to uphold their action. This sounds like a complaint against 'the decision itself'. Presumably it can be investigated to see if there are elements of maladministration in the handling of the complaint, or if there is any case for believing it to fall into the category of 'bad' decision. Presumably the department could be acting 'wrongly' or unreasonably without its decision being bad (i.e. 'thoroughly bad') and thereby constituting an example of maladministration. But if a decision is wrong or unreasonable without being thoroughly bad, there must be some explanation for this in the operations through which the decision was reached which could be detected if the case were closely scrutinized. Would these be 'elements' of maladministration? How far does the scrutiny of a case depend on the form of the complaint and whether there is any allegation of mishandling even of the most perfunctory kind? A complainant would seem unwise to allege that the decision in his case was wrong without saying that it had been mishandled. Can a complaint ever be dismissed without investigation as being only against the decision and not against the handling?

Legal Advice

The Commissioner places a good deal of reliance on the legal advice he gets from government departments. This seems less than satisfactory where the advice relates to jurisdictional points arising out of the Parliamentary Commissioner Act itself and its application to government departments. A good example is the legal advice of the Foreign Office about s 6(4) of the 1967 Act (1972 Annual Report, p. 6) which refers to 'rights or obligations which accrued or arose in the United Kingdom'. The department's legal advisers interpreted this as if the section had said '*legal* rights arising in the UK', so that the despatch of a letter to a government department would not as they alleged have the effect of creating a legal right in the correspondent wherever the letter came from. Though the Commissioner doubted (rightly) whether this section was intended to mean anything of the kind he did not contest it and discontinued action on the complaint against the Foreign Office without reaching a final view about s 6(4).[8]

Another example of restrictive governmental legal advice being given is that of the Attorney-General about the non-qualification of statutory instruments as examples of administrative activity. One cannot help but feel that at least on points affecting the Commissioner's jurisdiction the views of governmental legal advisers ought to be subject to a stiffer examination than they have had.

'Political complaints'

This is a queer category exemplified by the complaint against the Minister of Posts and Telecommunications about the distribution of broadcasting time during General Elections (see Annual Report for 1971, p. 6). The minister here, admittedly, exercises a discretion. But it was said that the considerations affecting its use are 'political'. What does this mean? That they have an impact on politics or political parties? So do many other ministerial discretions. Or is the suggestion that the decisions are made with an eye to the electoral fortunes of a particular party or parties rather than by an impartial consideration of the public interest? If that were so it sounds a very proper subject for enquiry. In what sense is such a discretion more 'political' than a discretionary decision about planning, education or the sale of council houses?

Complaints against the actions of statutory officers
This is one of a number of categories of complaints held to be outside the provisions of the Act because they are said not to constitute 'administrative' action by or on behalf of a department (e.g. Registrars of Marriages,[9] or Attendance Allowance Boards). Where an officer such as an examiner acting for the Comptroller General of Patents is not so detached from a department but is acting as part of an organization under the directions and superintendence of a Minister, he may still not, it is said, be exercising 'administrative' functions, but judicial functions or 'statutory' functions. Two things could be said about this. One is that a narrow view is being taken here of 'administrative' functions. The term 'administrative' has no single agreed meaning in either administrative law or the English language and there is no reason to be afraid of supposing that adjudicatory functions like rule-making functions can be an accepted part of the administrative process. As such their judicial or legislative character is not inconsistent with their also being administrative.

If this argument is not accepted, a second thing can still be said – namely that it is an issue for future Parliamentary consideration whether functions of this kind should fall within the purview of the Parliamentary Commissioner.

Complaints against legislation
A form of exclusion that has little to be said for it is that of

complaints about a specific hardship that arises from the terms of a statute. The original rationale for the exclusion has always been a feeble one. There is a good example at p. 15 of the 1972 Annual Report. S. 61 of the Friendly Societies Act 1896 prevents a Registered Society from paying out money on a life assurance policy without production of a death certificate. An enquiry into whether in some cases this causes hardship could hardly be described as a challenge to the sovereignty of Parliament. It would seem an entirely appropriate function for the Commissioner if he were permitted to draw the attention of ministers and of Parliament to such cases of hardship which may be unforeseen and unintended by the legislature so that they might be reviewed when amending or consolidation legislation is under consideration.

Executive action leading up to legislation

This category provides another instance of departmental action at present inconveniently excluded from the Commissioner's purview. The distinction drawn in relation to delegated legislation between the legislative act and the departmental processes leading up to it is equally apt in the case of primary legislation. It was in fact suggested in discussion between the Commissioner and the Select Committee in 1968 that the reasoning adopted in relation to statutory orders and the processes leading up to them might be applicable to decisions to promote or not promote a bill. Unfortunately, the Committee did not press this view and Sir Edmund Compton was reluctant to follow out its implications. But even if a complaint that a department had failed to promote a bill might be thought to be going rather wide, complaints about failures in departmental pre-legislative consultation – whether they relate to delegated or any other legislation – seem fairly referable to the administrative functions of a department. The process is traditionally referred to as 'Departmental' or 'Governmental' consultation. Indeed, the argument for admission of complaints prior to legislation is in some ways stronger than it is in relation to complaints about processes antecedent to the making of statutory rules and orders. The latter stand in a sense at the end rather than the beginning of the legislative process and flow indirectly from the authority of Parliament. But what a department does at an initial stage before promoting legislation is not in any sense at all a decision of or done under the authority of Parliament. It is pure executive or departmental action and the conventions of the constitution describe it as such. Certainly what a department fails to do can hardly be said to be under the control of Parliament. If any extension of existing practice is involved in admitting a complaint about these departmental processes it is one entirely consistent with common sense and the purposes of the 1967 Act.

Legal Proceedings

Yet another set of undesirable exclusions are those relating to legal proceedings, both where they may be possible as an alternative to an investigation by the Commissioner and where they may themselves be the subject matter of complaint.

Why should the Commissioner be ousted where a complainant might take legal proceedings (even allowing for the discretion given the Commissioner where he thinks such a course would be unreasonable)? We may want to know from the point of view of investigating and correcting maladministration why an administrator did what he did, even when it may turn out to be tortious or criminal. The courts are concerned with the remedy rather than with the background and explanation. If there is litigation we may never know the full facts about what went on and why, except in so far as may be necessary to determine the particular legal result. And litigation may be settled without the facts coming out at all.

Similar considerations apply if we consider the exclusion of the Commissioner from investigating the institution or conduct of criminal proceedings. The *conduct* of criminal or civil proceedings may perhaps be left to the legal process itself. But the legal process is not primarily concerned with the reasons for *instituting* proceedings if the proceedings themselves are well founded. Departments institute a great many legal proceedings and it is sometimes alleged that in particular cases the decisions to take action are unreasonable or amount to a vendetta. (See HC 490 of 1971–2, p. 5 – a purchase tax case.) A similar complaint about the motives behind a mooted prosecution was made in the Crichel Down case in 1954. The courts do not provide a forum or a remedy for such complaints. Who can investigate them if the Ombudsman cannot?

Sachsenhausen and Duccio

During the period of office of Sir Edmund Compton, the first Commissioner, some initial doubts as to the potency of the new machinery were, or at least should have been, dispelled when, with the approval of the Parliamentary Select Committee, he began to interpret his terms of reference more liberally.[10] In the Sachsenhausen prisoner-of-war compensation case in 1967 it became plain that the conduct of ministers, as well as that of civil servants might, if it were infected by departmental mishandling of evidence or information, be open to criticism.[11] In the following year similar interesting possibilities were revealed in the report on the Duccio affair – a complaint against the Board of Trade, alleging maladministration in its supervision of the law relating to auctions. In the course of his investigation Sir Edmund Compton took evidence from Mr Anthony Crosland against whom complaint had been made on the ground that a speech made by him in the House of Commons on 6 November 1968 had been damaging to the interests of two members of the Society of London Art Dealers. The Commissioner's special report[12] was critical of the Board of Trade for not making its role in relation to auctions clearer at an earlier date and vindicated the two complainants against Mr Crosland's criticisms of their actions in his Parliamentary Statement. The Commissioner was careful to add that he did not think that he could properly investigate the Parliamentary Statements themselves. An interesting constitutional question might have arisen had he done so since Article 9 of the Bill of Rights of 1689 declares that debates or proceedings in Parliament are not to be impeached or questioned in any place out of Parliament. A breach of Privilege by the Commissioner can however presumably be avoided if he confines his enquiries to the departmental briefing given to the minister on which his Parliamentary remarks are based.

Sir Alan Marre's Incumbency

In 1971 Sir Alan Marre took over as Parliamentary Commissioner. In his first annual report he remarked that there continued to be 'widespread misunderstanding about the scope of my office'. Complainants, he went on, 'not infrequently ask me to reverse decisions by departments (including Ministers) simply because they disagree with the decisions and not with the way they have been taken'.[13] The mystery of maladministration, in other words, had failed to make any impact on the public consciousness and aggrieved citizens who believed that they had suffered hardship because of wrong or unjust decisions taken by the administration persisted in believing that they were the victims of administrative injustice. Luckily, much that is objectionable can if necessary be called 'failure to give adequate consideration' to evidence germane to the decision. This is, we may suppose, a form of mishandling and in a wide sense a procedural fault. In many of his reports Sir Alan Marre did in fact characterize such faults not as 'maladministration' or even as 'elements of maladministration' but as 'shortcomings in the Departments' actions' or 'muddles' or 'inadequacy of response'.[14] Where some measure of maladministration occurred it was, he noted, generally the result of a mistake or human error rather than of serious maladministration. The Departments most prone to human error have, not surprisingly, been the Departments of Inland Revenue and Health and Social Security – the undisputed champions of the Commissioner's league tables. From 1970–3 complaints submitted against these departments numbered 115, 98, 94 and 96 (Inland Revenue), and 102, 79, 110, 106 (Health and Social Security). The Department of the Environment ran in third place with 88, 64, 83 and 95. Of the Inland Revenue's four-yearly total of 403 complaints only 288 were found to be within the Commissioner's jurisdiction. The figures for Health and Social Security were 397 received, 196 investigated; and for the Environment 330 with 208 investigated. The Inland Revenue has claimed to be suffering hardship and a measure of administrative injustice as the result of its exposed position in these numerical tables. Given the very large number of individual cases handled, its large absolute total of registered complaints is no cause for surprise. Possibly an index of complaints per thousand citizen-contacts would exhibit the Revenue in a fairer light as against, say, the Public Trustee or the Scottish Office. The average percentage for all departments of case reports in which there was 'maladministration leading to some measure of injustice' was 23 per cent in 1970, 37 per cent in 1971, 30 per cent in 1972 and 37 per cent in 1973.

In relation to the Inland Revenue Sir Alan Marre and the Parliamentary Select Committee secured a significant concession in 1971. An important category of cases in which hardship was felt to have been caused involved the collection of arrears of tax when the failure to make a correct assessment could be attributed to a fault on the part of the Revenue. The Revenue's attitude had been sometimes to assert that they had no power to remit arrears of tax, but sometimes to concede that extra-statutory concessions were possible where extreme hardship might result. In July 1971 the Government published a White Paper in which they agreed that the Revenue should remit tax arrears in such cases on the basis of 'comparative' rather than 'absolute' hardship – a welcome token of repentance for the Revenue's excusable though numerous human errors. The reports[15] of the Inland Revenue cases contain incidentally much fascinating and useful information for the taxpayer. They embody many invaluable insights into the department's motivation, tactics and prose style.

One striking feature of the Parliamentary Commissioner's jurisdiction is that it has not been much exploited by Members as a political weapon against ministers. Several of Sir Alan Marre's cases did however relate to matters in which ministers were involved and in which ministerial as well as departmental judgement was implicitly or explicitly criticized in his reports. One such case was the affair of the invalid tricycles. The motorized, three-wheel invalid carriage was the object of continual criticism by groups representing disabled drivers. The Commissioner's report on the Department of Health did not find that they had been guilty of indifference or a lack of concern for safety. But he did say that they were too slow to commission independent tests; that their initial refusal to publish the result of the tests was 'misconceived'; that their attitude of defensiveness was 'unwarranted and unwise' and that replies given by ministers to questions in the House had been 'less frank than they should have been'.[16] It seems clear that Ministerial policy judgements must have been involved in the formulation of the Department's attitude.

Another such issue was the Television Licences case of 1975. There the essence of the complaints was that the Post Office and the Home Office had acted unlawfully and unreasonably in attempting to prevent licence holders from holding overlapping licences, obtained before an announced increase in licence fees came into effect. The legality of the action taken was later disputed successfully in the courts[17] but the Commissioner in his report criticized the Home Office for causing needless distress and confusion by their administrative arrangements. His conclusion was that they had acted with 'both inefficiency and lack of foresight'. In reaching that conclusion the Commissioner said he had directed his mind to the question 'whether, within the framework of their view of the law, the Home Office's actions have been administratively sound and reasonable'.[18] This sounds perilously close to a consideration of the merits of the decision taken by the department in the exercise of its discretion – a consideration which we remember is specifically forbidden by Section 12 of the Parliamentary Commissioner Act.

Similar thoughts again might be suggested by the outcome of the Court Line case in August 1975. There the Commissioner blamed the Minister, Mr Benn, for giving misleading public assurances about the Court Line Company's holiday operations. Mr Benn and his ministerial colleagues rejected the Commissioner's findings. Mr Benn's speech was the result of a Cabinet meeting in which a decision had been made striking a balance between the need to inform holiday-makers, and the possible danger of undermining public confidence. In the House, the Prime Minister, Mr Harold Wilson, said that he and the Government accepted full responsibility for the decision and that Mr Benn's speech in the House had been made in support of it. Yet the Commissioner was willing to say (in effect) that the Cabinet decision was misleading and the statement unjustified. This seems to be getting into the merits with a vengeance. But was the faulty decision one that arose out of maladministration? Some of the terms in Mr Richard Crossman's original Parliamentary specification of the term might well have fitted it: 'Delay', 'incompetence' or 'ineptitude'[19] perhaps? Whatever it was, Opposition Members of Parliament may perhaps have drawn the encouraging conclusion that the Cabinet is capable of committing maladministration within the meaning of the 1967 Act.

In the Court Line case, the Commissioner was informed of the result of the Cabinet decision but he was not permitted to see Cabinet papers relating to it. Section 8 (4) of the Parliamentary Commissioner Act allows the Secretary to the Cabinet to certify that information or documents relate to the proceedings of the Cabinet or Cabinet Committees and such papers or information are privileged from production. It is not clear, however, that this precludes ministers from furnishing such documents. What the legislation says is that no person shall be required or authorized *by virtue of this Act* to furnish information in these categories. But it need not follow from that that there are no other powers under which it might be done or that it would be unlawful for ministers voluntarily to provide the Commissioner with Cabinet papers; or that he is precluded from asking them to provide them in the exercise of their discretion.

Proposed Amendments

In the aftermath of the Court Line case a private Member's
bill was introduced into the House by Mr Ian Gow, seeking
to amend the 1967 Act by giving the Commissioner access
to Cabinet documents unless the Attorney-General should
certify that their production would be prejudicial to the
security of the state.[20] The Bill also sought to alter the
method by which the Commissioner is appointed by requiring
future appointments to be made only after consultation by the
Prime Minister with the Chairman of the Parliamentary
Select Committee and after both Houses had given their
approval by affirmative resolution. This issue was revived in
1976 after the appointment of Sir Idwal Pugh as Sir Alan
Marre's successor. In reply to a Parliamentary question the
Prime Minister stated that he had not in fact consulted
Members of Parliament or members of the Select Committee
before making the appointment. Some MPs were inclined to
see in this position a threat to the concept of the Commissioner as a *Parliamentary* Commissioner. They concluded that
those who had been consulted on the appointment of the new
Commissioner must have been civil servants – 'the very
people whose activities the ombudsman has been appointed
to investigate'.[21]

Even more ambitious and forward-looking suggestions were
made – as, for example, that future Commissioners might not
always be civil servants but that the office might conceivably
be held by a politician, a former businessman or a lawyer.
If, however, rationality is to prevail in the matter, three other
possible revisions of the Act might well come into consideration. One would be to allow members of the Upper House
(who are no less members of Parliament) access to the Parliamentary Commissioner. Another would be to allow the Commissioner to initiate investigation on his own initiative if he
should think it necessary without having to be triggered or
propelled into action by a specific complaint. The third and
most radical (though eminently sensible) course would be to
permit complainants to have direct access to the Commissioner rather than compel them to use the inefficient and

undignified Parliamentary filter of submission through a Member of the House of Commons. There is nothing in the concept of a Parliamentary Commissioner that is inconsistent with this. Other Parliamentary systems allow it. It would not deprive any Member of his right to invoke the Commissioner's assistance. It would both cheer the citizen and stimulate the machinery of administrative justice. Like a Bill of Rights it would add a new and entertaining dimension to political life in England.

12 Whither the Commons?

S. A. WALKLAND

The first edition of this volume, *The Commons in Transition*, was written at the end of the 1960s, and despite a few dissenting voices some of the optimism of that reforming decade inevitably rubbed off on it. It would be a brave editor who could adopt the same approach in 1976. Less than ten years has served to demonstrate that neither the Commons nor the country as a whole was, in fact, in any transitional state, except to a worse condition, and that the multifarious social, educational, administrative and Parliamentary reforms of the 1960s have been ineffectual in securing any regeneration of Parliament, government or the economy, improvements in the functioning of which remain as elusive as ever. Failure in other areas of national life have inevitably affected our central representative institution; the decline of public confidence in liberal democratic processes, comparatively minor ten years or so ago, has become more marked, although certainly not yet to the point where the entire system is questioned. By the test of electoral participation, Parliamentary democracy in Britain is still reasonably healthy, but markedly less vigorous than it used to be – or is in most other West European countries. The main losers have been the two major parties. They have been steadily less successful in the last twenty-five years. In 1951 they got 97 per cent of the vote between them; in 1974 they got barely 75 per cent. But, as opposed to this, anti-Parliamentary parties in Britain have notably failed to make any headway whatsoever. What little support they have gained has tended to disappear when the Liberal party has put up candidates. We have been fortunate that the main vehicle for the protest vote against the dominance of the two main party organizations has been so pro-Parliamentary. This demonstrates the antipathy towards extremism which is widely felt in Britain, but also that what has recently been a substantial Liberal vote is very negative in its feelings towards the operation of the political system. It prefers to protest through moderate rather than extremist parties, when given the choice, but its main motivation is a negative one.

But if people have continued to vote in comparatively large numbers, it seems to be with resignation rather than optimism, more, one suspects, from ingrained habit than from enthusiasm. In the face of seemingly intransigent problems the British public is growing cynical and bitter, going through the motions of supporting a political system where, although traditional party politics may be the primary target of disillusionment, some of the disenchantment rubs off on Parliament. Close observers have questioned recently the degree of public attachment to Britain's representative institutions, and to the political system in general. The collapse of civil order in Ulster, the emergence of nationalism in Scotland and Wales, the strikes and demonstrations which have affected the stability of government, the emergence of direct action and the withdrawal to community politics have all been taken as testifying in different ways to a rejection of Parliamentary authority. It is small comfort to read with Bernard Crick and others that this authority has never been great in Britain, so cannot be restored. The fact remains that its ineffectuality in ordering or influencing the course of events, even in real crisis, is discerned as never having been lower.

A pronounced pessimism is now evident amongst practically all those whose professional interest brings them constantly into touch with Parliamentary politics. It was noticeable that the Study of Parliament Group, which entered the Parliamentary procedure debates of the mid-1960s with considerable vigour, and played a formative role in the developments of that period, viewed the prospect of a similar enquiry in 1976 with much reduced enthusiasm, and with a livelier appreciation of what little procedural adjustments could do to improve the current standing of Parliament. This pessimism is shared by many whose day-to-day concerns are with the British Parliament. As a colleague of the writer, a university lecturer in government and a contributor to this volume has remarked:

I imagine that most teachers of elementary courses in government have found serious difficulty in persuading all but their most naïve students to take Parliament seriously. And why should they? From the outset one is bound to confess that even as an observation platform from which to survey the places where real decisions are taken the House of Commons has limited value. One finds oneself countering the probing scepticism of such students by murmuring incantations about 'legitimation', or by suggesting, rather lamely, that although Parliament plays no part in policy formulation or even in the expert criticism of policy, potentially it does have a useful role as a ventilator of public issues which would otherwise remain shrouded in total darkness – admitting at the same time that it is too inexpert a body, and too much immersed in ritual party conflict, to perform even this modest task very well.

The symptoms of decline are obvious; to diagnose the disease is another and complex matter. The decline of the British Parliament has causes that go deep. Some are shared with most other democratic assemblies; others derive from purely domestic political circumstances. It may well be that in general throughout the West public policy is now the product of an untidy pluralism, in which representative assemblies cannot hope to play their former role. But there are signs in Britain that this pluralism is hardening fast into a rigid corporatism, both economic and political, and the problem of representative and responsible government is increasingly seen to be how the values once associated with a diffuse economic and social structure can be safeguarded in a situation which has become decidedly more monolithic. It is not just the development of direct state activity as reflected in the growth of public expenditure to the point where more than 60 per cent of GDP passes through governmental hands of one sort or another, although one Cabinet Minister, Mr Roy Jenkins, is on record as saying that further growth in the public sector would undermine the foundations of a plural society. It is also the case that at least since the early 1960s successive governments, with many hesitations and interruptions, have been developing a broad policy of economic corporatism, which owes little to conventional political ideology, whereby the state through the decisions of its economic agencies has largely superseded the working of the market economy in the private sector. The process can be characterized as an attempt at a comprehensive economic system in which the state at its discretion directs and controls predominantly privately owned business according to principles which are reckoned essential for national economic survival. The degree of flexible intervention which this requires is considerable, and at the time of writing is due for considerable expansion by planning agreements (and a substantial body of opinion in the Conservative Party is willing to see such developments continue). In these circumstances much of what was once seen as desirable restrictions on the executive – the need for detailed Parliamentary approval and the adherence to strictly limited roles defined through the rule of law and the requirements of specific Parliamentary assent become not just irrelevant but even embarrassing. Government of necessity has to be profoundly un-Parliamentary. Ministerial and departmental explanations to Parliament become more perfunctory; limitations are placed on the investigatory powers of Parliamentary committees; legislation, now largely in any case merely specifications for administrative action, is speeded up, and at the time of writing considerably more autonomy and flexibility is being sought by the Government by the introduction of 'framework' bills for major legislation.

Over and above this disjunction which economic corporatism imposes between the imperatives of government and the legitimate interests of Parliament there has developed an accompanying political corporatism, which recently has been refined to the point where it now threatens some of the traditional values of a free liberal society. Both of necessity and convenience government has found other arenas of consent and accommodation than the House of Commons, whether the NEDC or the various Labour Party–TUC liaison committees, and large groups of voters have grown accustomed to making their prime political demands through agencies other than Parliament. It is not merely the superficial evidence of political corporatism – the writing by the TUC of Government White Papers, the appearance of union leaders with ministers on party political broadcasts, etc. Nor is it simply a system which limits the unions to their own immediate interests of wages and working conditions, or the industrial climate. It is now commonly accepted that specific levels of public expenditure should be negotiated with the unions; that legislation should be pushed through at TUC behest; that the unions should determine by a process of economic bargaining levels of taxation and rates of allowances, to be mechanically ratified by Parliament. Any area of government policy, from the level of public expenditure and the rates of pensions and benefits to foreign affairs and overseas aid may now be determined by pre-emptive and extra-parliamentary bargaining, much of it in private. If these developments were the work of governments claiming majority support, or if their corporate partners were not so ludicrously unrepresentative of the electorate as a whole, and inherently undemocratic in addition, the system might, just, be squared with some of the requirements of political democracy. As it now operates it manifestly cannot, and considerable political change is needed if the House of Commons, as the main claimant to being the legitimate expressive agency of a liberal society, is to match them with any countervailing power and regain some authority as a central arena of economic and political accommodation and the guardian of the liberties of the mass of the electorate. Yet the present Commons, or rather the Government members of it, have collaborated in their supersession by other agencies; narrow considerations of party advantage have over-ridden their functions as Parliamentarians, and are likely to continue to do so while the present system of adversary Parliamentary politics persists. To take but one recent example, the Trade Union and Labour Relations (Amendment) Act of 1976, itself a large step on the road to corporatism, showed strikingly that in particular relation to the freedom of the Press in Britain the House of Commons as at present constituted provides no safeguard against encroachment on the fundamental liberties. What is needed if ground now lost is to be regained is political realignment to the point where no government is in a position to act as the political arm of a powerful minority interest, whether to the Left or the Right, and where its main allegiance is of political necessity and considerations of survival to a broader-based and representative House of Commons. Change of this nature cannot come from Parliament itself – it must reflect new social and political impulses relayed through the structure of the national party system, although much could be done to facilitate it through electoral reform. Procedural tinkering is in these circumstances irrelevant; the search for it dissipates energies which would be better employed in analysing the political problem.

It is against these depressing developments that the reforms of Parliament of the last ten years, which have so exercised the minds of members of the Study of Parliament Group, have to be judged, and from the outset it must be seen how puny they are in the extent to which they have failed to grip the essential problem. One thing stands out clearly with hind-sight (although some of us predicted it), which is that the main weakness of the Parliamentary reform movement is that it did not presuppose political change, without which its innovations have been weakened almost to the point of impotence. When one looks at the arguments which were deployed by the reformers one is constantly struck by how unpolitical they were, apparently unaware of the wider political context in which reforms would have to operate. Either by accident or design they left out of account some of the basic determinants of Parliamentary procedure – mainly the political structure of the Commons and the way in which it shapes fundamentally the relations of the House and the executive. All except a few Liberals assumed the desirability, even the inevitability, of a largely two-party model of Parlia-mentary politics, maintained by a plurality system of electoral voting. Whether this was because the system seemed so well-entrenched as not to attract basic criticism, or whether the academics and others who shaped reforming opinion had their own political axe to grind is not clear. But it is not without significance that Professors Hanson, Wiseman, Crick and Mackintosh, with their mentor, Professor Laski, were all

Labour supporters who could not be expected to canvass even the possibility of electoral change which might threaten the stability of their own party, and its chances under plurality voting of gaining governmental power. As a result all the significant contributors to the reform debate accepted and assumed a distinct model of twentieth-century Parliamentary government, in which 'strong' single-party executives maintained their authority at all times over a weak and supportive Parliamentary system. With but one or two exceptions all the reformers held deeply-rooted *a priori* assumptions about executive supremacy which even 'reformist' Members of Parliament seldom seriously questioned. The result inevitably was the adoption by the reformers of two fundamentally irreconcilable aims – the strengthening of Parliament without detracting from the power of government. There were those at the time, the present writer amongst them, who pointed out that it was inconceivable that any single-party government, secure in its voting strength on the floor of the House, would allow any significant scope to the powerful Parliamentary investigative agencies which were being proposed, or that associated reforms in Members' pay and facilities would add much to the efficacy of Parliament. For the essence of the problem is at bottom political – whether the Commons has the political power to make its views heeded in the decisions of government, or whether government can at all essential times control the decisions of Parliament. This was the awkward issue which the 1960s generation of reformers could only resolve by fudging.

Parliamentary committees of 'advice and scrutiny' were invented, with little discussion of what would happen if the advice went unheeded or the scrutiny proved ineffective. Some reformers, apparently resigned to the essential impotence of the Commons even when reformed, took refuge in a communications theory of Parliamentary power – the House of Commons, if incapable of influencing government directly, would mirror to the electorate the implications of government activity and reflect back the hopes and wishes of the voters, with the new committees the main instrument of analysis and dissemination. A few of the new investigative select committees of the House, such as the Select Committee on Science and Technology, have performed this function to some extent, but in respect of very small and highly specialized publics only. Given the exclusion of the new committees from central areas of public policy, they could do little to enhance this communicative role, which remains, so far as the Commons is concerned, more deficient in its operation than at any time in its history. If Parliament is to be likened to a two-way mirror, as the communicators tend to see it, then it is a distorting one. Political attitudes in an essentially unrepresentative Commons are geared up to an extent which produces a caricature of political feeling in the country. How, on the communications theory of Parliamentary politics, did it happen that for so long, and in a way which was gravely damaging to Britain's reputation as a serious and responsible nation, so many politicians misjudged the attitude of the electorate to British entry to the EEC? How is it that a potentially serious gap has grown between public opinion in the country and many aspects of permissive social policy espoused by 'progressive' back-benchers and Ministers? It might have been the case that patient all-party investigation of many recent such issues might have narrowed the gap between Parliament and public; the agencies were not created, the political climate of the House forbade it, and Parliament declined in public esteem as a result.

Ten years after the 'Crossman' innovations it is possible to gain some perspective on the course of reform. There is on the whole little fresh to report which was not included in *The Commons in Transition*. Since the earlier volume appeared, the Conservative Government in 1970 produced its Green Paper on Select Committees of the House of Commons, a reappraisal which it had inherited from the previous administration. It followed the trend of the Labour Government in cutting out 'departmental' select committees and restricting specialist committees to a few 'subject' areas. Its prime purpose was to make room for a new and comparatively large Expenditure Committee of the Commons, which it saw as fitting neatly into a packet of administrative reforms based on the reports of the Plowden and Fulton Committees. The new package was fervently described in a pamphlet by David Howell, MP, a former member of the Procedure Committee and subsequently Parliamentary Secretary to the Civil Service Department, entitled 'A New Style of British Government' in which a model of efficient British government employing both micro- and macro-economic techniques of expenditure planning and management was designed to usher in a new era of trans-Atlantic efficiency to Whitehall. The system it was destined to replace proved, however, particularly resilient; the Parliamentary Expenditure Committee either did not understand or showed little taste for its own role in the process and the reforms were never pushed through as fundamentally as had been proposed. The work of the Expenditure Committee is touched on below; the work of the few 'Crossman generation' committees remaining has continued quietly and unspectacularly. To succeed, even in the negative sense of being left alone by the government, the specialist committees have had to connect only peripherally with the main political processes of Parliament. They have avoided the fate of the earlier Agriculture Committee, which reached the limit of its effectiveness in the interests of the major parties in maintaining their executive privileges, but at the expense of a great deal of activity which has been largely purposeless, with little effect except in minor ways on government policy and without engaging to any great extent the attention of the parent House. As outlets for the frustrated energies of some back-benchers they obviously have a continuing function, but on the whole they exist and operate in a sort of bipartisan limbo, remote from the main House, unconnected with its procedures and deeply unsure of their role. To say this is not to undervalue either the quantity or quality of the work put in by committee members. In many ways their operations show the House of Commons at its best. The capacity of MPs for detailed work of a specialist kind, if limited by their experience, is nevertheless far greater than most ministers and officials would credit them with. But much of their effort has been wasted; the world has not been a different place as a result of their operations and in this respect the House remains much the same sort of body as it was in 1966.

The main innovation in the Commons since the first edition of this volume was published has been the creation of the new Expenditure Committee in 1971, following on the report of the Procedure Committee of Session 1968–9. The substantive work of this body has been dealt with in an earlier chapter,[1] but a few general points are worth making. It was designed to have a more intimate connection with important political processes and with some traditional activities of the House as a whole than were the earlier specialist committees. The analysis of the 1968–9 Procedure Committee which lay at the heart of the new body was complex. Conceived primarily as an agency whereby the House could modernize its procedures in the field of public expenditure planning and management it was also seen by its protagonists as a means of rescuing the specialist committee experiment from the deliberate de-emphasis and downgrading which it was receiving in the late 1960s at the hands of the Labour government. By linking its investigatory authority with legitimate concerns of the House of Commons with public expenditure it was hoped that the new committee and its sub-committees would gain an enhanced status and a significant role in some major political processes which had eluded the earlier Crossman committees. If in retrospect the functions allocated to the committee seem somewhat rigid and over-articulated they nevertheless rested on a rigorous analysis of a sort which was lacking in the earlier theorizing about specialist scrutiny of government by the House.

After two years or so of finding its feet and adjusting the relationships between the full committee and the sub-committees, the Expenditure Committee embarked eighteen months or so ago (this is written in May 1976) on a fruitful round of investigations and Reports which illustrate both the possibilities of specialist scrutiny of government action and the limitations put on it by the current political context of the House. One should ignore the spectacular 'political' investigations of some sub-committees, into private medicine and the NHS, or the practices of British firms in South Africa, which were light-years away from the Committee's original remit and served only to enhance the party-political reputation of their chairmen; one should also not pay too much attention to the low-keyed investigations by some sub-committees into matters of departmental administration, which are similar to and serve the same purpose as the work of the Committee's predecessor, the Estimates Committee. But recently the General, Defence and Trade and Industry Sub-committees have bitten off large chunks of raw meat, and have passed under critical review important aspects of the Government's budgetary, defence and industrial policies, to the point where it could be said that an unofficial bipartisan opposition, such as the reformers always hoped for, is emerging in the Commons.

The most significant work has been that of the General Sub-committee, aided by a number of specialist advisers drawn from the Department of Applied Economics at Cambridge, which, under its director, Mr Wynne Godley, has developed into a sort of alternative Treasury. The combination of skilled specialist advisers and capable chairmen and members has given its work a coherence and continuity which has been lacking in the case of some other sub-committees. From its initial role in improving the presentation of the annual Expenditure White Papers the General Sub-committee has moved on to query a number of fundamental aspects of government expenditure policy. In 1974 it made a general survey of the field of public expenditure, inflation and the balance of payments, an attempt at an explanation of the problems, terminologies and theories. In 1975 the Sub-committee published weighty criticism of the optimistic Treasury predictions concerning economic growth contained in the Expenditure White Paper, a skirmish which has now become a running battle between the Committee and the Treasury. A Report in 1975 on the expenditure implications of the Budget led to a dispute in the full Committee between Labour members and Conservative monetarists; the sub-committee and the full committee came together again in Session 1975–6 in a Report dealing with 'the missing £4 billion' – the fact that even allowing for inflation and policy changes public expenditure in 1975 was £4 billion up on the total planned in the 1971 White Paper. Treasury control over its own and local authority expenditure was heavily criticized. The most telling Report has been in this current year, when, again prompted by the Cambridge Group, the Sub-committee queried fundamentally the assumptions concerning economic growth which were contained in the 1976 White Paper, criticisms which were treated irresponsibly lightly by the Chief Secretary to the Treasury.

The Defence and External Affairs Sub-committee, despite the equally politically-sensitive area with which it deals, has managed also an impressive cohesion amongst its members. It has been critical of defence cuts, especially as they affect the British contribution to NATO, and has shown a markedly more conservative attitude towards defence policy than some members of the present Government. Perhaps the most critical Report on government policy has been that of the Trade and Industry Sub-committee on the British Leyland rescue operation, which is likely to be repeated by the Report of its current enquiry into the Chrysler Corporation. This Sub-committee, with membership ranging from far-Right to far-Left, has so far achieved almost complete unanimity.

The Expenditure Committee has provided a public platform for debates which have been altogether different from the charades which pass for economic and industrial debates on the floor of the House. Their effect, unfortunately, has been just about the same. The reactions of government have been tediously foreseeable – delay in replying to Reports, refusal to produce information, and, in the case of the Chrysler enquiry, the minister responsible for the policy. The rare debates on Reports have taken place long after the enquiries were held, and have been on take-note motions only – anything else would strain the loyalties of committee members intolerably. Low-keyed administrative and minor policy recommendations are often taken up by the executive, at a level where only officials and not Ministers are involved; the wider and more serious political criticisms are shrugged off. It is probably true to say that the work of the Expenditure Committee to date has not resulted in one penny of state spending being allocated differently, or budgetary policy being modified in any way. This may not be what it was set up to secure, but then questions must arise as to what its role sensibly is.

A senior Clerk of the House of Commons, with special responsibility for the Expenditure Committee, has described it, and select committees generally, apart from those established for a specific *ad hoc* enquiry, such as the wealth tax, as suffering from existential doubts, doubts about what they are for and what they are. That this should be so in the present Parliamentary context is not surprising, except perhaps to the original protagonists of these agencies. When all lip-service has been paid to the desirability of associating back-benchers with the work of government, the fact is that these bodies, no matter how competent, remain a sideshow of no political importance. The Commons as a whole, as at present constituted, and including select committee members except in relation to the committees to which they belong, is jealous of anything which might seem to derogate from the primacy of the House itself and which might seem to qualify the party warfare which is its staple diet. Given the present Parliamentary set-up there would seem no hope whatsoever of realizing the aims of the reformers of the 1950s and 1960s, and establishing select committee work as one of the main, if not the main, mode of Parliamentary activity. This would entail a distancing of the House of Commons from the executive and a diminution in the powers of ministers and party leaders which would only ensue from important alterations in the political structure of Parliament and consequent changes in the conventions which govern its relationships with the executive. This cannot be reconciled with the aims of many reformers of maintaining executive supremacy at all costs. It should now be obvious that so long as government is both in and of Parliament to the extent that it is, only minor and marginal procedural changes are to be expected, and these at the mercy of the government of the day. That this is leading to a crisis of confidence in representative institutions, where minority governments devoid even of a mechanical majority in the House of Commons manipulate every device to get their detailed programme through regardless of well-founded criticism, does not seem to register with the majority of politicians, although there are signs that it is registering with an increasing proportion of the electorate.

The same political constraints which operate in the case of select committees of the House have so far frustrated some of the would-be reformers of the legislative process in Parliament. As was reported in *The Commons in Transition*, most reforms of legislative procedures in the late 1960s were designed to enable government to get its legislation more swiftly, part of an implicit bargain whereby back-benchers would be compensated by more committee opportunities. The main features of reform were simplifications of the stages of most bills. Third Reading is now often taken without debate; non-contentious bills can be taken in committee for Second Reading and even on Report. Agreements on Allocation of Time Orders have also been speeded up. Since then little fresh has happened in this sphere, although much has been proposed. The Procedure Committee enquiry of Session 1970–1 into *The Process of Legislation*, although the most wide-ranging survey of this subject this century, made little progress. It made numerous minor recommendations, many of which were accepted, but where it would now seem that the legislative process in Parliament has been streamlined to the point where the last ounce of mechanical efficiency has been squeezed from it, serious doubts were raised in the Committee about some of its fundamental characteristics. Again they have to do with the deficiencies of the Commons' adversary procedures as applied to legislation; again, those would-be reformers who were most vocal have been reluctant to take their arguments to a conclusion and see their problems as being rooted in the present political structure of the House.

It is now fairly common ground amongst informed critics, including many MPs not necessarily of a reforming turn of mind, that the present totally adversary procedures for the examination in principle and detail of government legislation are deficient. The deficiencies are many, but combine to hinder adequate scrutiny by the Commons of government proposals. Some have to do with the equivocal role of back-bench members of standing committees, but they are mainly connected with the gross disparity of information available to ministers on the one hand and to back-benchers on the other, the government usually holding all the cards. One aspect of this is the degree to which essential information about the background and provenance of government bills is difficult to come by. Both at Second Reading and in committee there is a tendency towards vagueness, generality and secrecy which is advantageous to government and disadvantageous to the Opposition. The view of groping back-benchers facing secretive departments is widely held in the case of legislative proceedings, and is largely justified.

The need on the part of back-bench Members for more information and for more influence for themselves and interested publics lies behind the demand for an inquisitorial stage in the legislative process in Parliament, and in particular for pre-legislation committees of the House of Commons. Yet despite valiant attempts by a few members of the last Procedure enquiry into the process of legislation to argue for extensive use of pre-legislation committees in the case of important and politically sensitive bills, they made no progress. They were pushing too strongly at the bounds of the present political structure of the legislative process and the assumptions of the government/Parliament relationship. The superficially attractive idea of a trade-off, whereby, for example, the Opposition might agree to truncated debate on bills of a minor or administrative character, in exchange for more opportunities to delve in depth into major policy innovations, would meet with suspicion on all sides, fearful of upsetting the equilibrium of the *status quo* to their respective detriments. Even the comparatively minor proposal to allow standing committees more flexibility in their procedure to accommodate an investigative stage cannot be seriously contemplated as a feasible proposition. If the House is to be more involved in the legislative role, this can only come about through a diminution in the executive's power of initiative in this field. It postulates a different type of relationship between government and Parliament, and the development of specialization amongst MPs which given the present shape of the House does not seem feasible.

What else has happened in the field of reform? New

machinery and procedures for the scrutiny of both domestic and European secondary legislation have been devised. Members' accommodation and research facilities have again been improved. Their pay and allowances have been increased, but not enough to keep pace with living costs. It is likely that many MPs are now suffering some financial hardship, victims, with some rough justice, of an inflation which many of them did little to prevent and much to foster. Lacking any parallel development in their functions one can only comment, with John Mackintosh, 'Reforms may make life easier for MPs, but nothing will result from the use of these facilities, the role of the House of Commons will remain unaltered and the public will continue to ignore it.'[2] Parliamentary reform cannot be effective in a vacuum, or any longer within the confines of the present political structure of the House. Without wider reform the present House of Commons is impotent, and no amount of procedural or other tinkering will change this fact.

In all the current disquiet over the public image of Parliament, which recently has produced some high-level and expensive research in both the Study of Parliament Group and the Hansard Society, the dimension that is seldom mentioned is that of power. To contemplate a situation in which the House of Commons could determine some of the decisions of government, produce an effective legislative role and penetrating scrutiny of expenditure which would affect the level and allocation of public resources seems anathema to most reformers. Yet it is power which attracts publicity, guarantees interest and promotes respect. Anything else designed to enhance the public relations of Parliament which misses this essential fact is likely to be merely cosmetic. The reluctance of most Parliamentary reformers to admit this leads to many ingenious theories of the role of Parliament and much misplaced comparative criticism. For example, most reformers who resist any transfer of power from the executive to Parliament usually pray in aid the Congressional experience of the USA, equating it with slow, weak and comparatively unstable government. Bernard Crick puts the classic comparison in his *The Reform of Parliament*. If, as he avers, both American Republicans and Democrats looked ten years ago with envy on 'strong' British national executives and a disciplined Parliamentary legislative machine, it seems incredible to this writer that these sentiments could now still be held with any conviction. They take no account of the interruptions and discontinuities which an over-long adherence to a system of adversary politics has produced, or the loss of real political choice for many voters which the system entails. When one regards the reality of American democracy it is hard to prefer the drab syndicalism which passes for political democracy in Britain today. The famed independence of British MPs, lauded by many commentators, is in any case a myth. Collectively they can offer nothing to compare with Congress's fierce scrutiny of the executive, not surprisingly since government back-benchers act individually as delegates not from their constituents but from the executive branch of government itself. Congressmen acting as representatives of the people who elected them are a far more sensitive index of public opinion than the tightly controlled band of government MPs from a party rejected by 70 per cent of the electorate. Undistracted by considerations of ideology, American government is carried on by a constantly self-renewing and self-adjusting set of majority coalitions across a wide spectrum of political agencies, resulting in a government much more sensitive to fine representative tuning than the British system and marked by a capacity to produce constructive unity rather than chronic division in the governmental process. One does not have to go to the USA for this sort of comparison. All recent reformers seem to have missed the common experience of many West European states, where multi-party legislatures, supporting coalition governments elected on proportional systems, are able, by virtue of the complex political linkages between government and assembly, to impose fairly consistent discipline on their respective executives. If Parliamentary government has traditionally been the pride of Britain, on this criterion it has been honoured more in the breach than the observance, and has been practised more effectively in other West European democracies.

There have been many watershed periods in the life of Parliament when the political impulses which sustain its energies diminish and run out, when Parliamentary politics reach the end of their creativeness and when the only way to renewed vigour is fundamental political reform. Such watersheds were reached in 1832, and in the 1880s when the electoral basis of the present system of Parliamentary politics was laid down. The classic case for single-party majority government was formulated then, at a time when interventionist politics had stringent limits and when the House of Commons could function as the central agency of political accommodation. The major parties then were loose associations with widely shared beliefs about the nature of British society and few ideological barriers. The Commons this century has had to attempt to fit this structure to radically changed national and party circumstances, and to fashion out of it a continuing national consensus. In this it has been only partially successful. Particularly since 1945, when ideological differences between the parties became essentially incapable of resolution, the balance that has been struck has been seldom more than an uneasy compromise, in no case supported by a majority of the electorate and providing the worst possible framework for the development of long-term national policy. It is the contention of this essay that with the decline in support for the two major parties the electoral situation has become unacceptable. It is now doubtful whether either of the main parties is any longer capable of performing the representative function. What is urgent for the country as a whole and Parliament in particular is a realignment of politics to produce a lasting and more compelling consensus. The need for this has recently been recognized by a large and diverse number of commentators: yet many of them, when it comes to the point, actively oppose the electoral reform which could be the catalyst of such a transformation.

The detailed case for electoral change has recently been argued with vigour and insight,[3] although its Parliamentary dimension has not had the attention which it deserves. But at the time of writing the outlook is not encouraging. It is the final disservice of the governing parties that as they become less relevant they grow ever more self-protective, whatever the cost to the nation. Very few politicians are prepared even to examine the consequences of their decline into sectarian minorities. The dream of total power, of perpetual zero-sum politics, persists, manifestly though it ignores public demand. It blocks for the present any chance of changing our institutions to take account of new realities. Even the opportunities presented by the Scottish devolution debate have so far been missed. Designed with the sole aim of saving Labour seats in Scotland, the policy has been cynically opportunistic, desperately trying in all essentials to preserve the *status quo*. The hope is that this will be self-defeating, and that the advance of nationalism will cause government at last to espouse radical constitutional, including electoral, change, from which developments it will prove impossible for Westminster to be insulated. Fundamental political change occurs more through the force of events than the logic of argument, and the SNP might, oddly enough, prove to be the needed catalyst. For this we must wait – much will be clearer by the time this volume is published.

Notes

Chapter 1

1 See particularly, Chapter 11 of his *Reform of Parliament*, Weidenfeld & Nicolson, 2nd edition, 1970.
2 For a detailed proof of the relatively limited extent of amendment of government bills resulting from the Parliamentary process and of the almost total absence of amendments made against the wishes of government, see Professor J. A. G. Griffith's *Parliamentary Scrutiny of Government Bills*, Allen & Unwin, 1974.
3 Erskine May, 18th edition, p. 281; 19th edition. p. 287.
4 Second Report of the Procedure Committee, 1970–1, HC 538, paras. 27–9.

Chapter 2

1 David Butler and Dennis Kavanagh, *The British General Election of February 1974*, Macmillan, 1974, p. 275.
2 David Butler and Dennis Kavanagh, *The British General Election of October 1974*, Macmillan, 1975, p. 208.
3 For a detailed description and discussion of the selection process see Michael Rush, *The Selection of Parliamentary Candidates*, Nelson, 1969.
4 ibid., pp. 61–4 and 222–3.
5 Butler and Kavanagh, *The British General Election of October 1974*, p. 212.
6 David Butler and Anthony King, *The British General Election of 1966*, Macmillan, 1966, p. 207.
7 Anthony Barker and Michael Rush, *The Member of Parliament and his Information*, Allen & Unwin, 1970, figure 45, pp. 380–1.
8 Anthony Barker and Michael Rush, *Political Socialisation in the British House of Commons: A 'Generational' View*, paper presented to ECPR Workshop, Mannheim, April 1973.

9   See Michael Rush and Malcolm Shaw (eds.), *The House of Commons: Services and Facilities*, Allen & Unwin, 1974, and Janet Morgan, *Reinforcing Parliament*, PEP, 1976.

10   *Review Body on Top Salaries: Ministers of the Crown and Members of Parliament*, Cmnd 4836, December 1971, Appendix A, Table 7.

11   Barker and Rush, *The Member of Parliament and his Information*, pp. 383–6, and Barker and Rush, *Political Socialisation . . ., passim.*

Chapter 3

1   But the first few days were occupied with the formalities of choosing a Speaker and with Members taking the oath and affirming. For purposes of comparability these four days are ignored in the table and the Session is regarded as starting with the Queen's Speech on 29 October.

2   198 if the extra four days are included. (See note 1.)

3   For other compilations of how the House has spent its time, see Lord Campion, *An Introduction to the Procedure of the House of Commons*, London, 1958, Appendix III; P. G. Richards, *The Backbenchers*, Faber & Faber, 1972, p. 95; and R. M. Punnett, *British Government Politics*, Heinemann, 1971, p. 222.

4   Richards, op. cit., p. 95. (See notes 1 and 2.)

5   This explains the apparent absence of debates on Europe in 1972–3.

6   S.O. no. 13.

7   Technically this ought perhaps to be included in the government legislation total but it seems more sensible to list it separately to emphasize its place as one of the opportunities for back-benchers to raise topics of their choosing.

8   Occasionally it is more than half an hour; in practice it is frequently a few minutes less.

9   This debate is interesting also in that the first three days were conducted on the basis of a motion for the adjournment of the House, while the last was on a motion (and amendments to it) to 'take note' of the Government's

White Paper on the subject.

10 As with the final day of the Devolution debate of January 1976.

11 In 1975–6 it occupied only five days.

12 Prior to 1939 it was usual for Liberal or other minority party amendments to be called. For details see *Second Report from the Select Committee on Procedure 1974–5*, HC 372, Annex.

13 ibid., para. 4.

14 This, of course, does not include the time spent debating Finance Bills on the floor of the House: that is subsumed under the government legislation heading.

15 For the establishment of this Committee see HC Debs 853, cols. 680–95.

16 For more discussion of this see Chapter 10.

17 For a discussion of some of the problems see M. Ryan and P. Isaacson, 'Parliament and the European Communities', *Parliamentary Affairs*, Vol. XXVIII, pp. 199–215.

18 For an analysis of the content of adjournment debates see V. Herman, 'Adjournment Debates in the House of Commons', *Parliamentary Affairs*, Vol. XXVI, pp. 92–104.

19 The Speaker can use it as a consolation prize for an unsuccessful S.O. No. 9 applicant: e.g. on 8 May 1975 he chose a topic on which he had declined to allow an S.O. No. 9 debate just a week earlier.

20 See *Second Report from the Select Committee on Procedure 1966–7*, HC 282, para. 5.

21 The change did not forbid the giving of reasons – Speakers could give them if they wished – but since then they seem to have acted as though they were forbidden to do so.

22 Others might count the 1974–5 total slightly differently: three applications included here were not technically refused by the Speaker but were ruled out of order by him: for infringing the rules of notice or, in one case, because the matter was *sub judice*.

23 HC Debs 852, col. 1500.

24 See Chapter 6.

25 See p. 113.

26 The suggestion for skeletal legislation is but the latest response to this problem.

27 The major exception to this was the rather unhappy experiment with morning sittings in the late 1960s. Significantly they were essentially hangovers from previous sittings rather than the start of new sittings. The House has not properly faced up to the prospect of beginning its work at a less gentlemanly hour than 2.30 p.m.

28 *Fourth Report from the Select Committee on Procedure 1974–5*, HC 671, para. 23.

29 A. L. Lowell, *The Government of England*, New York, 1920, first published 1908, Vol. 1, p. 314.

30 Even when a back-bencher seems content to make a career as a vigorous Select Committee chairman he may be tempted by a government post as, for example, Mr Pat Duffy in 1976.

31 For a good statement of this point of view see J. Mendelson, 'The Chamber as the Centre of Parliamentary Scrutiny' in A. Morris (ed.), *The Growth of Parliamentary Scrutiny by Committee*, Pergamon, 1970, pp. 109–24.

Chapter 4

1 HC 539, 1966–7.

2 Bernard Crick, *The Reform of Parliament*, Weidenfeld & Nicolson, 2nd edition, 1968, p. 226.

3 HC 538, 1970–1. For this writer's views on the Report and the response to it see *Modern Law Review*, Vol. 35, 1972, pp. 289–94.

4 Cmnd 6053 of 1975. For this writer's views on the Report see *Political Quarterly*, Vol. 46, 1975, pp. 443–6.

5 Hansard, Vol. 904, cols. 964–78.

6 See *The Process of Legislation*, op. cit., p. 267. This estimate takes no account of time spent on delegated legislation or on private legislation or (since the Report was published) European secondary legislation. And it

excludes the vast amount of legislative business trans-
acted off the floor of the House.

7 S. A. Walkland, *The Legislative Process in Great
Britain*, Allen & Unwin, 1968, p. 20.

8 ibid., p. 71.

9 See John P. Mackintosh, 'The House of Commons and
Taxation', *Political Quarterly*, Vol. 42, 1971, pp. 75–86;
and this writer's remarks on the Immigration Bill, *post*.

10 P. Bachrach and M. S. Baratz, 'Two Faces of Power',
American Political Science Review, Vol. 56, 1966, pp.
947–52.

11 It is no coincidence that the period chosen here is the
same as that in respect of which this writer has collaborated with Dr Ivor Burton in producing sessional surveys
of public bill legislation, published in successive issues
of *Parliamentary Affairs*. This seems an appropriate
place to acknowledge my debt in writing this essay to our
collaborative work.

12 Conversely, the passing of an Act, for example the Child
Benefit Act 1975, does not always mark the successful
realization of a policy objective. And some Acts (the
Industrial Relations Act 1971, *post* is a spectacular
example) although implemented, simply do not work as
intended.

13 The general issue of amendment is discussed in detail by
J. A. G. Griffith, *Parliamentary Scrutiny of Government
Bills*, Allen & Unwin, 1974, *passim*.

14 V. Herman has usefully taken this approach one step
further by using the promise in the Queen's Speeches at
the beginning of each Session as a measure of intended
'input': 'What Governments Say and What Governments Do: An Analysis of Post-War Queen's Speeches',
Parliamentary Affairs, Vol. XXVIII, 1974–5, pp. 22–30.
Of course, we can only guess at the number of prospective and intended inputs which are killed or mutilated at
an earlier and less visible stage.

15 For a fuller account see Ivor Burton and Gavin Drewry,
'Public Legislation: A Survey of the Session 1970–1',
Parliamentary Affairs, Vol. XXV, 1972, pp. 129–34.

16 ibid., pp. 134–7. See also Hannen Rose, 'The Immigration Act 1971: A Case-Study in the Work of Parliament', *Parliamentary Affairs*, Vol. XXVI, 1972–3, pp. 69–91.

17 See Burton and Drewry, '1971–2 Legislation Survey', *Parliamentary Affairs*, Vol. XXVI, 1973, pp. 149–53.

18 See Philip Norton, *Dissension in the House of Commons*, 1975, pp. 404 ff. Norton also notes, at p. 610, that there was a remarkably high level of cross voting by Conservative MPs throughout the 1970–4 Parliament.

19 See Burton and Drewry, '1971–2 Legislation Survey', op. cit., pp. 155–9.

20 See Burton and Drewry, '1974 Legislation Survey', *Parliamentary Affairs*, Vol. XXIX, 1976, pp. 155–89.

21 A procedure which avoids the need for sick or disabled MPs to be physically present in the division lobbies to have their votes received.

22 It is now the practice for government to even out the work-loads of the two Houses by introducing at least one or two of its major bills into the Lords each Session (quite apart from the increasing number of consolidation bills, which always begin in the Lords, though scrutiny takes place in joint committee). Thus, the National Health Services Reorganization Bill, 1972–3, was started in the Lords. Sometimes (though rarely) a really controversial measure will begin in the upper House, as with the Galleries (Admissions Charges) Bill in 1971–2.

23 The case turned ultimately on whether a vessel being built at a shipyard not included in the Bill was in fact an oil rig or a ship.

24 op. cit., para. 42.

25 HL 188, HC 407, 1972–3. For a general view of the Brooke Committee's work see J. M. Grey, 'Delegated Legislation in the United Kingdom Parliament: The Work of the Brooke Committee', *The Table*, Vol. XLII, 1974, pp. 47–60.

26 The concept is explained and discussed in J. Blondel *et al.*, 'Legislative Behaviour: Some Steps towards a Cross-National Measurement', *Government and Opposi-*

tion, Vol. 5, 1969–70, pp. 67–85.

27   Hansard, Vol. 904, col. 984.

28   See note 11.

29   The original definition of the distinction, subsequently elaborated upon in successive annual surveys of legislation (see note 11), can be found in the first (1968–9) survey, *Parliamentary Affairs*, Vol. XXIII, 1970, pp. 161–2. Alternative methods of classifying bills, and some of their practical implications for reform, are discussed by this writer in 'Reform of the Legislative Process: Some Neglected Questions', *Parliamentary Affairs*, Vol. XXV, 1972, pp. 286–302.

30   Though an administration bill is by no means always controversial.

Chapter 5

1   I am grateful to George Allen & Unwin and Political and Economic Planning for allowing me to reproduce in this chapter some passages from my *Parliamentary Scrutiny of Government Bills*, 1975.

2   The position on private Members' bills is different and requires separate analysis.

3   For fuller explanation of such phrases see my *Parliamentary Scrutiny of Government Bills*.

4   HC 538, 1970–1, Appendix 1, para. 89.

5   *The Diaries of a Cabinet Minister*, Vol. 1, p. 561.

Chapter 6

1   See J. A. G. Griffith, *Parliamentary Scrutiny of Government Bills*, for a detailed examination of how far government bills are amended.

2   The 1967 Act sponsored by Leo Abse to amend the law on homosexual offences was introduced under this Standing Order and given government time. Such cases are rare. They will only occur when ministers wish an issue to be brought before Parliament but do not care to take the initiative themselves.

3   HC Debs 480, col. 976.

4   In November 1969, Robin Maxwell-Hyslop (Con., Tiver-

ton) stayed at the Commons overnight to be first in the queue when the Public Bill Office opened to receive Ten-minute Rule Bills for the 1969–70 Session. He handed in seventy notices on behalf of himself and other Con-servative Members to pre-empt all the time available under SO No. 13 for the whole Session. After protests in the Chamber, Opposition leaders intervened and it was agreed that fourteen days should be left vacant for the use of Labour Members. This is a good example of how a smart trick can fail because it gives general offence to the House. HC Debs 792, cols 639–50.

5   HC Debs 873, col. 851.

6   This incident caused a Parliamentary storm. It was alleged that Government supporters had stayed outside the Chamber to obstruct the measure, although they were not willing to oppose it. HC Debs 1884, cols. 2196–2208. Subsequently the Bill was allowed to pass.

7   For full discussion see Peter G. Richards, *Parliament and Conscience*, Allen & Unwin, 1970.

8   HC Debs 887, col. 887. The Bill was given an un-opposed second reading and subsequently became law.

9   Macdonald, 1973.

10   ibid., pp. 193–9. Churchill introduced a successful Bill which made minor changes in the law of motor insurance.

11   HC Debs 835, col. 1015.

12   HC Debs 810, col. 1547.

13   *Procedure on Public Business, Special Report*, Q 1530; 1930–1 (161), viii.

14   ibid., Q 718.

15   *Parliament*, Cambridge University Press, 2nd edition, 1957, p. 373.

16   E.g. the article by Ronald Butt in *The Times*, 23 October 1969.

17   Cmnd 247, 1956–7.

18   HC Debs 851, col. 996.

19   Conservative Member for Kidderminster 1950–64 and for Worcestershire South 1966–73.

20   A. Barker and M. Rush, *The Member of Parliament and his Information*, Allen & Unwin, 1970, p. 52, *et seq.*

Chapter 7

1   Paul Einzig, *The Power of the Purse*, London 1959. Andrew Hill and Anthony Whichelow, *What's Wrong with Parliament?*, Penguin, 1964. Hill and Whichelow claim that 'the control of the Nation's money is at the heart of our Parliamentary system', p. 15.

2   If a motion to reduce an estimate is carried, the government regards this as a rejection of that estimate.

3   John Mackintosh, 'The House of Commons and Taxation', *Political Quarterly*, Vol. XLII, 1971. Also David Millar, 'Parliamentary Control of Taxation in Britain', in David Coombes *et al.*, *The Power of the Purse: The Role of European Parliaments in Budgetary Decisions*, Allen & Unwin, PEP, 1976.

4   This is a common problem in many countries. See David Coombes *et al.*, op. cit.

5   Select Committee on Public Expenditure, 1807.

6   A. H. Hanson, 'The House of Commons and Finance', in A. H. Hanson and Bernard Crick (eds.), *The Commons in Transition*, Fontana, 1970. Also Gordon Reid, *The Politics of Financial Control*, Hutchinson, 1966.

7   See especially the opening speech by the Liberal economic spokesman, John Pardoe, HC Debs, 22 March 1976. This topic was selected by the Liberals who formed part of the Opposition.

8   HC Debs, 9 April 1976, col. 811.

9   See especially the speeches by John Cartwright (Woolwich East) and David Weitzman (Hackney North and Stoke Newington). These Members represent areas with serious housing shortages and great pressure on the social services.

10   By 1975–6 the growth of public spending had run far ahead of the ability and willingness of taxpayers to support it. About 20 per cent of all public expenditure in these years was financed from borrowing from the domestic and foreign money markets. To cover such a large Public Sector Borrowing Requirement (PSBR) by raising income tax would require a standard rate of about 65p.

11   *Public Expenditure to 1979–80*, Cmnd 6393.

12   The fullest analyses (but of social policy only) are pro-
     vided by the Centre for Social Policy. Its publications
     include: *Social Policy and Public Expenditure 1974*,
     Rudolf Klein (ed.); and *Social Policy and Public
     Expenditure*, Rudolf Klein (ed.).

13   HC Debs, 10 March 1976, col. 547.

14   ibid., col. 550.

15   ibid., col. 506.

16   In 1976 the Budget statement was also about the Pay
     Policy.

17   HC Debs, 10 March 1976, col. 512.

18   John Pardoe, HC Debs, 22 March 1976. Also C. Sand-
     ford and A. Robinson, 'Public Expenditure', *The Banker*,
     November 1975, p. 1255.

19   HC Debs, 29 April 1976 written answer.

20   HC Debs, 4 May 1976 written answer.

21   *Fourth Report of the Public Accounts Committee*,
     1974–5, HC 502.

22   ibid.

23   This type of enquiry is undertaken by the General Sub-
     Committee. See *Public Expenditure to 1979–80*, op. cit.

24   A number of sub-committees have undertaken this type
     of enquiry. Reports include: *Employment Services and
     Training*, HC 214, 1972–3; *Accident and Emergency
     Services*, HC 115, 1973–4; *Further and Higher Educa-
     tion*, HC 48, Vols 1 and 2, 1972–3; *Urban Transport
     Planning*, HC 57, Vols 1, 2 and 3, 1972–3.

25   The work of the Defence and External Affairs Sub-
     Committee is largely of this nature. See, for example,
     Defence Cuts, HC 308, 1974, and *The Defence Review
     Proposals*, HC 259, 1974–5. The Education and Arts
     Sub-Committee has investigated *Decision-Making in the
     DES* (Report pending).

26   *Diplomatic Manpower and Property Overseas*, HC 473,
     1974–5, and *The Motor Vehicle Industry*, HC 617 (188),
     1974–5.

27   *Wages and Conditions of African Workers Employed by
     British Firms in South Africa*, HC 116, 1973–4.

28 The civil service provides the greatest single source of witnesses to the Expenditure Committee. See *Specialist Committees in the British Parliament: The Experiences of a Decade*, by members of the Study of Parliament Group, PEP, Vol. XLII, No. 564, June 1976, p. 26, table 3.

29 ibid., pp. 28–31.

Chapter 8

1 This paper, while based on *Questions in Parliament*, Oxford, 1962, by Sir Norman Chester and N. Bowring, takes account of changes and developments since then.

2 Altered in 1904 first to No. 51 and then to No. 45.

3 Strangely enough, it is not mentioned in Erskine May until the 19th (1976) edition.

4 Question days were Monday, Tuesday, Thursday and Friday; Wednesday replaced Friday in 1902.

5 Nevertheless, Members will occasionally put down starred Questions for answer on a day when the minister concerned is not on the list, even putting them down to the Prime Minister for answer on Monday or Wednesday.

6 On 3 February 1976 the whole of Question Time was lost in the proceedings for the resignation of the Speaker and the election of his successor. The 46 starred Questions about Education and Science were converted into W Questions. This meant that during the first four months of 1976 Members had only two, instead of three, real chances to obtain answers in the Chamber from the ministers responsible for Education and Science.

Chapter 9

1 See this writer's 'Select Committees as Tools of Parliamentary Reform', in *The Commons in Transition*, Fontana, 1970, especially pp. 241–8.

2 ibid., p. 244.

3 See the *Sessional Returns for Select Committees*. The figures quoted do not, of course, include multiple membership of committees by a substantial number of MPs. They also include domestic and procedural committees.

4   *The 13th Report of the Expenditure Committee 1974–5*,
    HC 616, on new towns was accompanied by 4 volumes
    of evidence; the 14th Report from the same committee
    in the same session on the Motor Vehicle Industry was
    backed up by 3 volumes of evidence; the Science and
    Technology Committee's 1970–1 Report on Prospects
    for the UK Computer Industry in the 1970s was sup-
    ported by two large volumes of evidence. These, not
    untypical, examples underline the scale of the information
    demands now imposed by several select committees.

5   *The Report of the Select Committee on Procedure
    1968–9 on Scrutiny of Public Expenditure* remains the
    last broad treatment of how the select committee struc-
    ture should develop. In essentials, its scheme for an
    Expenditure Committee was adopted by Mr Heath's
    Government in late 1970.

6   This is particularly true of the Race Relations and
    Immigration Committee which has reported on Housing,
    Education and Employment, all topics involving other
    departments than the Home Office.

7   The distinction between financial supervision and
    scrutiny of policy implementation is anyway fraught with
    difficulty and in some degree unreal. And though one
    may for some purpose regard the European Secondary
    Legislation etc. Committee as one of administrative
    contrôle, it also examines contentious policy proposals.

8   A very clear case of party controversy taking over was
    in the course of the enquiry into private practice in the
    NHS by this Sub-Committee in 1971–2 (NHS Facilities
    for Private Patients, HC 172, 1971–2). The Employ-
    ment and Social Services Sub-Committee split on
    straight party lines on the major issues.

9   Committee reports and volumes of evidence show print-
    ing costs (which nowadays can run to £6000 or more for
    a fat volume). But no attempt has ever been made to cost
    an enquiry fully – i.e. wage and salary costs, travelling,
    etc.

10 I am very much indebted to Mr David Pring, Clerk of
    Committees, for advice and information on administra-

tive support for select committees.

11 In the five years 1970–5 turnover of membership on the Science and Technology Committee averaged two per year, on the Committee for the Parliamentary Commission for Administration 2·5 (though only one per year 1970–3), on the Nationalized Industries Committee 4·5 per year, on the Public Accounts Committee seven per year (very high), and on the General Sub-Committee of the Expenditure Committee five. Bearing in mind the small size of most committees and sub-committees, these proportions are substantial.

12 The number of addresses varies from committee to committee: the Race Relations and Immigration Committee obviously has more addresses than the Committee on the PCA.

13 Select Committee on Science and Technology, *1st Special Report 1971–2*, HC 181, text of a letter from Mr Airey Neave (Chairman) to Mr E. Heath.

14 There is also the complicating factor of state investment in or acquisition of private companies, as well as the role of the National Enterprise Board set up in 1975. It appears that any Parliamentary supervision of these developments will fall to the Expenditure Committee rather than to the Nationalized Industries Committee. The PAC also has authority to scrutinize the accounts of the NEB, though the extent of the C and AG's power is in doubt.

15 The European Secondary Legislation etc. Committee presents many interesting problems and undoubtedly it has a scrutiny task which is more difficult than that of other committees. Unfortunately, further discussion must be omitted.

16 See note 11 for some examples.

17 The reference here is, of course, to select committees only.

18 One day per year is still allocated to PAC reports and two to Expenditure Committee reports. For other committees it is very much a matter of luck whether a debate can be secured and the odds are against it. Even

individual Sub-committees of the Expenditure Committee must expect rare attention on the floor. Between 1971 and 1974 only one report out of seventeen published by the Defence and External Affairs Sub-committee of the Expenditure Committee was debated. I owe this point to a valuable forthcoming article in *Public Administration*, 'Parliament and Defence Affairs: The Defence Sub-Committee of the Expenditure Committee', by M. Hyder, University College, Aberystwyth. This example illustrates the neglect referred to above, though in my view there are also perfectly straightforward reasons for this. The conception of the House being regularly fed with learned select committee Reports, and then engaging in well-informed debate of them has always belonged to the ivory tower.

19 The party Whips do, however, exert a powerful influence on nominations to select committees.

20 This opinion echoes that expressed ten years ago in my book, *Parliament and Administration: The Estimates Committee 1945–65*, Allen & Unwin, 1966. I trust that I do not reveal myself as a Bourbon by continuing to subscribe to it.

21 It is hard to know whether to laugh or cry over the dialogue of the deaf which took place between the Trade and Industry Sub-committee of the Expenditure Committee and Mr Reg Birch and his colleagues in the course of the enquiry into the motor vehicle industry 1974–5.

22 The 1974–5 Select Committee on a Wealth Tax provides an interesting example of how a committee failed even to present a proper Report (merely reporting its failure to agree) largely owing to internal party divisions. Despite this, it published several valuable alternative draft reports and that of the Chairman showed how much bipartisan agreement had been reached. For this reason a Chancellor is unlikely to ignore the findings should he decide to legislate on the matter.

23 It is worth recalling that the Wilson Government's proposals for an elected Scottish Assembly with legislative

powers foresaw permanent legislative committees in the Assembly and *not* something like the Westminster select committees.

24 There is indeed a tradition reaching back into the last century that the House of Commons does refer taxation issues to select committees: there have been many examples of this.

Chapter 10

1 I am most grateful to officials of the House of Commons and the House of Lords for providing a great deal of valuable information and comment on the subject of this article. The views expressed are entirely my own.

2 The author is chairman of a working party, set up by the Hansard Society as part of a programme financed by the Ford Foundation, enquiring into 'The Effects on British Representative Institutions of Membership of the European Community'. The working party hopes to publish its report in the second half of 1976.

3 Although *directives* may be put into effect by means of Parliament passing enabling legislation, in practice there is usually little room for manœuvre within the terms of a *directive*. Parliament's failure to adopt 'form and methods' is not accepted as an excuse for failing to obey a *directive*.

4 Treaty establishing the European Economic Community, articles 138, 201, 235, 236, 237.

5 ibid., article 138.

6 Second Report from The Select Committee on European Community Secondary Legislation, session 1972–3, 25 October 1973. HC 463, I, especially paras. 33–7, 60–79.

7 The Committee's terms of reference, however, do not direct it to consider the merits of particular proposals, but 'to consider draft proposals by the Commission . . . for secondary legislation and other documents published by the Commission for submission to the Council of Ministers, and to report their opinion as to whether such proposals or other documents raise questions of legal or political importance, to give reasons for their opinion,

to report what matters of principle or policy may be affected thereby, and to what extent they may affect the law of the United Kingdom, and to make recommendations for the further consideration of such proposals and other documents by the House'.

8   The explanatory memoranda are made available along with copies of the document concerned for all Members at the Vote Office.

9   Based on the proposals of a Select Committee chaired by Lord Maybray-King (Second Report by the Select Committee on Procedures for Scrutiny of Proposals for European Instruments, 25 July 1973, HL 194). This Committee had initially suggested a joint committee of both Houses.

10 Its terms of reference are: 'To consider Community proposals, whether in draft or otherwise, to obtain all necessary information about them, and to make reports on those which, in the opinion of the Committee, raise important questions of policy or principle, and on other questions to which the Committee consider that the special attention of the House should be drawn.' The Committee is not, therefore, confined to draft secondary legislation and may consider merits.

11 The Committee has become an important authority on the legal aspects of Community business through the work of its sub-committee on Law assisted by a Legal Adviser. The process of sifting documents is performed mainly by the Chairman of the Committee, who is salaried and treated as officer of the House.

12 First Special Report, session 1974–5, 26 November 1974, HC 46; Second Special Report, session 1974–5, 25 February 1975, HC 234; First Special Report, session 1975–6, 15 March and 28 April 1976, HC 336 and 53, v.

13 First Report, session 1974–5, 25 March 1975, HC 294.

14 HC Debates (1974–5), 1014, cc. 28–107.

15 This understanding followed from the so-called 'Luxembourg Agreement' in January 1966, when under pressure from the French government, the other governments

agreed to continue discussion in the Council until unanimous agreement could be reached when any matter affecting a state's 'vital national interest' was in question. However, the treaties provide for most decisions to be made by a qualified majority vote in the Council.

16 This undertaking was first given on 2 May 1974 (HC Debs, 1974, vol. 872, col. 525 w.) and has been repeated since.

17 No proposal goes to the Council without having been considered first by the Committee of Permanent Representatives, consisting of the governments' official representatives to the Community with ambassadorial rank. That Committee itself usually submits new proposals to a working party of national officials for preliminary negotiation.

18 HC Debs, 1975–6, vol. 911, 19 May 1976, cols. 1561–1620. If the Minister had not accepted the proposal, the decision on agricultural prices, aspects of which were highly favourable to British farmers, would not have been taken.

19 HC Debs, 1974–5, vol. 1014, cols. 37–8.

20 HC 336–53, v, 1974–5, para. 25.

21 ibid., para. 21. This was before the 'skimmed milk powder' affair.

22 HC 294, 1974–5, paras. 13–16. A debate can now be held over for the next sitting if Mr Speaker feels that the time for closure pre-empts adequate debate.

23 Submission to a standing committee is by a motion of the House, and twenty Members can defeat such a motion (as happened on 10 February 1976, to keep treatment of documents on nuclear safety on the floor: HC Debs, 1975–6, vol. 905, cols. 247–8). The motion to take note of a document is taken on the floor of the House usually on the day following the debate in standing committee, which is probably too short a time for Members to consider the Official Report of debate in committee and table amendments, see HC 336–53, v, 1975–6, para. 30. The possibility of giving further consideration to documents in standing committee has

probably increased the number of documents recommended by the Scrutiny Committee for further consideration.

24   Opposition amendments were accepted by the Government on three occasions in the first half of 1976: on the farm price review, 12 February; on nuclear safety, on 23 February; and on energy, 17 March.

25   HC Debs, 1974–5, vol. 1014, cols. 101–7. Even Mr Enoch Powell criticized the Government's defence of keeping matters on the floor.

26   In Denmark a similar reaction also led to stringent parliamentary controls, but mainly by means of taking major issues in committee, see John Fitzmaurice, 'National Parliaments and Community policy-making' in *Parliamentary Affairs*, Summer 1976.

27   Commission officials have told me that British ministers and official representatives are frequently embarrassed by the need to delay Community business on the grounds of the Government's undertaking to hold debates in Parliament before a Council decision. This has put them at a negotiating disadvantage. One suspects that the need for prior Parliamentary consideration is often invoked by officials as an excuse for delaying decisions which are undesirable on other grounds.

28   See, for example, HC 463, I, 1972–3, paras. 9–11.

29   HC 336–53, iv, 1975–6, paras. 10–11.

30   See pp. 214–15.

31   European Parliament, 'Elections to the European Parliament by direct universal suffrage', January 1975.

32   HC 336–53, v, 1975–6, pp. 149–94.

33   See, for example, HL Debs, 11 March 1976, vol. 368, cols. 1413–21, and HC Debs, 1975–6, vol. 911, cols. 1595–1601.

Chapter 11

1   Mr Lionel Cohen has examined the practice of Members in his article 'The Parliamentary Commissioner and the "MP Filter"', 1972, *Public Law*, 204.

2   See HC 334, pp. 69, 71.

3 Or cf. Case C111/195/G. 3rd Report 1972–3, HC 178, p. 43, where it was alleged that the Secretary of State for the Environment 'did not give adequate and proper consideration to all the issues involved' (Oxford School case). In Case C.173/G, HC 178, 1972–3, p. 63, the allegation was that the complainant's arguments had been heard but not 'heeded'.

4 HC 334, p. 13.

5 Cf. HC 406, 1972–3, p. 103, Case C 419/9 (Refusal to compensate for expenses in travelling to hospital).

6 For a case in which the Commissioner does appear to have criticized the merits of a departmental review of its rule see HC 406, 1972–3, p. 163 (a refusal to reimburse a taxpayer for exceptional expenses incurred through an error made by the Inland Revenue).

7 HC 490.

8 See the comments of the Select Committee on this case (HC 379, 1972–3). They suggest that 'whatever the technical position . . . a British subject, wherever resident, has a proper expectation that a Government Department will handle his or her correspondence efficiently' (p. vii).

9 See Case C 412/D. 4th Report 1971–2, HC 490, p. 194. (Failure of a Registrar to attend a marriage ceremony.)

10 See *The Commons in Transition*, 1970, pp. 122–7.

11 See HC 54 (1967–8). Also chapter 11 of R. Gregory and P. Hutchison, *The Parliamentary Ombudsman* (1975).

12 HC 316 (1968–9) made under Section 10(4) of the 1967 Act.

13 HC 116 (1971–2), p. 9.

14 See cases C.283/G. and C.431/G. in the 4th Report for 1972–3, HC 290 (1972–3) at pp. 65, 72 and 82. On the notion of 'maladministration' see Gregory and Hutchison op. cit. Chapter 8; Marshall 'Maladministration' [1973] *Public Law*; and K. C. Wheare, *Maladministration and its Remedies* (1973), Chapter 1.

18 In August 1972 the Commissioner initiated the practice of publishing all his case reports in quarterly volumes. Analytically speaking the cases are laid out so as to

secure maximum inconvenience to the user. Cases in which there are findings of maladministration are not grouped together; nor is there any guide or key to the cases to identify those in which such findings appear. The cases are also 'anonymized'. It is not clear whether the heavy responsibility for the invention of this practice rests upon Sir Alan Marre or Sir Edmund Compton.

16   HC Deb. 529 (1974–5).
17   *Congreve* v *Home Office* [1976] 2 WLR 291.
18   HC 680 (1974–5), p. 14.
19   In 1967, in the Parliamentary debate on the 1967 Act, Mr Crossman had said that maladministration might encompass 'bias, neglect, delay, incompetence, ineptitude, perversity, turpitude, arbitrariness and so on', 734 HC Deb. 5s. col. 51 (1966).
20   The New Zealand Parliamentary Commissioner Act provides for certification by the Attorney-General that information should not be disclosed on the ground of its involving disclosure of Cabinet or Cabinet Committee proceedings. (Other grounds for such certification are prejudice to security, defence, New Zealand's international relations or the investigation or detection of crimes.)
21   Mr Leon Brittan, MP, *The Times*, 25 February 1976.

Chapter 12

1   See Chapter 7.
2   Professor John Mackintosh, on an earlier round of similar reforms. See his *The British Cabinet*, p. 499, note 46.
3   See especially S. E. Finer (ed.), *Adversary Politics and Electoral Reform*, Anthony Wigram, 1975.

Notes on Contributors

The Study of Parliament Group

The Study of Parliament Group was established in 1964. Membership is confined to senior members of universities working specifically in the Parliamentary field and officers (or ex-officers) of both Houses of Parliament and is restricted to about 50. The Group has on several occasions prepared evidence for Select Committees on Procedure. It has undertaken original studies of many Parliamentary matters and has published several books and pamphlets in this field. An earlier collection of essays by members of the Group, entitled *The Commons in Transition*, was published by Fontana Books in 1970.

R. L. Borthwick is lecturer in Politics at the University of Leicester. He has also taught in the USA. He has contributed articles on Parliamentary organization to *Parliamentary Affairs*, etc.

Sir Norman Chester has been Warden of Nuffield College, Oxford, since 1954. His publications include *Control of Passenger Transport* (1936), *Central and Local Government: Financial and Administrative Arrangements* (1951), *Lessons of the British War Economy* (Editor 1951), *The Organisation of British Central Government* 1945–51 (Editor 1957), *Questions in Parliament* (with Nona Bowring) (1962), *The Nationalisation of British Industry* (1975). He was Editor of *Public Administration*, 1943–66, and is a past-President of both the International Political Science Association and the UK Political Studies Association. He is currently President of the Study of Parliament Group.

David Coombes is currently directing the Hansard Society's programme on *The Future of Parliamentary Institutions in*

Europe, and is Visiting Professor of Politics, Birkbeck College, University of London. He was formerly Professor of European Studies at Loughborough University, and is the author of *The Member of Parliament and the Administration*; *Politics and Bureaucracy in the European Community*; *State Enterprise – Business or Politics*; *The Power of the Purse in the European Community*.

Gavin Drewry is Lecturer in Government at Bedford College, University of London. His main publications are *Final Appeal* (co-author 1972), *Law, Justice and Politics* (1975), *Law and Morality* (co-editor 1976). He is a regular contributor of articles to legal and political journals, and is currently researching in the field of the legislative process.

J. A. G. Griffith is Professor of Public Law in the University of London and editor of *Public Law*. He is the Honorary Secretary of the Council for Academic Freedom and Democracy. His publications include *Principles of Administrative Law* and *A Casebook of Administrative Law* (both with H. Street); *Central Departments and Local Authorities*; *Parliamentary Scrutiny of Government Bills*; *Government and Law* (with T. C. Hartley). He is currently preparing *Politics of the Judiciary*.

Nevil Johnson has been Nuffield Reader in the Comparative Study of Institutions at Oxford since 1969, and is a Fellow of Nuffield College. Before holding academic posts in the Universities of Nottingham and Warwick he spent some years as an administrator in Whitehall. He is the author of *Parliament and Administration: The Estimates Committee 1945–65* (1966), *Government in the Federal Republic of Germany* (1974), as well as of numerous articles, reports and memoranda in the fields of government, public administration, and the comparative analysis of political institutions. He has been Hon. Editor of *Public Administration* since 1967 and became a member of the Study of Parliament Group shortly after its founding.

Geoffrey Marshall is Fellow and Tutor in Politics, Queen's College, Oxford. He has published *Parliamentary Sovereignty and the Commonwealth* (1957), *Some Problems of the Constitution* (with G. Moodie, 1959), *Police and Government* (1965), *Constitutional Theory* (1971).

P. G. Richards has been on the staff of the University of Southampton since 1946, and has been Professor of British Government since 1969. He has published *Patronage in British Government* (1963), *Parliament and Foreign Affairs* (1967), *Parliament and Conscience* (1971), *The Reformed Local Government System* (1973), *The Backbenchers* (1972). He has been Chairman of the Study of Parliament Group.

Ann Robinson is a graduate of the Universities of Oxford and McGill, and has taught at the Universities of Durham, Bristol and Bath. She is currently lecturer in Politics at University College, Cardiff. She has written numerous articles on public expenditure and is currently researching in the field of taxation policy-making in the UK.

Michael Rush is Lecturer in Politics at the University of Exeter and has taught at Universities in Canada. He has published *The Selection of Parliamentary Candidates* (1969), *Parliament and the Public* (1976). He is also the co-author of *The Member of Parliament and his Information* (1970) and *The Introduction to Political Sociology* (1971). He was joint-editor and contributor to *The House of Commons; Services and Facilities* (1974). He is currently joint honorary secretary to the Study of Parliament Group.

Michael Ryle is a Deputy Principal Clerk in the House of Commons, where he has served in the Clerk's Department since 1951. He has written, lectured and broadcast on many aspects of Parliamentary practice and procedure. He was a founder member of the Study of Parliament Group and has been Chairman of the Group since 1975.

S. A. Walkland has been Senior Lecturer in Politics at the University of Sheffield since 1965. He has published *The Legislative Process in Great Britain* (1968) and numerous articles and sections of books on Parliamentary government in Britain. He has been vice-Chairman of the Study of Parliament Group since 1975.

Index

The Modern Britain Series
Readers in Sociology

This original series is designed to show how the sociologist analyses and describes the main features of a complex, modern, industrial society. Each book contains extracts by British and foreign sociologists, and each chapter has a short introduction by the editors which discusses the main issues and problems and links the extracts together. This series is of great value to all those interested in contemporary society, and not only those engaged in formal courses.

The general editors of the series are Eric Butterworth, Reader in Community Studies at York University, and David Weir, Lecturer in Sociology at the Manchester Business School.

The Sociology of Modern Britain
Edited by Eric Butterworth & David Weir

This work introduces students to the study of their own society. The chapters cover the main institutional areas of contemporary Britain – the family, community, work, class and power. The book also includes a chapter on the values implicit in British society, around which much political and social conflict is inevitably centred.

Social Problems of Modern Britain
Edited by Eric Butterworth & David Weir

This book discusses such problems as inadequate housing, environmental depreciation, poverty, immigration, racial discrimination, crime, deviant behaviour and sets them in the context of the social attitudes and perspectives of the 'social problem' groups themselves.

Men and Work in Modern Britain
Edited by David Weir

Readings on organisational types, occupations and social status, recruitment, selection and training, career patterns, ideologies and values, deviance, leisure and unemployment, linked by critical editorial introductions.

Understanding American Politics

R. V. Denenberg

In this concise guide to American politics, R. V. Denenberg offers an up-to-the-minute account of the workings, functions and relations of American institutions, from the Constitution and the Presidency, through Congress and the Supreme Court, to the bureaucracy and the mass media.

'Three cheers . . . for this brief, lucid, accurate and exceedingly informative study of a difficult and important subject.'
Hugh Brogan, *New Society*

'. . . a splendid introduction which avoids the patronizing tone that experts often assume when describing an unfamiliar political system, and also succeeds in being humorous without cynicism – not always an easy task.' *Sunday Telegraph*

'. . . a quick, illuminating and often edgy account of some of the things in danger of falling apart.' Martin Hillman, *Tribune*

Unended Quest: An Intellectual Autobiography

Karl Popper

Internationally hailed as one of the most outstanding philosophers writing at present – on politics, on science, on human knowledge, on society – this unique book is Sir Karl Popper's own account of his life and of the development of his ideas. In fascinating detail he traces the genesis and formulation of his major works: *The Open Society and Its Enemies, The Logic of Scientific Discovery, The Poverty of Historicism, Objective Knowledge,* and *Conjectures and Refutations: The Growth of Scientific Knowledge.*

'. . . a splendid introduction to the man and his ideas.'
Martin Gardner, *The New Leader*

'. . . a remarkable document of intellectual history.'   Lewis S. Feuer

'This autobiography is part discussion on method; part intellectual history of Popper's major ideas; and part a continuing discussion of his ruling preoccupations.'   Tyrrell Burgess, *New Society*

'. . . few broad areas of human thought remain unillumined by Popper's work.'   Bryan Magee